The Old South

Endowed by

Tom Watson Brown

and

The Watson-Brown Foundation, Inc.

The Old South

A Brief History with Documents

DAVID WILLIAMS

MERCER UNIVERSITY PRESS
MACON, GEORGIA

MUP/ P486

Published by Mercer University Press, Macon, Georgia 31207

1400 Coleman Avenue
Macon, Georgia 31207

9 8 7 6 5 4 3 2 1

Books published by Mercer University Press are printed on acid-free paper that meets the requirements of the American National Standard for Information Sciences—Permanence of Paper for Printed Library Materials.

ISBN 978-0-88146-484-9
Cataloging-in-Publication Data is available from
the Library of Congress

Contents

For my students

Introduction

This collection of essays and documents sheds new light on Southern history for students and general readers alike. The book's five chapters—one each dealing with the colonial period, Revolutionary era, westward expansion, late antebellum period, and Civil War era—show how the South's people acted on each other, reacted to each other, and responded to forces beyond themselves in ways that affect the region's people and the nation to this day. Though I cover time periods broadly, my narrative and selected documents often emphasize lesser-known but significant aspects of Southern history that have been traditionally marginalized or ignored. In this way, I hope to reveal the region's people to be historically more diverse and complex than is generally known, even among Southerners. And I hope to go some way toward explaining why the South evolved as it did.

Beginning with the earliest Native American migrations, the story tells of first contacts between area natives and Europeans, resulting in a clash of cultures that rapidly transformed societies and economies. Struggles for land and power, strategies to subdue and enslave, and efforts to resist and survive all laid the foundations of what would become what we call the South—a region I define as those states in which chattel slavery persisted through the mid-nineteenth century.

During the American Revolution, the Southern states became part of a new nation, the United States, birthed in a painful conflict that was as much a civil war as a war for independence, especially in the South. Over the following decades, Native Americans were relentlessly driven out as the South moved west, establishing an agriculturally based society dominated by a slaveholding minority.

Facing pressures against them from within the South as well as without, slaveholders sought to make slavery perpetual by means of a war that pitted not only North against South, but Southerners against each other. The new Confederacy could hardly survive this two-front war. Some predicted as much. Barely a year into the war, an Atlanta newspaper wrote, "If we are defeated, it will be by the people at home." And so the Confederacy was defeated, not simply by the Union armies–

in which nearly half a million men from the slave states served–but also by opposition on the home front. Only in the postwar period did the Confederacy begin take on an aura of unity that it never enjoyed during its brief existence.

The documents in this collection have been edited for ease of reading and comprehension. Spelling, capitalization, and punctuation have been altered frequently, but never the words or their meanings. Those who wish to view the documents in original form should consult the sources I cite.

For the many ways in which they have all contributed to making this book possible, I owe numerous debts of gratitude, especially to Dr. Paul Riggs, head of the History Department at Valdosta State University; Dr Jay Rickman, chair of the department's scheduling committee; Dr. Chris Meyers, professor of history at VSU; Dr. Connie Richards, dean of VSU's College of Arts and Sciences; Dr. James LaPlant, assistant vice president for research and dean of the Graduate School; Dr. Alan Bernstein, university librarian and dean of the Master of Library and Informational Science Program; Deborah Davis, university archives director; Denise Montgomery and VSU's interlibrary loan staff; Rex Devane and his staff at the VSU media center; Dr. David Carlson, professor of history at Troy State University; Marc Jolley, Marsha Luttrell, Mary Beth Kosowski, and the staff of Mercer University Press; and the many fine historians upon whose work I have relied.

My most heart-felt gratitude goes to Teresa Crisp Williams, my wife of more than three decades and a fine historian in her own right, who read early versions of the manuscript and has been a pillar of support throughout.

1

Clash of Cultures: Race, Class, and Conflict in the Colonial South

First Peoples of the Southeast

As North America lay in the grip of our planet's most recent Ice Age, the first humans known to inhabit the continent migrated from Asia. By at least 13,000 years ago they arrived in what is today the southeastern United States. These Paleo-Indian (Old Indian) peoples were hunter-gatherers, living in small bands of 20-30 people, who followed large herds of migratory game animals such as woolly mammoth, mastodon, and giant bison.

With the end of the Ice Age 12,000–10,000 years ago came a warmer climate and extinction of the large beasts upon which the Paleo-Indians had depended for their survival. They adapted well to their changing environment during this 2000-year transitional era, ushering in a new phase called the Archaic period that stretched from 10,000 to 3,000 years ago. Archaic peoples used new hunting tools and techniques aimed at bringing down smaller game animals such as deer, rabbit, possum, and squirrel. The spear-throwing stick (atl-atl by its Aztec name) and bow and arrow became essential, as did hooks, nets, and baskets for catching fish. But most of their food came from more easily gathered sources like nuts, acorns, and freshwater shellfish called mussels. Twice-yearly migrations were common among the South's Archaic peoples, spending springs and summers at base camps along rivers and streams taking advantage of abundant mussels, then moving to upland areas in the falls and winters where they harvested nuts and acorns. In coastal regions, where mussels, clams, and fish were plentiful, people developed more permanent villages. Some of their remains can be seen to this day on

Georgia's Sapelo Island, where for thousands of years Archaic peoples piled huge rings of discarded shells around their settlements.

Toward the Archaic period's close, the development of pottery led to a significant change in lifestyle. Now easily able to boil water, people could leech tannic acid out of acorn meal, produce and store more food, and remain more settled. They also began to care for natural stands of local fruits, berries, and grain, pulling weeds to increase yields and saving seeds to ensure the next year's harvest. Planting and cultivation (all human power since there were no horses or cattle until the coming of Europeans) made food production even more stable and abundant, completing the change to an agriculturally based lifestyle, still supplemented by hunting and gathering, called the Woodland period.

Lasting from about 3000 to 1000 years ago, the Woodland era saw Native Americans developing domestic varieties of vegetables and grains such as maize (corn), beans, squash, and melons that were much larger and more productive. More food meant that villages could support populations of several hundred. And it meant people could spend more time on non-agricultural activities–spinning and weaving cotton cloth, making jewelry, fashioning specialized tools, and producing new forms of pottery both for utilitarian and ceremonial purposes. Much of their time was also devoted to spiritual activities and the construction of ceremonial sites. Most common of these communal projects were burial mounds containing dozens of graves, usually centered around higher-status individuals, both men and women, who may have served as chiefs or priests.

So skilled were Woodland farmers and artisans that they usually produced more than their villages alone could use. This surplus encouraged trade from one village to the next across routes that stretched the length and breadth of the continent. Cotton was traded from the South. Copper came from the Great Lakes region, red pipe stone from Wisconsin and Minnesota, abalone from the Pacific coast, obsidian (a volcanic glass) from the Rockies, crystalline mica and steatite (soapstone) from Appalachia. Pearls came from coastal regions and jewelry made its way from all points of the compass. As trade increased, villages located at the intersection of trade routes attracted merchants and artisans from surrounding areas and saw their populations rise to many thousands. Over time, these larger towns came to exert not only economic influence over smaller villages, but cultural and political influence as well. In effect, they became the capital cities of chiefdoms that encompassed hundreds of square miles and dozens of towns. The first of these large chiefdoms came to prominence along the Mississippi River and gave rise to a new cultural phase called the Mississippian period.

By a thousand years ago, Mississippian culture had become the dominant lifestyle among the South's Native Americans. It was an agriculturally based culture in which large amounts of surplus food, in addition to trade goods, flowed into larger towns to support their huge populations. A hierarchical elite class of chiefs and priests, developed mainly around kinship ties, organized the storage and redistribution of this surplus, ensuring that no town within the chiefdom suffered unduly during times of drought or pestilence. Elites were also responsible for conducting rituals and ceremonies, interceding with the spirit world for continued blessings of abundant harvests. The most important of these rituals were performed atop large platform or temple mounds, so called because they were flattened on top with temples built on the elevated surface. These were much larger than the burial mounds of the Woodland era. Some reached heights of 60 feet or more and covered as much as an acre or more at the base. Though most were destroyed by European settlers seeking buried treasure, some still remain. Among the best preserved are Moundville in Hale County, Alabama; Etowah Mounds near Rome, Georgia; and the Ocmulgee Mounds in Macon, Georgia.

Around the thirteenth century, Mississippian rituals began to fail. Earth entered a series of cooling phases known as the Little Ice Age that lasted several centuries. Global temperatures on average dropped by only 1 to 3 degrees Fahrenheit, but the impact was far-reaching. Shortened growing seasons brought famine to northern Europe and destroyed the Anasazi culture of the American Southwest. In the Southeast, large Mississippian chiefdoms broke into smaller regional chiefdoms, though they retained much the same social structure and agricultural economy. What might have developed from this later Mississippian culture will never be known, for that world was devastated in the sixteen and seventeenth centuries by invading Europeans.

The Spanish Incursion

The first European expedition to set foot in the Southeast was led by Ponce de Leon, who landed in 1513 near St. Augustine, Florida. He established no permanent settlement, but represented the first wave of Spanish slave traders from the Caribbean who raided coastal communities as far north as Virginia. In 1526, Lucas Vazquez de Ayllon, a financial backer of these slave raids, tried to establish a permanent settlement on the Georgia coast called San Miguel de Gualdape near Sapelo Sound. The colony of 600 included the first known African slaves brought to what is now the United States. Starvation, disease, attacks from local natives, an uprising among the African slaves, and the death of Allyon himself all brought the venture to an end after just six weeks. Only 150 survivors returned to the Spanish Caribbean.

In 1539, a Spanish army of nearly 700 led by Hernando de Soto landed at Florida's Tampa Bay. The next year it made its way through Georgia looking for gold, plunder, and slaves. The Spaniards continued in a long loop through the Carolinas and Tennessee before turning back south into the Coosa chiefdom of northern Georgia and Alabama. In central Alabama, the Spaniards ran into stiff resistance at the Battle of Mabila, a fortified town under Chief Tuskaloosa. Two hundred Spaniards fell, but with their guns, lances, horses, and war dogs inflicted perhaps ten times that number of casualties by Spanish claims.

After recovering from the encounter, De Soto's army continued toward the Mississippi River, where De Soto himself died of fever. His men went as far as Texas before turning back toward the Mississippi. There they built seven boats and floated down river, harassed by local natives as they went. They reached the Gulf Coast in 1542 and headed for Mexico with less than half the men who began the journey three years earlier.

Other than to make them wary of Europeans, De Soto's men had little immediate effect on Native Americans. But they brought invisible enemies whose long-term impact would be devastating. Old World

Indians greeted Spaniards as potential trading partners, but the newcomers were more interested in territorial conquest and religious conversion than mutual commerce. Natives who refused to submit were pronounced demon-possessed and sentenced to such tortures as purification by fire, during which the victim was roasted to death.

Engraving by Theodor de Bry, 1598.

diseases such as bubonic plague and small pox, to which the Native Americans had no immunity, spread from one town to the next along a well-established network of trade routes. Within a generation, tens of thousands were dead. The Southeast's native population, estimated to be perhaps 5 million at the time of European contact, was reduced by over 90 percent by the late seventeenth century.

In 1559, 1500 Spaniards under Tristan de Luna established a colony near modern Pensacola, Florida. In need of food, they set out into the interior looking for the great towns described in the De Soto journals. They did not find what they had expected. After an arduous journey through Alabama and into northern Georgia, they found the once thriving Coosa chiefdom in decline with little food to spare. Its capital, the site of at least 500 households twenty years earlier, now had less than fifty. The temples atop its earthen mounds were in decay. Most of the surrounding cornfields were overgrown and deserted. De Luna's men headed back to the Gulf Coast and abandoned their colony.

The first permanent Spanish settlement in the Southeast was established in Florida. In 1565, Pedro Menendez and his men destroyed the French outpost of Fort Caroline at the mouth of the St. Johns River where modern Jacksonville is now located. To ward off further French incursions on Spanish territorial claims, just to the south Menendez built what would become the oldest surviving European settlement in the United States, the town of St. Augustine. The next year during an exploration up the coast, Menendez landed on the island of Santa Catalina (St. Catherines) and met the principal headman of a chiefdom that covered much of Georgia's coastal region and perhaps many miles inland. The chief's name was Guale, pronounced "Wally" by the Spanish, and they began to refer to the region as Guale.

Over the next few years, Menendez sent soldiers to establish small forts called presidios in the interior of northern Florida and southern Georgia among the Timucuans, Appalachees, and Guales. The soldiers were accompanied by Catholic priests whose job it was to set up missions, convert the locals to Christianity, and make them more compliant to Spanish demands. As subjects of the Spanish crown, the natives were expected to pay taxes in the form of food and other goods to support the missions and presidios. Some natives, hoping for trade with the Spanish or fearing their soldiers, paid the taxes. Others saw little benefit in cooperating with the invaders. Sporadic rebellions occurred, the most significant of which was the Guale or Juanillo Revolt of 1597. The trouble started when two priests intervened to prevent Juanillo, the son of a Guale chief, from succeeding his father. They deemed Juanillo too uncooperative and favored a more submissive chief. Guales who opposed Spanish rule flocked to Juanillo's side. They attacked missions along the coast, killing several priests, and seemed bent on driving the Spanish all the way back to St. Augustine. They were finally stopped on San Pedro (Cumberland) Island when a Spanish-supporting chief ordered his men to turn back the attackers. Still, the mission system north of Cumberland Island was entirely broken.

Florida's Spanish governor responded with a series of raids north along the coast and into the interior, burning crops and villages and killing so ruthlessly that soon the Guales were begging for the priests and their missions to return. In 1606 the bishop of Cuba toured Guale and reported that the natives were fully subdued.

The following decades saw Spain expand its presidio and mission system west from the coast into southern Georgia, establishing outposts near Folkston, Valdosta, and Lumber City. They also pushed north from their strongholds near Tallahassee, Florida, setting up missions in southwestern Georgia along the lower reaches of the Flint and Chattahoochee rivers. The threat of Spanish raids kept rebellions suppressed, but a greater threat to Spanish control was looming far to the north.

The British Challenge

In 1607, England established the Virginia colony with its first permanent settlement at Jamestown. From Spain's perspective, this was an invasion of its territory since it claimed all of North America. But Spain did not press the claim. Neither did the British immediately press their own claims any farther south. Then in 1663 Britain's Parliament granted a charter for a colony south of Virginia to be called Carolina. Two years later the new colony's southern boundary was, at least on paper, extended well south of St. Augustine, nearly halfway down the Florida peninsula.

Spain at first ignored British claims since there were no actual settlements in Carolina. That changed in April 1670 with the founding of Charles Town (modern Charleston). In May, Spain and England signed the Treaty of Madrid in which each side recognized the possessions of the other. But there was a problem. At the time, Spain had no knowledge of Charleston. Some Spanish officials urged an attack. Others, including the viceroy of New Spain, argued against such a move. Although the English may have been deceptive, technically the treaty still covered Charleston. Spain finally decided to launch an expedition against Charleston, but the fleet turned back because of rough seas.

The British soon moved to undermine Spain's regional dominance by establishing trade with the natives west and south of Charleston stretching into what is now Georgia. Dr. Henry Woodward made an agreement with the Westoes in which Charleston would supply them with guns, powder, ammunition, and metal tools in exchange for Native American slaves and deerskins. British traders made similar agreements with the Savannahs, Yamassees, and "Chiluques" (believed to be Cherokees). Many of the natives had long sought firearms, denied them by the Spanish, both to combat Spain's control and to break the influence of its Native American allies.

In 1680 Chief Altamaha led his Yamasees in a major raid against Spain's northernmost mission on St. Catherines Island. More raids by slave catchers and freelance pirates, who were often employed by the British, forced Spain to abandon all of Guale by 1686 and withdraw south of the St. Marys River, the modern coastal boundary between Georgia and Florida. Spain tried to shore up its regional claims with the establishment of Pensacola in 1698 but were cut off by the French, who had made their way down the Mississippi from Canada, established an outpost at Biloxi in 1699, and in 1702 set up a fort on Mobile Bay. A few years later, in 1718, the French Mississippi Company founded New Orleans.

The Spanish suffered another series of blows with the outbreak of Queen Anne's War (War of Spanish Succession) in 1702. In August, Carolina's Governor James Moore and Deputy Governor Robert Daniell sailed an army of nearly 500 soldiers and 370 Native Americans, mostly Yamasees, down the coast. Their intent was to drive the Spanish out of Florida. They destroyed the missions around St. Augustine, burned the town itself, and laid siege to its fort, the Castillo de San Marcos. The Spanish defenders were saved only by a relief expedition from Havana, Cuba, which arrived on 30 December.

In 1704, during a massive raid that came to be called the Appalachee Massacre, fifty Carolinians and a thousand of their Native American allies swept down the Flint River, destroyed nearly all the Spanish missions in southern Georgia and northern Florida, killed most of the region's Appalachee inhabitants and sold hundreds into slavery. Continued raids over the next few years almost depopulated the area of its native peoples, leaving only a few Appalachee, Timucua, and Calusa survivors huddled around St. Augustine for protection.

The Treaty of Utrecht in 1713 brought an end to Queen Anne's War, in part reiterating the 1670 Madrid Treaty's agreement that each side recognize the other's colonial possessions. But the war's end brought only more misery for Native Americans. Increasingly dependant on trade with the British, they became more vulnerable to being cheated and abused. Whites set the terms of trade, and prices were going up. They demanded more deerskins and slaves for fewer goods. Upwards of 100,000 skins were exported from Charleston annually, and the natives were in debt to the traders for as many more. A census from the period shows that Native American slaves accounted for 15 percent of Carolina's population, not including those exported to New England and the West Indies.

The Native American slave trade was not without controversy among British colonists. Supporters argued that slavery was the best way to Christianize the natives. They also saw slavery as saving the Native Americans from the Spanish, the French, or each other. But an opponent of Native American enslavement lamented that whites generally, and white slave catchers especially, endeavored "to ravish the wife from the husband, kill the father to get the child and to burn and destroy the habitations of these poor people into whose country we were cheerfully received by them, cherished and supplied when we are weak, or at least never have done us hurt; and after we have set them on work to do all these horrid wicked things to get slaves to sell the dealers in Indians, call it humanity to buy them and thereby keep them from being murdered."

Finally the Tuscaroras of eastern North Carolina had had enough. After years of having their lands stolen and their people sold into slavery, the Tuscaroras struck back. In 1711, a faction led by Chief Hancock, together with local Native American allies, struck plantations along the Roanoke, Neuse, and Trent rivers as well as the town of Bath. Hundreds of white settlers were killed. Militia forces along with Native American allies, including some Tuscaroras, responded violently in 1712, slaughtering more than 300 natives on the Nuese River and selling 100 survivors, mostly women and children, into slavery. The next year, a thousand more natives were killed or captured at Fort Neoheroka in Greene County, breaking the back of Tuscarora resistance. Those who escaped fled to New York, later becoming part of the Iroquois Confederation.

Struggles for the Debatable Land

Farther south, Yamasees felt the heavy hand of British oppression. Some had allied with the whites against the Tuscaroras to gain better treatment, but no better treatment came. In 1715, joined by the Cherokees and a collection of other groups, some of which would soon form the Creek Nation, the Yamasees led a coordinated assault on Carolina. They killed South Carolina's agent to the natives along with dozens of traders. They burned the trading posts, then moved east to sack tidewater plantations. Charleston was flooded with refugees, and it seemed that the city might fall. Carolina whites soon gained the upper hand by resorting to their old tactic of setting Native Americans against each other. They bribed the Cherokees with gifts and favorable trade agreements then set them against their former allies. When a band of Creeks came to confer with the Cherokees, they were put to death, an incident that caused mistrust between the two nations for years. In 1717 Charleston made peace with the Creeks, bringing the Yamasee War to a close. The Yamasees themselves fled to Spanish Florida, but were hunted down by English slave catchers. Most were killed or captured and enslaved.

The Yamasee War taught Native Americans a hard lesson about safety in numbers, and most of them took that lesson to heart. Beginning with the Coweta and Cusseta bands on the Chattahoochee River near modern Columbus, Georgia, groups including the Hitchiti, Yuchi, Eufaula, Tuskegee, and Alabama formed a political and military alliance that whites called the Creek Nation, after the Ochese Creeks who had a major trading post near Macon. The alliance soon encompassed nearly all native peoples of central and southern Georgia and eastern Alabama. Most were native speakers of the Muskogee language, but the alliance included other linguistic groups. With such an alliance, numbering at its outset around 10,000 people (roughly the same white population as British Carolina), the Creeks could ward off white slave catchers and negotiate from strength with the British, French, and Spanish for more favorable trade agreements.

Charleston learned a lesson too. Carolina's vast southwestern claim, mostly the region that would later become Georgia, was at the center of a three-way international tug-of-war. It was, as historians have called it, the Debatable Land. During the Yamasee War, with the British distracted, Spain began to push out from St. Augustine and re-established some of its old presidios and missions. The French moved into the heart of Alabama and built Fort Toulouse near the present city of Montgomery. What Charleston needed was a militarized buffer zone to the south.

After two abortive attempts to establish such a buffer, James Oglethorpe arrived in 1733 with a hundred new settlers to found the colony of Georgia. For their town site, Oglethorpe selected a patch of high ground overlooking the Savannah River called Yamacraw Bluff after a small band of local natives. Oglethorpe asked their chief, Tomochichi, for permission to settle there. Owing at least in part to the intercession of white trader and interpreter James Musgrove and his half-Creek wife Mary, Tomochichi agreed for the time being. The matter would eventually have to be taken up with the Creek National Council.

In May, with Tomochichi's support, Oglethorpe negotiated his first treaty with the head men of Coweta and Cusseta towns representing the Creek Nation. The resulting "Articles of Friendship and Commerce" made clear that trade would be conducted with set rates and prices. The treaty also stipulated that although the land still belonged to the Creeks, they consented to Britain's use of it. As the Creeks saw it, the treaty was not a land cession but an expression of willingness to share what they had with their British neighbors. They issued no land titles and viewed land as held collectively, never individually. Georgia's charter, on the other hand, gave the colony all lands between the Savannah and Altamaha rivers, northwest to their headwaters, then west all the way to the Pacific Ocean. At the time, eastern Georgia was populated by so few Creeks, and even fewer colonists, that there were no immediate difficulties. But the treaty represented a growing economic dependence on the part of the Native Americans and a pattern of deception on the part of the whites that would eventually lead to the loss of Native American lands across the South.

Oglethorpe soon began building a string of forts down the Georgia coast as far south as Fort St. George near present-day Jacksonville, just 35 miles north of St. Augustine. Spanish threats forced him to abandon Fort St. George but, for the time being, Spain did not contest his forts farther north. Oglethorpe's efforts were well timed. Trouble was brewing with Spain not only over land disputes but also Britain's right to the slave trade in Spanish America. British smuggling in Spanish waters served only to increase tensions.

Spain exacerbated tensions over slavery by promising freedom to any British slaves who might escape to Florida. Oglethorpe increasingly anticipated war with Spain. If it came, he meant to take St. Augustine, and he hoped to have help from the Creeks. At the Coweta Conference in 1739, Oglethorpe and Mary Musgrove tried to bring the Creeks into a military alliance with Britain. The Creeks refused, but promised that they would not ally with the Spanish or French either.

That same year, the conflict came to a head. Members of Parliament who supported war latched on to an incident that had occurred a few years earlier when British sea captain Robert Jenkins had his ear cut off by a Spanish officer who accused him of piracy. Jenkins was summoned to Parliament and displayed his ear, preserved in a jar, for all to see. This affront to British honor became the excuse for a declaration of war on Spain. The conflict was sometimes called King George's War and later became part of Europe's War of Austrian Succession, but it was most popularly known as the War of Jenkins' Ear.

Oglethorpe gathered a force of about 1500 men in May 1740 and sailed for St. Augustine. He planned a combined land-sea assault against the town, but Spanish ships blocked the water approach. Oglethorpe suffered another blow near Fort Mose, an outpost just north of St. Augustine settled by free blacks who had escaped slavery in Carolina. On 15 June a band of blacks and Spaniards wiped out a nearby British camp. With word that Spanish reinforcements were coming and that his naval support would soon depart, Oglethorpe retreated to Fort Frederica on Georgia's St. Simons Island.

Now St. Augustine took the offensive. Governor Manuel Montiano amassed an army of 2000 and in June 1742 landed on the southern end of St. Simons Island. He occupied Fort St. Simons, but did not move against Oglethorpe's main force at Fort Frederica for a week. That gave Oglethorpe time to lay his own plans and to call for Scots reinforcements from Darien. With his regular forces supplemented by the Highlanders, Oglethorpe blocked the Spanish advance at Gully Hole Creek and ambushed a Spanish relief force at Bloody Marsh. Montiano made probing forays over the next few days, but when British ships appeared on the horizon he quickly set sail for St. Augustine.

Oglethorpe tried to get more British troops for another expedition, but his requests were ignored. Still, he mounted a second campaign against St. Augustine in early 1743. His strategy this time was to draw the Spanish out of their defenses, but they refused to take the bait. Again, Oglethorpe withdrew to Frederica. Discouraged and angered by lack of support from London, Oglethorpe returned to England in July, never to set foot in Georgia again.

Though the war in Europe dragged on for another five years, there was no further action on the Georgia-Florida boarder. For the time being, Georgia remained the anchor of British North America's southern frontier.

The Chesapeake Region: Natives, Intruders, and Indentured Servants

Farther north, Virginia was Britain's mainmast in the colonial South and had been since its founding over a century earlier. Even so, its beginnings had been rocky and its survival far from certain. Founded as a joint stock venture by the Virginia Company of London, the primary role of Virginia's first colonists, who were essentially company employees, was to make money for company investors. They expected to do so just as the Spanish initially had—by enslaving the natives and mining for gold.

In 1607 the Virginia Company sent over 100 colonists under Christopher Newport, a veteran privateer who had been raiding Spanish treasure ships for twenty years, to establish the settlement of Jamestown. Their first task was to find gold, though no one had ever seen it in raw form. According to Captain John Smith, "there was no talk, no hope, nor work, but dig gold, wash gold, refine gold, load gold." Newport soon left Smith in charge of the colony and returned to England with a ship full of "yellow dirt." It was pyrite—fools gold—and absolutely worthless.

Back in Virginia, the colonists were starving. One account told how they were "driven through insufferable hunger to eat those things which nature most abhorred, the flesh and excrements of man." One corpse was "digged by some out of his grave after he had lain buried three days and wholly devoured him; others, envying the better state of body of any whom hunger had not yet so much wasted as their own, lay wait and threatened to kill and eat them; one among them slew his wife as she slept in his bosom, cut her in pieces, salted her, and fed upon her till he had clean devoured all parts saving her head."

Chief Powhatan and his people tried to help the English, first by feeding them and then by teaching them to farm. Still they had trouble feeding themselves. Many abandoned Jamestown to live among the Powhatan Indians. Seeing his workforce melt away, John Smith demanded that the refugees be returned. Powhatan, puzzled by such a demand, replied that they were not prisoners. He remained willing to feed any who came and welcomed them to stay as long as they liked.

Smith, who had been saved from execution by Powhatan's daughter Pocahontas after an earlier dispute with the natives, now attacked a nearby Powhatan village. He set fire to the houses, cut down the corn, killed at least sixteen and captured the wife and children of the village headman. He threw the children into the James River and, according to one witness, "shot out their brains in the water." Their mother was stabbed to death.

Smith then swept through neighboring villages, taking Native American captives and enslaving them. The effort failed mainly because natives could easily escape. Unable to enslave them, Smith determined to kill as many as he could and force the survivors into the interior. In a pattern that would repeat itself throughout British North America, Smith attacked native villages just before harvest time when most of the men were out hunting. He would burn homes, destroy crops, and kill the women and children. With nothing left of their homes or families, the men joined other villages farther west.

Powhatan begged Smith for peace, but Smith and the English did not want peace. They wanted land. That land became particularly valuable after 1612 when John Rolfe pioneered the successful cultivation and marketing of tobacco. King James I, famous for commissioning the Biblical translation that bears his name, disliked tobacco and discouraged its use. But so many Englishmen took to the noxious weed that it became the foundation of Virginia's plantation economy.

Because of primogeniture and entail laws in Britain restricting inheritance of landed estates to the eldest surviving son, younger sons eagerly sought their own land holdings in America. The more influential their families, the more readily land grants came their way. To work their new estates, they purchased indentured servants by the thousands. Such a large labor force was made available by one of the most significant developments in British-American history, the Enclosure movement.

In the sixteenth century, as landed nobility began to fence off or "enclose" much of their land to raise sheep for new woolen markets, hundreds of thousands of peasant farmers were driven off. They migrated to the rising towns and cities of Britain's nascent Industrial Revolution looking for work, but there were not enough jobs to meet the need. Many displaced peasants fell deep into debt. Some turned to petty theft. Simply being a "masterless" peasant was itself a violation of British law. All were equally criminal, and many thousands were sentenced to indentured servitude in America. So lucrative was the trade in indentured servants that ship captains with a bit of remaining space

Nathaniel Bacon's rebel army, which included blacks and whites held in servitude as well as tenant farmers and small freeholders, sets fire to Virginia's capital of Jamestown in 1676.

Illustration from *Harper's Encyclopedia of the United States* (1905).

often ordered their men to "nap" children off the streets and haul them on board. Kidnappers were especially eager to grab attractive young women since they brought good prices in America for sexual services as well as their labor.

Once on the docks, servants were auctioned off to the highest bidder and indentured for a term of service, usually seven years, though many served much longer. They were underfed, poorly housed, and overworked. In the seventeenth-century Chesapeake region, nearly half died during their first year of servitude. Those who managed to survive faced similar hardships in a nominal freedom. Since they had no money and few skills other than farming, most became tenant farmers. Charged rent on, and extended credit for, the land they worked, the tools they used, and the seeds they planted, all at prices set by landlords, they nearly always ended the harvest season in debt and trapped in a new state of servitude from which few could ever escape.

Power, Resistance, and the Origins of Chattel Slavery

In 1619, new kinds of servants arrived on the docks at Jamestown, auctioned off by a Dutch merchant vessel. They had been captured in Africa and sold as slaves, but under British law there was no provision for slavery. So they were treated as indentured servants and acquired the same nominal freedom that white servants did. The servants themselves were, as historian Kenneth Stampp put it, "remarkably unconcerned about their visible physical differences." They were very familiar with the confines of their class system, but rigid caste lines based on race were unknown. Black and white servants worked together, played together, lived together, and married each other. The brand of racism that would become all too familiar to later generations of Americans was absent through most of the seventeenth century.

That began to change as colonial elites, fearing rebellion from below, took steps to divide poor whites and blacks socially and economically. The threat of rebellion was very real in a society where most people were servants, landless tenants, or small farmers holding marginal lands that the gentry did not want. Few held enough land or wealth to vote or hold office. Those privileges were restricted by wealth throughout the colonies. Virginia's House of Burgesses, founded in 1619 as the first representative assembly in British America, was dominated by fifty families by the end of the century. The situation was similar in Maryland. Though the Calvert proprietors held nominal authority, as did the royal governors in Virginia, it was the assemblies that levied taxes. No governor could succeed without their financial backing.

The taxes colonial assemblies levied were most often directed at smaller farmers and artisans who could neither vote nor hold office in those assemblies. High taxes kept them not only poor but also in constant danger of losing what little land they had. Their resentment, along with that of tenants and servants, was almost a sure formula for rebellion. Virginia's Governor William Berkeley himself recognized the danger when he wrote, "How miserable that man is that governs a people where six parts of seven *at least* are poor, indebted, discontented, and *armed*."

As early as 1661, the Virginia assembly took a major step toward heading off rebellion through social division by defining blacks who had not already acquired freedom as "servants for life." It was not enough. In 1676, the underclasses of Virginia, black and white, united against their oppressors during what came to be known as Bacon's Rebellion. Nathaniel Bacon himself was a member of the minor nobility bent on seizing control, but his attempted coup soon took on wider dimensions. Landless servants and tenants wanted land and saw violence as the only way to get it. They established fortifications along the James River, marched against the capital of Jamestown, burned it to the ground, and came close to seizing control of the colony before Crown forces put them down. Among the last to surrender was a band of eighty blacks and twenty whites.

Bacon's Rebellion sent shock waves through the ranks of the ruling elites. Many feared that some future insurrection, perhaps larger and better organized, might succeed. What could be done to avert such a calamity? Their strategy became one of divide and conquer. In the words of historian Edmund Morgan, "for those with eyes to see, there was an obvious lesson in the rebellion. Resentment of an alien race might be more powerful than resentment of an upper class." Creating a social distance between poor whites and blacks, assigning whites the superior social position, might make the two less likely to unite.

In the late seventeenth and early eighteenth centuries, colonial legislatures throughout British North America passed a series of laws designed to do just that. They outlawed interracial marriage. They amended criminal codes to deal more harshly with blacks than whites. In 1705 Virginia defined black servants as chattel slaves outright, the absolute property of slaveholders. At the same time, Virginia mandated payment in cash and/or in kind for whites on completing their term of indenture and restricted the practice of most skilled trades to whites only. Elites in other colonies followed suit. None of this resulted in meaningful political reform for lower-class whites. But it did instill in whites of all classes a sense that they were somehow "better" than those with even a drop of African blood—though many had a few such drops in their own bloodlines whether they knew it or not.

The strategy worked, and worked even better than elites had hoped. The new racism was a self-perpetuating thing passed on from generation to generation, keeping the poor divided and more easily controlled. Lower-class whites still resented their tax burden, their tenancy, their marginal lands, and lack of political power. And they occasionally rebelled, driving off tax and rent collectors. Slaves too sometimes rose in rebellion. But never again did poor whites unite with blacks against their common oppressor as they had in 1676 Virginia.

The Carolina-Georgia Lowcountry: New Directions, Old Attitudes

The lessons of social control established in Virginia were applied in Carolina and Georgia as well. There were nominal rights for many white males, though politically these proved to be more apparent than real. The original Carolina colony was essentially a land grant to eight noble families who governed their trust as lords proprietor. Their governing document, the Fundamental Constitutions, authored in part by British political philosopher John Locke, granted voting rights to white males with at least 50 acres of land, but 500 acres were required for membership in the legislature. Even then, assemblymen could discuss and vote only on those matters already approved by the proprietors.

Still, small land grants served to attract farmers, who were required to serve in the militia in exchange for their land. Though officially Anglican, Carolina extended land grants and political rights to all religious dissenters except Catholics. This brought not only British religious refugees but also mainland Europeans, such as French Huguenots and German Palatines. Most colonists still came as indentured servants, and most of the good tidewater land went to a few large landgraves, equivalent to barons, and to lesser gentry who set up huge rice plantations worked by slave labor. By 1710, more than half the population of what would become South Carolina was held in slavery.

Heavy taxes levied on small farmers, whether they held enough land to make them voters or not, tended to keep upward mobility limited. So did land rents for tenant farmers, many of them former small landholders who had lost their lands at the auction block over their inability to pay the taxes imposed. Whether small landholders or tenants, most whites found themselves locked in a system of poverty from which few could escape. The pattern of upper-class control and lower-class division was well established by 1729 when the lords proprietor sold their rights and holdings to Parliament and the colony was officially split north and south.

Georgia originally took a much different socioeconomic path. It was designed as a charity colony where unfortunates could make "a comfortable subsistence" for themselves and help relieve Britain's unemployment problem. In 1732 James Oglethorpe and twenty other prominent men acquired a charter for the new colony, and they governed it as an absentee board of Trustees, Oglethorpe being the only Trustee ever to set foot in Georgia. The colony was to be populated mainly by yeoman farmers, together with small merchants and craftsmen, who could also serve as a militia force. Toward that end, no one, including the Trustees, could own land outright, meaning that land grants could not be mortgaged or sold. Such grants would be limited to 50 acres for most colonists, though about half the land granted by the Trustees went to a class of affluent "adventurers" who could receive up to 500 acres each (raised to 2,000 acres in 1740). The Trustees would rule by decree, though none could hold any title of office in the colony. Local magistrates, usually constables and justices of the peace, would enforce

Trustee rule, answerable only to the Trustees. Lawyers were forbidden to practice in the colony.

Also forbidden was slavery, though the prohibition was more practical than altruistic. Oglethorpe himself never argued against slavery in other colonies. As a director and later deputy governor of the Royal African Company, Oglethorpe promoted the institution and profited by it. But in Georgia, slavery would not do. Oglethorpe needed militiamen, and slaves could not serve that purpose. They might even seek freedom among the Spanish or, worse yet, they might rise in bloody insurrection. Already slaves from South Carolina were using Georgia as an escape route into Florida. In 1739, during the Stono Rebellion, an armed band of South Carolina slaves killed nearly two dozen whites and headed for the Savannah River before Carolina militiamen cut them off. Oglethorpe wanted no such trouble in Georgia.

Though Georgia succeeded as a military buffer colony, as a charity colony it failed miserably. The main problem for most colonists was the same that they had faced in Britain—deep and continuing debt. Of the 2,831 colonists transported to Georgia during its first decade, at least a third came with unrelieved debt hanging over their heads. Most of the rest became indebted the moment they set foot in Georgia. The vast majority of colonists had no way to pay for their passage from Britain, and the Trustees would not transport them for free. Nor would they take steps to relieve their prior debts. So immigrants indentured themselves for years of service, often to the Trustees themselves.

Restrictions on land use and the generally poor soils made life difficult for most Georgia colonists. Much of the coastal lands were flooded at high tide, and the rest was too sandy for most crop varieties. The inland pine barrens were good for little more than growing trees. That the Trustees tried to impose wine and silk production only made matters worse. Food was so scarce during Georgia's first decade that crops had to be imported from other colonies.

Some Georgians abandoned their unproductive land grants entirely and turned to trade with the natives. Deer, otter, and beaver skins were in high demand among the British, as were guns and other manufactured goods among Native Americans. Earlier Scots immigrants to Carolina as well as more recent Scots arrivals to Georgia were among the most active traders. Many took wives among the Creeks and Cherokees. Because native societies were matrilineal, the children identifying with their mother's extended family, men with names like McIntosh, McGillivray, and Ross became some of the wealthiest and most influential among the natives.

Slavery Debated and Resisted

After Oglethorpe left Georgia in 1743, the Trustees gave the colony's new presiding officer, William Stephens, authority to grant land. This act marked a major shift away from Georgia's mission as a charity colony. Stephens made clear that he favored larger land grants and wealthier immigrants. Within a few years, plantations were being established along the Georgia coast.

With larger land grants came increased pressure on the Trustees to lift their ban against outright (or fee-simple) land ownership and slavery. For years South Carolina rice planters had sought land in Georgia, and they wanted to bring their slaves with them. Many Georgia landholders, especially those with larger estates, wanted the ability to sell portions or mortgage it all to raise cash. And they wanted to use that cash to buy more land and slaves. Pressure also came from Savannah merchants who hoped to enhance their fortunes by trading in slaves or becoming slaveholding planters themselves.

Other Georgians were just as determined to keep slavery out. Georgia's free laborers had among the highest wages in colonial America, mainly because they were not competing with slaves. Working class women who earned a living as cooks, laundresses, and housekeepers worried that slavery would end their employment. Artisans and craftsmen too feared what slavery might mean to their trades. The Scots Highlanders at Darien drew up a petition begging the Trustees to continue their ban on slavery. After listing various disadvantages of slavery to the colony, they concluded by stressing, "It is shocking to human nature that any race of mankind and their posterity should be sentenced to perpetual slavery; nor in justice can we think otherwise of it, than that they are thrown amongst us to be our scourge one day or other for our sins."

The Darien petition also pointed to other dangers of slavery. With the Spanish in Florida promising freedom to escaped slaves, the danger seemed real enough. Already that promise had sparked slave rebellion in South Carolina during the Stono Rebellion. Many other slaves succeeded in escaping and making their way to Florida. Any attempt to establish slavery in Georgia would invite more rebellion and escapes.

Still, the Stephens administration implicitly encouraged slavery by issuing Georgia's best land to wealthy men in grants of hundreds of acres. In 1745, there were complaints that the poor were being crowded out and pushed off onto marginal lands. "Merchants and other gentlemen," one Georgia resident complained, now had in their hands "all good and convenient ground at the sea coasts and banks of rivers." Poorer folk were "forced to possess lands, remote from the conveniency of rivers and from town."

Despite its illegality, slavery soon followed in the wake of large land grants. Under Stephens, Carolina planters began to get land in Georgia, and they brought slaves with them. Georgia planters brought in more slaves to work their land. Finally in 1750, with so many slaves already in Georgia, the Trustees relented and lifted their ban on slavery and on fee-simple land ownership. Stephens and his council quickly tied large land grants to slavery. The more slaves a man owned, the more land he could get.

In 1752 the Trustees gave up on their Georgia project and turn it over to Parliament as a royal colony. Thereafter Georgia took on much the same character as South Carolina. Rice planters dominated the coastal regions as well as the legislature. Charity colonists retained their 50-acre grants, which would have qualified them for voting, but debt forced most to sell all or part of their holdings at bargain prices to wealthier immigrants. These small farmers, like those in other Southern colonies, tended to be pushed onto marginal lands in the backcountry where taxes and rents kept them poor.

Discontent in the Backcountry

Lower-class folk pushing westward from the lowcountry often found non-natives already living in the backcountry. Some were earlier refugees from tidewater Virginia who had fled south and west to escape indentured servitude, tenancy, or slavery. Some formed biracial communities and even tri-racial communities whose descendants were referred to as Melungeons. Central and western North Carolina served as a popular haven for these people long before there was a Carolina colony. Others pushed farther west into what is now eastern Kentucky and Tennessee.

White immigrants from the east were almost all from the British Isles, mostly English, Welsh, and Scots. Other backcountry immigrants followed the Shenandoah Valley from Pennsylvania and Maryland into western Virginia and southward beyond. Immigration from the North tended to be more diverse, including Germans and Swiss. The most prevalent group from this northern wave was Scots-Irish, refugees mainly from Scotland who sought to escape English dominance by moving first to Northern Ireland, then to America.

Backcountry Southerners, whatever their origins, faced the common difficulties of high taxes, heavy rents, and little or no political representation. Tidewater gentry dominated Southern legislatures and paid little attention to the plight of backcountry folk. Tax and rent collectors from the tidewater regularly patrolled their colonies' western frontiers, taking the fruits of the people's hard work. Rarely did those fruits return in any form to the backcountry. What difficulty they had with Native Americans or outlaws was their own affair. They were left to form their own irregular militias without government support. Government of any kind in the backcountry was nearly non-existent except for what was necessary to enforce tax and rent payments.

Westerners got little better treatment from the Church of England, or Anglican Church, which was the official government-supported religion in each of the Southern colonies. Anglican ministers typically nestled comfortably in tidewater towns like Williamsburg, Charleston, and Savannah, serving the gentry but rarely venturing among their parishioners in the backcountry whose taxes largely paid their salaries. Though religion was not an overriding concern on the frontier, where few adhered to any particular denomination, frontier settlers resented the Anglican Church for the taxes they paid to it and the neglect they received in return.

That resentment made the backcountry fertile ground for cultivating new ideas about the relationship between humanity and God, and between God and government. The notion of separation of church and state, pioneered by Baptists like Roger Williams in New England, was especially attractive to backcountry folk who resented taxation to support an Anglican Church that ignored them. Also influential were John Wesley and George Whitefield, two reform-minded Anglican ministers who advocated a more direct relationship with God than was prevalent in the Church.

Wesley served in Savannah in the 1730s, where he was influenced by Moravians, a group of German-speaking Protestants from the modern Czech Republic. Their Anglican neighbors viewed them with suspicion for their unusual practices, among them allowing women to preach and hold religious office. On his return to England, Wesley began to advocate missionary evangelism, open-air preaching, and the concept of free will. Though he never officially broke with the Church of England, his writings laid the groundwork for Methodism in England and America as well as heavily influencing Holiness churches worldwide.

George Whitefield, a close friend of Wesley's and an early adherent of Methodism, carried missionary evangelism into the colonial backcountry during a 1740s rival movement, called by later generations the Great Awakening. Stressing a fiery emotionalism through which worshipers were said to experience direct contact with the Holy Spirit, Whitefield and others emphasized the individual over the institutional Church, an approach that had considerable appeal to a relatively isolated and largely illiterate backcountry population.

By the mid-eighteenth century, Anglican clergymen became worried about the rising influence of strange new doctrines and practices in the backcountry. Among them was Charles Woodmason of Charleston, South Carolina, who set off in the 1760s to bring frontier folk back into the arms of Anglicanism. But by then, it was too late. The Great Awakening had been nearly as much a political as a religious movement, playing on frontier resentments and linking Anglicanism inexorably to the tidewater gentry in the minds of backcountry folk. Main-line Anglican ministers like Woodmason were so firmly viewed as supporting oppression from the east that they received a chilly reception in the west. Handbills announcing Woodmason's sermons were torn down or had their dates altered. On one occasion, Presbyterians freely distributed whiskey when Woodmason managed to attract a crowd. He was booed at and shouted down so often that he was hardly ever heard. Woodmason soon returned to Charleston, thoroughly disgusted with his experience among what he called the "wild peoples" of Carolina's backcountry.

Documents

1. Guale Game and Ceremony (ca. 1595)

A castaway Spaniard, shipwrecked along what would later be the Georgia coast, experienced a welcoming ceremony that was typical of Southeastern natives. They used such ceremonies in hopes of establishing friendly relations with strangers and to cement bonds of affection with neighboring peoples. At the time, Spaniards claimed the entire Southeast and referred to the whole region as Florida.

They received us with happy faces and affable expressions and words that we did not understand just as they did not understand us. They soon attempted to entertain us with a certain game. To start it off, they all assembled together in one section of the plaza together with their cacique [chief], each one with a pole or a piece of a sharp-pointed lance.... The chief had a stone in his hand of the shape and size of a half-real bread roll. On beginning the game, the one who held it threw it rolling with all his strength, and they threw their poles after the stone all at one time and without any order. They took off after them at a run at the same time. I did not understand the game very well. But it appeared to me that the one who ran the best and arrived first took his pole and the stone and, without hesitating for a moment, threw it back again in the direction from whence it had come. They took it again in the same manner and threw it once again. They spent a great deal of time in this exercise and became so involved in the chase that the sweat ran from all over their bodies. Once the entertainment had ended, we all entered into the council house together and we all sat down, Spaniards, chiefs, and leading men, on the bed made of tree branches, which was raised more than a yard from the ground. In the council house and close to the door on its right side, there was a little idol or human figure badly carved. For ears it had those of a coyote and for a tail that of the coyote as well. The rest of the body was painted with red ochre. Close to the idol's feet there was a wide-mouthed jar full of a drink that they call *cacina* and around the jar and the idol was a great number of two-liter pots, also full of *cacina*. Each Indian took one of these in his hand, and with reverence they went about giving it to those who had played, who were each seated on a bench. Each one took and drank his. As a result of this their bellies became like a drum and as they went on drinking, their bellies kept on growing and swelling. They carried this on calmly for a while, and we [were] waiting to see how that fiesta would come to an end, when we saw that, on opening their mouths with very great calmness, each one began ejecting by way of them a great stream of water as clear as it was when they drank it, and others, on their knees on the ground with their hands, went about spreading the water that they had ejected to one side and the other. All those who did this were leading men. That solemn fiesta ended in this fashion.

Fray Andres de San Miguel, *An Early Florida Adventure Story*, translated by John H. Hann (Gainesville: University Press of Florida, 2001) 66–67.

2. Cheating the Carolina Indians (ca. 1700)

It was a common thing for white traders to cheat their Native American customers, driving them far into debt, only to have colonial governments demand land cession in payment of those debts. Violent conflicts were sometimes the result, as Surveyor-General John Lawson makes clear in his 1709 report to the Carolina proprietors.

They are really better to us than we are to them. They always give us victuals at their quarters, and take care we are armed against hunger and thirst. We do not do so by them (generally speaking) but let them walk by our doors hungry, and do not often relieve them. We look upon them with scorn and disdain, and think them little better than beasts in human shape, though if well examined, we shall find that, for all our religion and education, we possess more moral deformities and evils than these savages do....

We reckon them slaves in comparison to us, and intruders, as oft as they enter our houses, or hunt near our dwellings. But if we will admit reason to be our guide, she will inform us that these Indians are the freest people in the world, and so far from being intruders upon us, that we have abandoned our own native soil to drive them out and possess theirs.... We trade with them, it's true, but to what end? Not to show them the steps of virtue and the Golden Rule, to do as we would be done by. No, we have furnished them with the vice of drunkenness, which is the open road to all others, and daily cheat them in everything we sell, and esteem it a gift of Christianity not to sell to them so cheap as we do to the Christians, as we call ourselves. Pray let me know where is there to be found one sacred command or precept of our Master that counsels us to such behavior?... All the wars which we have had with the savages were occasioned by the unjust dealings of the Christians towards them.

John Lawson, *A New Voyage to Carolina; Containing the Exact Description and Natural History of That Country: Together with the Present State Thereof* (London: n.p., 1709) 235–36. North Carolina Collection, University of North Carolina at Chapel Hill.

3. Oglethorpe's "Articles of Friendship and Commerce" with the Creeks (1733)

Native Americans understood treaties with whites as little more than inviting trade. Yet, although this treaty between James Oglethorpe and Lower Creeks contains no hint of it, Georgia's 1732 charter laid claim to all lands between the Savannah and Altamaha rivers and westward across the continent to the Pacific Ocean. Though the Creeks did not yet know it, as far as the English were concerned, their land was no longer their own.

Articles of Friendship and Commerce between the Trustees for establishing the colony of Georgia in America and the Chief Men of the Nation of the Lower Creeks....

The Trustees bearing in their hearts great love and friendship to you, the said Head Men of the Lower Creek Nation, do engage to let their people carry up into your towns all kinds of goods fitting to trade in the said towns at the rates and prices settled and agreed upon before you the said Head Men....

We the Head Men of the Coweta and Cussita Towns, in behalf of all the Lower Creek Nation, being firmly persuaded that He who lives in Heaven and is the occasion of all good things has moved the hearts of the Trustees to send their beloved men among us for the good of us, our wives, and children...do therefore declare that we are glad that their people are come here, and though this land belongs to us, the Lower Creeks...do consent and agree that they shall make use of and possess all those lands which our Nation hath not occasion for to use and we make over unto them, their successors, and assigns all such lands and territories as we shall have no occasion to use, provided always that they upon settling every new town shall set out for the use of ourselves and the people of our Nation such lands as shall be agreed upon between their beloved men an the head men of our Nation and that those lands shall remain to us forever.

John T. Juricek, editor, *Early American Indian Documents: Treaties and Laws, 1607–1789, Volume 11, Georgia Treaties, 1733–1763* (Washington DC: University Publications of America, 1989) 15–17.

4. Powhatan's Plea for Peace (1609)

By the time the British arrived at Jamestown in 1607, the Spanish had already attempted a settlement on Chesapeake Bay. Chief Powhatan's brother Opechankanough, who had been captured by the Spanish, escaped and led a raid that destroyed the Spanish outpost. Now Captain John Smith and the English were asking for food, taking it at times by force when opportunity allowed. Powhatan was willing to help, but not with a gun to his head.

Captain Smith, ... some doubt I have of your coming hither, that makes me not so kindly seek to relieve you as I would. For many do inform me [that] your coming hither is not for trade, but to invade my people and possess my country, who dare not come to bring you corn, seeing you thus armed with your men. To free us of this fear, leave aboard your weapons, for here they are needless, we being all friends.... You may understand that I having seen the death of all my people thrice, and not any one living of those three generations but myself; I know the difference of peace and war better than any in my country. But now I am old and ere long must die.... What will it avail you to take by force what you may quickly have with love, or to destroy them that provide you with food? What can you get by war, when we can hide our provisions and fly to the woods, whereby you must famish by wronging us, your friends.... Think you I am so simple not to know it is better to eat good meat, lie well, and sleep quietly with my women and children, laugh and be merry with you, have copper hatchets, or what I want, being your friend, than be forced to flee from all, to lie cold in the woods, feed upon acorns, roots, and such trash, and be so hunted by you that I can neither rest, eat, nor sleep; but my tired men must watch and if a twig but break every one cryeth there cometh Captain Smith. Then must I flee I know not whether, and thus with fear end my miserable life, leaving my pleasures to such youths as you, which through your rash unadvisedness, may quickly as miserably end for want of that you never know where to find? Let this therefore assure you of our loves, and every year our friendly trade shall furnish you with corn, and now also if you would come in friendly manner to see us, and not thus with your guns and swords as to invade your foes.

Edward Arber, editor, *Travels and Works of Captain John Smith, Part II* (Edinburgh, Scotland: John Grant, 1910) 451–52.

5. James Revel's "Sorrowful Account" of Servitude in Virginia (ca. 1660)

James Revel, like so many thousands, was sentenced to servitude in the colonies. Unlike most, he was literate and was able to make his way back to England after being set free. Few ever lived to see home again. About half died during their first year in the colonies. Some time after his return, Revel wrote a poetic and depressing portrait of a typical servant's experience in Virginia, part of which appears below.

Down to the harbor I was took again,
On board of a sloop bound with an iron chain,
Which I was forced to wear both night and day,
For fear I from the sloop should run away.
  My master was a man but of ill fame,
Who first of all a transport thither came,
In Rapahannock country we did dwell,
In Rapahannock river known full well.
  When the ship with lading home was sent,
An hundred miles we up the river went,
The weather cold, and hard my fate,
My lodging on the deck both hard and bare.
  At last to my new master's house I came,
To the town of Wicowoco called by name,
Here my European clothes were took from me,
Which never after I could see.
  A canvas shirt and trousers me they gave,
A hop-sack frock, in which I was a slave,
No shoes or stockings had I for to wear,
Nor hat, nor cap, my hands and feet went bare.
  Thus dressed unto the field I next did go,
Among tobacco plants all day to hoe,
At day break in the morn our work begun,
And lasted till the setting of the sun.
  My fellow slaves were five transports more,
With eighteen negroes, which is twenty-four,
Besides four transport women in the house,
To wait upon his daughter and his spouse.
  We and the negroes both alike did fare,
Of work and food we had an equal share,
And in a piece of ground that's called our own,
That we eat first by ourselves was sown.
  No other time to us they will allow,
But on a Sunday we the same must do,
Six days we slave for our master's good,
The seventh is to produce our food.

And when our hard day's work is done,
Away unto the mill we must begone,
Till twelve or one o'clock a-grinding corn,
And must be up by day-light in the morn....
At length it pleased God I sick did fall,
Yet I no favor did receive at all,
For I was forced to work while I could stand,
Or hold the hoe within my feeble hand.
Much hardship then indeed I did endure,
No dog was ever nursed so before,
More pity the poor negro slaves bestowed,
Than my brutal and inhuman master would....
At length my fourteen years expired quite,
Which filled my very soul with fond delight,
To think I should not longer there remain,
But to Old England once return again.
My father and my mother well I found,
Who to see me with joy did abound,
My mother over me did weep for joy,
My father cried once more to see my boy.
Whom I thought dead but does alive remain,
And is returned to me now once again....

James Revel, *The Poor Unhappy Transported Felon's Sorrowful Account of His Fourteen Years Transportation, at Virginia, in America* (York, England: C. Croshaw, ca. 1800). Special Collections Library, Duke University.

6. Elizabeth Sprigs's Deplorable Condition of Servitude (1756)

We know nothing of Elizabeth Sprigs beyond this brief letter. Why she was banished from her home, what her "bad conduct" might have been, and how she came to Maryland is a mystery. Neither do we know whether her serving at "master's pleasure" involved rape, but for many female servants it certainly did.

Honored Father Maryland Sept'r 22'nd 1756

My being ever banished from your sight, will I hope pardon the boldness I now take of troubling you.... O, Dear Father, believe what I am going to relate, the words of truth and sincerity, and balance my former bad conduct [with] my sufferings here, and then I am sure you'll pity your distressed daughter. What we unfortunate English people suffer here is beyond the probability of you in England to conceive. Let it suffice that I, one of the unhappy number, am toiling almost day and night, and very often in the horse's drudgery, with only this comfort that you bitch you do not half enough, and then tied up and whipped to that degree that you'd not serve an animal, scarce anything but Indian corn and salt to eat, and that even begrudged. Nay many Negroes are better used. Almost naked, no shoes nor stockings to wear, and the comfort after slaving during master's pleasure, what rest we can get is to rap ourselves up in a blanket and lie upon the ground. This is the deplorable condition your poor Betty endures, and now I beg if you have any bowels of compassion left, show it by sending me some relief. Clothing is the principal thing wanting, which if you should condescend to, may easily send them to me by any of the ships bound to Baltimore Town, Patapsco River, Maryland.

Public Record Office, London, High Court of Admiralty, in Isabel M. Calder, editor, *Colonial Captivities, Marches and Journeys* (New York: Macmillian, 1935) 151–52.

7. Nathaniel Bacon and His Army Destroy Jamestown (1676)

The high-water mark of Bacon's Rebellion came in September 1676 when the rebel army of about 300 went up against Governor William Berkeley's force of 1000, well secured behind the walls of Jamestown. This account is from a Royal Commissioner's Report of 1677.

About day-break next morning six of Bacon's soldiers ran up to the palisades of the town and fired briskly upon the guard, retreating safely without any damage....But by their movings and drawings up about town, Bacon understood they intended a sally and accordingly prepares to receive them, draw up his men to the most advantageous places he could, and now expected them (but they observed to draw off again for some time) and was resolved to enter the town with them, as they retreated, as Bacon expected and foretold they would do. In this posture of expectation Bacon's forces continued for a hour till the watchman gave notice that they were drawn off again in town, so upon this Bacon's forces did so too. No sooner were they all on the rebel's side gone off and squandered but all on a sudden a sally is made by the governor's party, yet in this great hurry and disorder on the other side they so received them as that they forced them to retreat in as much confusion as they found them…

So great was the cowardice and baseness of the generality of Sir William Berkeley's party (being most of them men intent only upon plunder or compelled and hired into his service) that of all, at last there were only some 20 gentlemen willing to stand by him, the rest (whom the hopes or promise of plunder brought thither) being now all in haste to be gone to secure what they had got; so that Sir William Berkeley [was]…forced to leave the town to the mercy of the enemy.…

Bacon having early intelligence of the governor and his party's quitting the town the night before, enters it without any opposition, and soldier like considering of what importance a place of refuge that was, and might again be to the governor and his party, instantly resolves to lay it level with the ground, and the same night he became possessed of it, set fire to town, church and state house.…

Charles M. Andrews, editor, *Narratives of the Insurrections* (New York: Charles Scribner's Sons, 1915) 130–35.

8. Virginia's Act Concerning Servants and Slaves (1705)

Virginia's elites had for decades, in piecemeal fashion, tried to legislate a social distance between poor blacks and whites, making it less likely that they would join together in rebellion. That effort reached its apex with this act, which was soon copied in part or whole by legislatures in other colonies.

IV. All servants imported and brought into this country, by sea or land, who are not Christians in their native country, (except Turks and Moors in amity with her majesty, and others that can make due proof of their being free in England, or any other Christian country, before they were shipped, in order to transportation hither) shall be accounted and be slaves, and as such be here bought and sold notwithstanding a conversion to Christianity afterwards....

VII. All masters and owners of servants...shall not, at any time, give immoderate correction; neither shall, at any time, whip a Christian white servant naked, without an order from a justice of the peace....

XI. No negros, mulattos, or Indians, although Christians, or Jews, Moors, Mahometans, or other infidels, shall, at any time, purchase any Christian servant, nor any other, except of their own complexion, or such as are declared slaves by this act....

XIII. There shall be paid and allowed to every imported servant...at the time of service ended, by the master or owner of such servant, viz: To every male servant, ten bushels of Indian corn, thirty shillings in money, or the value thereof, in goods, and one well fixed musket or fuzee, of the value of twenty shillings, at least: and to every woman servant, fifteen bushels of Indian corn, and forty shillings in money, or the value thereof, in goods....

XIX. Whatsoever English, or other white man or woman, being free, shall intermarry with a negro or mulatto man or woman, bond or free, shall, by judgment of the county court, be committed to prison, and there remain, during the space of six months, without bail or mainprize; and shall forfeit and pay ten pounds current money of Virginia....

XXXIV. If any slave resist his master, or owner, or other person, by his or her order, correcting such slave, and shall happen to be killed in such correction, it shall not be accounted a felony; but the master, owner, and every such other person so giving correction, shall be free and acquit of all punishment and accusation for the same, as if such accident had never happened....

XXXVI. Baptism of slaves doth not exempt them from bondage; and all children shall be bond or free, according to the condition of their mothers....

William Wallar Hening, *The Statutes at Large; Being a Collection of All the Laws of Virginia, from the First Session of the Legislature, in the Year 1619, Vol. 3* (Philadelphia: Thomas Desilver, 1823) 447–51, 453–54, 459–60.

9. Call for Help from Enslaved Virginians (1723)

This anonymous letter came on the heels of a series of conspiracies that so unnerved Virginia planters that they sold the ringleaders abroad. They also passed a series of acts for "more effectual" control of slaves, a move that may have prompted such a dangerous letter. The writer belongs to his or her own brother, illustrating the interracial sexual relations that were so common in the colonies.

To the Right Reverend Father in God my Lord Arch Bishop of London.

This comes to satisfy your honor that there is in this land of Virginia a sort of people that is called mulattos which are baptized and brought up in the way of the Christian faith and follows the ways and rules of the Church of England and some of them has white fathers and some white mothers and there is in this land a law or act which keeps and makes them and their seed slaves forever....

We your humble and poor petitioners do beg Sir your aid and assistance in this one thing...which is that your honor will, by the help of our sovereign lord King George and the rest of the Rulers, will release us out of this cruel bondage, and this we beg for Jesus Christ's his sake who has commanded us to seek first the kingdom of God and all things shall be added unto us....

Here it is to be noted that...I am my brother's slave ....

We are commanded to keep holy the Sabbath day and we do hardly know when it comes for our task masters are as hard with us as the Egyptians was with the Children of Israel.... We are kept out of the Church, and matrimony is denied us, and to be plain they do look no more upon us than if we were dogs, which I hope when these strange lines comes to your Lordship's hands will be looked into....

And Sir we, your humble petitioners, do humbly beg...that our children may be brought up in the way of the Christian faith and our desire is that they may be learned the Lord's prayer, the [Apostle's] Creed, and the Ten Commandments, and that they may appear every Lord's day at Church...for our desire is that godliness should abound amongst us and we desire that our children be put to school and learned to read through the Bible....

We dare not subscribe any man's name to this for fear of our masters. For if they knew that we have sent home to your honor, we should go near to swing upon the gallows tree.

Fulham Papers, American Colonial Section, Lambeth Palace Library, London, in Thomas N. Ingersoll, "'Releese Us Out of This Cruell Bondegg': An Appeal from Virginia in 1723," *William and Mary Quarterly* 51,4 (October 1994): 777–82.

10. William Bull's Account of the Stono Rebellion (1739)

Lieutenant Governor William Bull of South Carolina gives us the only eyewitness account we have of the Stono Rebellion. In his report to the British Board of Trade, which oversaw colonial affairs, Bull notes that slaves' attempts to reach freedom in Spanish Florida were common and not infrequently successful.

My Lords,

I beg leave to lay before your Lordships an account of our affairs; first in regard to the desertion of our negroes, who are encouraged to it by a certain proclamation published by the King of Spain's order at St. Augustine declaring freedom to all negroes who should desert thither from the British colonies; since which several parties have deserted and are there openly received and protected. Many attempts of others have been discovered and prevented, notwithstanding which on the 9th of September last at night a great number of negroes arose in rebellion, broke open a store where they got arms, killed twenty-one white persons, and were marching the next morning in a daring manner out of the province, killing all they met, and burning several houses as they passed along the road. I was returning from Granville County with four gentlemen and met these rebels at eleven o'clock in the forenoon, and fortunately discerned the approaching danger [in] time enough to avoid it, and to give notice to the militia who on that occasion behaved with so much expedition and bravery, as by four o'clock the same day to come up with them and killed and took so many as put a stop to any further mischief at that time. Forty-four of them have been killed and executed. Some few yet remain concealed in the woods expecting the same fate, seem desperate.

Sainsbury Transcripts, Records in the British Public Record Office Relating to South Carolina, vol. 20, 179–80, South Carolina Department of Archives and History, Columbia, in Mark M. Smith, editor, *Stono: Documenting and Interpreting a Southern Slave Revolt* (Columbia: University of South Carolina Press, 2005) 16–17.

11. Antislavery Petition from Freeholders of Darien, Georgia (1739)

By the late 1730s, wealthy Savannah merchants were demanding slavery in Georgia. They were opposed by common folk who were just as determined to keep slavery out. The Scots Highlanders at Darien opposed slavery as well and listed its various disadvantages in a petition to General James Oglethorpe.

We are informed that our neighbors of Savannah have petitioned your Excellency for the liberty of having slaves. We hope, and earnestly entreat, that before such proposals are hearkened unto, your Excellency will consider our situation, and of what dangerous and bad consequence such liberty would be to us, for many reasons.

1. The nearness of the Spaniards [in Florida], who have proclaimed freedom to all slaves who run away from their masters, makes it impossible for us to keep them without more labor in guarding them than what we would be at to do their work.

2. We are laborious, and know a white man may be, by the year, more usefully employed than a Negro.

3. We are not rich, and becoming debtors for slaves, in case of their running away or dying, would inevitably ruin the poor master, and he become a greater slave to the Negro-Merchant, than the slave he bought could be to him.

4. It would oblige us to keep a guard duty at least as severe as when we expected a daily invasion [from the Spanish]. And if that was the case, how miserable would it be to us, and our wives and families, to have one enemy without and a more dangerous one in our bosoms!

5. It is shocking to human nature, that any race of mankind and their posterity should be sentenced to perpetual slavery; nor in justice can we think otherwise of it, than that they are thrown amongst us to be our scourge one day or other for our sins. And as freedom must be as dear to them as to us, what a scene of horror must it bring about! And the longer it is unexecuted, the bloody scene must be the greater. We therefore for our own sakes, our wives and children, and our posterity, beg your consideration, and entreat that instead of introducing slaves, you'll put us in the way to get us some of our countrymen, who, with their labor in time of peace, and our vigilance, if we are invaded, with the help of those, will render it a difficult thing to hurt us, or that part of the province we possess. We will for ever pray for your Excellency, and are with all submission, etc.

John Mackintosh-Moore
John Mackintosh-Linvilge
John Mackintosh-Son to L.
John Mackintosh-Bain
Jo. Cuthbert
James Mackay
Archibald McBain, his mark AMB
Ranald Macdonald
John Macklean
Jos. Burges, his mark BE
Donald Clark-first
Alex. Clark, Son of the above
Donald Clark-second
Donald Clark-third, his mark X
Hugh Morrison, his mark HM
Alex. Monro

John Macdonald Will Monro

Sir John Perceval Egmont Papers, Hargrett Rare Book and Manuscript Library, University of Georgia Libraries, Athens.

12. Indentured Servants and Slaves Escape Bondage (1764)

Indentured, or "indented," servants and slaves escaped often, sometimes together, as numerous advertisements in colonial newspapers attest. Rewards for their capture could range from 2 to 10 pounds each, a tidy sum when working folk might average only 30 pounds a year.

RUN away from the subscriber in King and Queen [County], Virginia, two white indented servants, a man and his wife. The man is English, about 5 feet 5 inches high, of a red complexion, wears his hair, is much sun-burnt, steps short and quick in his walk, is a brick maker by trade, and has a set of shoemaker's tools...his name is James Marrington. His wife is about 30 years of age, about 5 feet high, very thick, looks well, and has got good clothes; she is an Irish woman, and her name is Mary Marrington.

Run away likewise 4 Negroes, viz. Jack, a black thick fellow, about 30 years old, about 5 feet 6 inches high, speaks broken English; has been used to go by water, but of late to plantation business.... Dick, a dark mulatto, very lusty, and 25 years old, about 5 feet 8 inches high, a carpenter and painter by trade.... Daniel, a well set black fellow, about 5 feet 10 inches high, has been used to plantation business.... Dorcas, a small wench, about 5 feet high, has been used to house business.... They have all large bundles, as they stole several sheets and blankets, with other things. They were supposed to be seen crossing from Point Comfort to Little River in a small boat with a blanket sail last Saturday morning, and I imagine will make for North Carolina. Whoever apprehends the above servants and slaves, and delivers them to me, shall have ten pounds reward if taken in Virginia, if out thereof twenty pounds.

Pennsylvania Gazette (Philadelphia), 29 November 1764, in Billy G. Smith and Richard Wojtowicz, compilers, *Blacks Who Stole Themselves: Advertisements for Runaways in the Pennsylvania Gazette, 1728–1790* (Philadelphia: University of Pennsylvania Press, 1989) 73.

13. Rev. Devereux Jarratt on "Simple" People and "the Richer Sort" (ca. 1750)

Devereux Jarratt was born in Virginia, New Kent County, in 1733. He learned to read and write, made his way into the Anglican priesthood, and became a preacher of considerable reputation. He had three volumes of sermons published as well as an autobiography, which appeared five years after his death in 1801. Here Jarratt gives us some sense of rural life and class relations during his childhood in the colonial South.

My grandmother, as I was told, was a native of Ireland. Both she and my grandfather died before I was born, and I have no account of them, except that they were poor people, but industrious, and rather rough in their manners....

My father was brought up to the trade of a carpenter, at which he wrought till the very day before he died. He was a mild, inoffensive man, and much respected among his neighbors. My mother was the daughter of Joseph Bradley, of Charles City, a county bordering on New Kent. None of my ancestors, on either side, were either rich or great, but had the character of honesty and industry, by which they lived in credit among their neighbors, free from real want, and above the frowns of the world. This was also the habit, in which my parents were. They always had plenty of plain food and raiment, wholesome and good, suitable to their humble station, and the times in which they lived. Our food was altogether the produce of the farm...except a little sugar, which was rarely used; and our raiment was altogether my mother's manufacture, except our hats and shoes, the latter of which we never put on, but in the winter season. We made no use of tea or coffee for breakfast, or at any other time; nor did I know a single family that made use of them. Meat, bread and milk was the ordinary food of all my acquaintance. I suppose the richer sort might make use of those and other luxuries, but to such people I had no access. We were accustomed to look upon what we called gentle folk as beings of a superior order. For my part, I was quite shy of them, and kept off at a humble distance. A periwig, in those days, was a distinguishing badge of gentle folk—and when I saw a man riding the road near our house with a wig on, it would so alarm my fears and give me such a disagreeable feeling that, I dare say, I would run off as for my life. Such ideas of the difference between gentle and simple were, I believe, universal among all of my rank and age....

My parents neither sought nor expected any titles, honors, or great things, either for themselves or children. Their highest ambition was to teach their children to read, write, and understand the fundamental rules of arithmetic. I remember also they taught us short prayers and made us very perfect in repeating the Church Catechism. They wished us all to be brought up in some honest calling that we might earn our bread by the sweat of our brow as they did. Two of their children died in infancy, before I was born, and only four lived to years of maturity, three sons and a daughter. I was a great favorite, as being the youngest.

The Life of the Reverend Devereux Jarratt, Rector of Bath Parish, Dinwiddie County, Virginia, Written by Himself (Baltimore MD: Warner and Hanna, 1806) 13–16.

14. Reverend Charles Woodmason on the "Wild Peoples" of the Backcountry (1768)

Charles Woodmason presents another view, an English gentleman's view, of the South's common folk. A newly ordained Anglican minister, he took the unusual step of leaving the comforts of Charleston to become an itinerant backcountry minister. Though often condescending toward South Carolina's backcountry folk, he blamed their plight, especially their lack of adherence to the Anglican Church, largely on a legislature that failed to support church efforts in the region.

It is impossible that any gentleman not seasoned to the clime could sustain this. It would kill 99 out of 100. Nor is this a country or place where I would wish any gentleman to travel or settle, although religion and the state requires a number of ministers. Their ignorance and impudence is so very high as to be past bearing. Very few can read—fewer write.... They are very poor, owing to their extreme indolence, for they possess the finest country in America, and could raise but every thing. They delight in their present low, lazy, sluttish, heathenish, hellish life, and seem not desirous of changing it.... They will commit the grossest enormities, before my face, and laugh at all my admonition.....

Few or no books are to be found in all this vast country.... Nor do they delight in historical books or in having them read to them, as do our vulgar in England, for these people despise knowledge, and instead of honoring a learned person or anyone with knowledge be it in the arts, sciences, or languages, they despise and ill treat them, and this spirit prevails even among the principals of this province....

Set off this morning with a guide for Flatt Creek. Here I found a vast body of people assembled. Such a medley! Such a mixed multitude of all classes and complexions I never saw.... Most of these people had never before seen a minister, or heard the Lord's Prayer, service or sermon in their days. I was a great curiosity to them, and they were as great oddities to me. After service they went to reveling, drinking, singing, dancing, and whoring—and most of the company were drunk before I quitted the spot....

Ought such to be without the Word of God...? How lamentable to think, that the legislature of this province will make no provision—so rich, so luxurious, polite a people! Yet they are deaf to all solicitations, and look on the poor white people in a meaner light than their black slaves, and care less for them....

It will require much time and pains to new model and form the carriage and manners, as well as morals of these wild peoples.... The men with only a thin shirt and pair of breeches or trousers on—barelegged and barefooted. The women bareheaded, barelegged, and barefooted with only a thin shift and under petticoat. Yet I cannot break [them] of this, for the heat of the weather admits not any [but] thin clothing. I can hardly bear the weight of my wig and gown during service. The young women have a most uncommon practice, which I cannot break them of. They draw their shift as tight as possible to the body, and pin it close, to show the roundness of their breasts, and slender waists (for they are generally finely shaped) and draw their petticoat close to their hips to show the fineness of their limbs—so that they might as well be in Puri Naturalibus. Indeed nakedness is not censurable or indecent here, and they expose themselves often quite naked, without ceremony—rubbing themselves and their hair with bears oil [partly as an insect repellant] and tying it up behind in a bunch like the Indians—being hardly one degree removed from them....

Woodmason Manuscript Journal, New-York Historical Society, in Richard J. Hooker, *The Carolina Backcountry on the Eve of the Revolution: The Journal and Other Writings of Charles Woodmason* (Chapel Hill: University of North Carolina Press, 1953) 52–53, 56, 60–61.

2

Rebels, Tories, and Victims: The South's First Civil War

War, Taxes, and the Expansion Dispute

Woodmason was not alone among outsiders in disparaging backcountry folk in the mid-eighteenth century. Though tidewater gentry who owned land to the west usually welcomed even uninvited tenants who could pay them rent, growing populations meant more competition for good land and a corresponding increase in poverty rates. Poorer settlers continually pushed south through the piedmont and along the eastern slopes of the Appalachian range looking for better lands. Georgia was the last stop for these economic refugees, many of whom ended up as impoverished squatters unable to afford rent payments. Worsening poverty led Georgia to enact a vagabond law designed to discourage poor people from entering the colony. Those who could not pay land rents were subject to imprisonment or impressment into the British navy.

Still, Georgia and other Southern colonies needed more residents for militia service. The Seven Years War had broken out in 1756 between Britain and France, which claimed lands in North America from the Appalachians west to the Rockies and from Canada south to the Gulf of Mexico. Spain allied with the French. So did most Native Americans, which is why British settlers called it the French and Indian War. Although relations between the French and Native Americans were sometimes strained, natives tended to favor the French because they came mainly to trade. The British came not only to trade but also to take land.

Governor Henry Ellis of Georgia used diplomacy to keep peace with the Creeks, who were generally reluctant to take sides in any case. Not so with the Cherokees. In 1758, land disputes from Georgia to Virginia led to the Anglo-Cherokee War, which lasted until 1761. Cherokee resistance, together with French and Spanish raids along the coast, made clear to Southern governors that they needed stronger militias.

To get more men they needed more land, but the Native Americans were reluctant to give up more. That changed when the Treaty of Paris (1763) ended the Seven Years War. France lost its claims in North America. French Canadians were exiled, some ending up in Louisiana to become the later Cajuns. Spain got New Orleans as a result of the treaty, as well as virtually all areas west of the Mississippi. In exchange, it gave up Florida to Britain. Now the Native Americans were more dependent than ever on British trade, and Southern governors took full advantage. With the Treaty of Augusta, also signed in 1763, the governors of Virginia, the Carolinas, and Georgia forced major land cessions from native peoples.

Though the French and Indian War secured Britain's claim to North America east of the Mississippi, it left the royal treasury exhausted. Continued conflict with natives over land threatened to further drain the empire. Britain acted on these difficulties in two ways. First, to secure peace with the Native Americans, it announced the Proclamation of 1763 establishing a boundary running down the Appalachian Mountains, then cutting across Georgia's backcountry to the St. Marys River. All areas west and south of that line would be reserved to the Native Americans. Second, to rebuild the treasury, Parliament for the first time began imposing direct taxes on the American colonies.

Colonial upper classes generally resented both these moves. Some had already granted themselves land beyond the Appalachians and hoped to sell those lands or move settlers onto them who would pay rent. They balked at the taxes as well with the refrain "no taxation without representation." Since the colonies were not directly represented in Parliament, then that body should have no power to impose taxes on them. Parliament responded with the doctrine of virtual representation, arguing that every member of Parliament represented the interests of the empire, and America was part of that empire. Besides, the colonies had benefited enormously from the recent war by having the French and Spanish threats removed. They should help pay the war's cost as well as the cost of maintaining British armed forces in America. And the cry of "no taxation without representation" rang hypocritical in any case.

Colonial legislatures had for generations been taxing people who had neither land nor wealth enough to vote or hold office.

Wealthy Americans complained the loudest because the new taxes were aimed mainly at them. The first tax, the Revenue Act of 1764, targeted sugar, a relatively expensive import. It was followed in 1765 with the Stamp Act, which required that all kinds of written material—books, newspapers, legal documents, bills of lading, permits—be printed on embossed paper bearing a royal seal. The tax had little direct effect on most colonists because illiteracy rates were so high, especially in more rural and isolated Southern communities. A few church-sponsored and locally supported schools existed in the larger towns, but funding was so meager that good teachers were hard to keep.

Most colonial legislatures protested the new taxes, and all but one governor refused to enforce the Stamp Act until protests could be heard in London. Only Governor James Wright of Georgia tried to enforce the Stamp Act. He refused to call the legislature into secession to discuss the issue, and for several weeks closed the port of Savannah until the stamped paper arrived. A mob composed mainly of Savannah merchants, along with Stamp Act opponents from Charleston who had come to egg them on, hanged and burned a stamp master in effigy. They demanded that the port be opened with the Stamp Act ignored. Wright opened the port, but cleared shipping only with stamped paper. So eager were they to get the ships moving that most merchants and planters supported Wright's action.

Differing Directions of Discontent

Parliament repealed the Stamp Act in 1766 and reduced the tax on sugar, but a year later imposed new taxes with the Townshend Acts. These acts placed taxes on a variety of imported goods such as paper, paint, lead, glass, and tea. In response, the lower house of Massachusetts's legislature sent a circulating letter to all the colonies asking them to resist the Townshend Acts and boycott British goods. Virginia sent out a similar letter. The Carolinas supported a boycott, but opinions were more divided in Georgia. In 1768, Georgia's lower house passed resolutions supporting the right of protest and called the

Townshend Acts a violation of British constitutional principles, but stopped short of imposing a boycott. The next year Savannah merchants held two meetings calling for a boycott, but little came of the move.

Other colonies had more success with their boycott movements. In 1769 British imports dropped by 38 percent. The next year Parliament again relented and dropped most of the taxes. But it retained the tax on tea as an assertion of its right to raise revenue. Throughout the crisis over the Townshend Acts, only in Georgia did British imports continue to flow freely. Legislators in South Carolina were so upset with their neighbor to the south that some suggested invading the colony and closing its ports. They settled for a boycott of Georgia instead.

The South's upper classes also responded to the Townshend taxes by passing higher costs on to lower-class folk, many of whom did not qualify to vote or hold office. Land rents and taxes were going up as well. But most Southerners, especially those in the much-neglected backcountry, saw little benefit from the taxes they paid. The tidewater-dominated legislatures spent most public funds for their own benefit and ignored the needs of those farther inland. So did the state-supported Anglican Church. Few Anglican ministers ventured into the backcountry, leaving vast regions devoid of parishes and schools. Their apathy left the way open for Presbyterians, Methodists, and especially Baptists, who forcefully preached separation of church and state.

So high did taxes become that many yeomen who could not pay lost their land and were forced into tenancy. In the Carolinas, backcountry farmers began refusing to pay increased taxes and rents. By the late 1760s many had organized themselves into armed bands of "Regulators," and drove off tax and rent collectors—sometimes wearing tar and feathers. In North Carolina, when two of the movement's leaders were arrested, 700 armed farmers forced their release. At its height, in the three western North Carolina counties where it was concentrated, the Regulator movement enjoyed as much as 80 percent support.

In 1771, with backing from the North Carolina legislature, an eastern militia led by Governor William Tryon invaded the backcountry and crushed the rebellion at the Battle of Alamance. Six Regulators were hanged. Frightened refugees scattered across the Southern backcountry. Some ventured west across the Appalachians, joining Scots-Irish folk

The Proclamation Line of 1763, imposed by Britain to limit white expansion and keep peace with the Indians, infuriated colonial elites who wanted, and had already claimed, Indian land for themselves.

Map from Dixon Ryan Fox, *Harper's Atlas of American History* (1920).

who had earlier settled along the Watauga, Nolichucky, and Holston river valleys of present-day eastern Tennessee. At the time all of what is now Tennessee was claimed by North Carolina, though settlement there was technically prohibited since it was beyond the 1763 Proclamation Line. The settlers were ordered out, but refused to leave.

In 1772, the region's "Overmountain Men," as they were collectively called, negotiated a land lease with a faction of local Cherokees, though others led by Dragging Canoe opposed the lease. The settlers also established their own government under the Articles of the Watauga Association. No copy survives, but later documents suggest that the Overmountain Men assumed their independence from North Carolina while still considering themselves British subjects. Still, Britain refused to recognize their right to be there. With Dragging Canoe and his Cherokee followers claiming protection of the 1763 Proclamation, the future of Watauga was uncertain and tensions remained high.

Tensions were brewing in far-off Boston as well that would have consequences for all the colonies. In 1773, the British East India Company lowered prices on its tea, making it cheaper than tea smuggled in by Boston merchants trading illegally with the Dutch. The smugglers and their supporters, some disguised as Native Americans, dumped their competitor's tea in Boston Harbor and called it a protest against the tea tax. Parliament responded the next year with a series of laws known in America as the Coercive Acts or, as some called them, the Intolerable Acts. They temporarily closed the port of Boston and dissolved the Massachusetts legislature, allowing the royal governor direct rule. Merchants and political leaders in Massachusetts and other colonies howled in protest.

In September 1774, twelve colonial legislatures sent delegates to Philadelphia to form a united front against the Intolerable Acts. They declared their objection to the acts, petitioned Parliament for redress, and organized a boycott of British goods called the Continental Association. They also agreed to meet again the next spring should their efforts prove ineffective.

Reaction to the Intolerable Acts was more muted in Georgia. As the youngest of the thirteen colonies, Georgia's most prominent families still had strong family and economic ties to Britain. They had religious ties as well, being members of the Anglican Church. A major exception was St. Johns Parish, centered around the Midway settlement, which was populated mainly by South Carolina immigrants whose families had largely come from New England and had been in America for generations. Though nominally Congregationalist, nearly all of their ministers were Presbyterian.

Like the Midway planters, Savannah merchants most directly affected by the tax issue were among early leaders of the resistance in Georgia. In July and August of 1774, they and other resistance leaders met in Savannah at Peter Tondee's tavern and drew up the Tondee's Tavern Resolutions. They protested the Intolerable Acts and denied Parliament's right to tax the colonies. They also urged the planter-dominated General Assembly to send delegates to Philadelphia, but no response was forthcoming.

Making and Resisting the Break

Planters in other Southern colonies, most of whose families had been colonials for generations, were more prone to protest, though not unanimously so. Anglicanism was one factor that kept protest more muted among Southern elites, but economics ultimately trumped religion. Debt had much to do with who supported protest and who did not. Entail laws ensured that debts were passed on from one generation to the next. High interest rates from British financial institutions and import taxes worked against debt relief, especially for the lesser gentry.

The Navigation Acts also played a part in making debts harder to pay off. Under these laws, colonial exports could be sold only to British merchants, and it was British firms licensed to trade in the colonies that set prices for colonial goods. Many of these houses extended credit to colonial planters and merchants, then set prices that made it difficult to repay that debt. By 1775, Southern planters were collectively £2,000,000 in debt to Britain despite a £90,000 positive trade balance. Virginians George Washington and Thomas Jefferson, two early leaders of the resistance movement, were both heavily indebted to British firms. The further in debt a planter was, the more he tended to support resistance and rebellion.

Beginning in 1775, Whigs conducted a reign of terror as Committees of Public Safety tortured, exiled, and sometimes killed anyone who refused to swear allegiance to the independence movement. In this scene, Tory suspects are hauled up on a "liberty pole" and a goose is plucked in preparation for the victims being tarred and feathered.

Engraving from the Library of Congress.

In May, a month after fighting broke out at Lexington and Concord in Massachusetts, the Second Continental Congress met to oversee armed resistance. Again, Georgia's Assembly sent no representatives. In July, a competing body calling itself the Provincial Congress met in Savannah. It declared Georgia no longer subject to acts of Parliament, though still nominally loyal to King George, and sent representatives to Philadelphia.

That same month, the Continental Congress drew up a document laying out its rationale for rebellion, the "Declaration of the Causes and Necessity of Taking Up Arms." Congress also authorized the formation of an army and placed George Washington in command. Washington was seen as a figure who might bring more Southerners into the fray. And his appointment may have helped. By winter 1775-76, every one of the South's royal governors had been driven from office, though the region's assemblies might have disowned them in any case. Most assemblymen were already leaning toward resistance and had taken to calling themselves Whigs after Britain's liberal Whig Party, which generally opposed the more authoritarian Tory Party. Now in armed rebellion, Whigs were called simply rebels by British loyalists, or Tories as they came to be known.

Whig assemblies throughout the South established councils of safety to act as executive bodies, enforce the ban on British trade, and support rebellion generally. Through late 1775 and into 1776, these state councils set up local committees through which they instituted a reign of terror. Southerners suspected of loyalty to Britain were forced to sign an oath of allegiance to the Continental Association. Most complied to preserve their lives and property. "If a Tory refused to join," recalled Savannah resident Elizabeth Johnston, "he was imprisoned, and tarred and feathered."

Though armed and dangerous, the Whigs inspired little genuine loyalty among common folk. The Continental army itself reflected that ambivalence. It was a small force of mostly middle-class soldiers led by upper-class officers and was beaten every time it dared challenge the British army. Most lower-class folk, who largely felt they had nothing to fight for, were staying out of the conflict. But without more men, the Continental cause could not hope to succeed. By early 1776, Whig leaders were increasingly using words like "freedom" and "equality" in an effort to draw common folk into what by then had become an independence movement.

The culmination of that effort came in July 1776 when Congress issued the Declaration of Independence. Though generally viewed as a statement of grievances, the Declaration's main purpose was to draw more common folk into active support for independence and into the Continental army. By stating in vague terms "that all men are created equal, that they are endowed by their Creator with certain unalienable rights, that among these are life, liberty, and the pursuit of happiness," delegates hoped to cast the war as a fight for equality without taking firm steps toward establishing genuine equality.

Though Thomas Jefferson was the Declaration's primary author, the phrase "life, liberty, and pursuit of happiness" was not entirely original to Jefferson. British political philosopher John Locke had used a similar phrase in his *Second Treatise of Government* (1689) to justify Parliament's ouster of King James II. In doing so, he argued that governments were established to protect life, liberty, and property. King James, he asserted, had become destructive of those ends, giving Parliament the right to replace him. That right was well established in British tradition by the time of the American Revolution. Now Thomas Jefferson used it to justify ousting the king's government in America. But he removed the word "property" because the document was aimed largely at drawing people into the independence movement who held little or no property.

Ironically, among the grievances listed was that the British had "endeavoured to bring on the inhabitants of our frontiers, the merciless Indian Savages." In fact, the British had since 1763 tried to keep peace with Native Americans by limiting white settlement to areas east of the Appalachians. It was colonial elites, eager for new lands and rents, who were pushing for white settlement beyond the Proclamation Line. For that reason primarily, most Native Americans favored maintaining the British Empire in North America. They well knew that if British authority collapsed, the Proclamation Line would also fall and their lands would be claimed by Congress, which, though professing that all men were created equal, seldom treated Native Americans with much regard.

Nor did Congress treat women with much regard. Equality of any sort was beyond the pale for women as far as Congress was concerned, even for upper-class women. The founding fathers generally assumed, or wished to believe, that right-thinking women wanted no part of public life in any case. Jefferson represented the founders' attitudes when he wrote that women had "the good sense to value domestic happiness above all" and were "too wise to wrinkle their foreheads with politics."

Created Equal?

Few if any delegates to the Continental Congress held freedom or equality as principles in themselves. Many, including Jefferson, had claimed ownership of black people their entire adult lives and would continue to do so until the day they died. Nor had they ever shown much sympathy for equality among whites. Most had for years been members of their respective colonial legislatures and had made no moves toward extending political representation to lower class folk. On the contrary, when farmers and tenants fought back against mistreatment, such as they did during the Regulator movement, they were brutally suppressed by the very men who were now asking them to take up arms for an undefined equality.

Though the Declaration proclaimed equality, at least among men, it said nothing about what that meant or how it would be established. Nowhere did the document promise even soldiers the right to vote. Small wonder that so few responded to the call. Many of those who did were motivated mainly by the opportunity for social and economic advancement. Whig promises of confiscated Tory property led some poorer men to join the fight. A chance to advance through the ranks prompted others to enlist. Still, recruits were relatively few. In his study of that era, *A People Numerous and Armed,* historian John Shy estimates that perhaps a fifth of the entire colonial population was actively rebellious against the British Empire. At least as many opposed independence, and Tory loyalists were most numerous in the Southern colonies. Even so, most colonists, Southerners included, simply tried to stay out of the war, seeing little benefit in it for themselves no matter which side prevailed.

Whigs in most Southern colonies did throw a bone to religious dissenters by disestablishing Anglicanism as the official church, though this was more a symbolic cutting of ties with England than anything else. Some colonies went further than that. With strong backing from Baptist ministers, Thomas Jefferson led the effort for complete separation of church and state in Virginia. Georgia not only disestablished Anglicanism but also wrote into its new state constitution that "no clergyman of any denomination shall be allowed a seat in the legislature."

As to who should sit in Southern state legislatures and elect their members, radical and conservative Whigs often disagreed. Conservatives tended to want voting and office holding restricted to men of considerable property. Radicals usually supported broader political rights as a way of drawing more common folk into the independence movement. In something of a compromise, state constitutions typically split the difference, granting the vote to free men over the age of twenty-one who owned property or paid taxes while imposing much more substantial requirements for office holding. In no case did any Southern state grant unrestricted white male suffrage.

For voting rights, South Carolina and Maryland required ownership of 50 acres. Virginia stipulated 25 acres of improved land or 500 acres unimproved. Only in Georgia and North Carolina were there no land ownership requirements, but they did mandate tax payment. To qualify to run for a seat in the state legislatures, requirements were much higher. North Carolina mandated that senators own 300 acres of land. Maryland required its senators to own property worth £2,000 sterling. In Maryland's lower house, membership was somewhat less restrictive at £500. Georgia's unicameral legislature was limited to men with 250 acres or property worth £250, a small fortune at a time when schoolteachers might earn £60 annually and unskilled workers considerably less.

Aside from property qualifications for voting and office holding, the gentry secured its traditional power in the state legislatures by counting slaves as persons for legislative apportionment. Doing so meant that tidewater voters, where slaveholders dominated, had greater proportional representation than the backcountry with its larger population of poorer whites. Still, many conservative Whigs were far from satisfied. Joseph Clay, a Savannah conservative, complained that

Georgia's new constitution was too "democratical" in giving political voice to "those whose ability or situation in life does not entitle them to it." With such attitudes so common among Whig leaders, it seems little wonder that most common whites felt that they had little at stake in the conflict. Neither side promised them much more than they already had, which was not much to begin with.

Race, Class, and Questions of Liberty

The British tried to establish a standing alliance with the Cherokees and Creeks to supplement their forces in the Southern backcountry. Though most Native Americans tended to favor continued British control, unsure of who might win and not wanting to alienate trading partners, most adopted a neutral stance early in the war. But fear of a British-Native American alliance led to several Rebel attempts to drive both Cherokees and Creeks farther into the backcountry during 1777-78. The resulting famine spoiled British plans, though some Cherokees and Creeks did later join Tory bands in their raids against Whig militia.

The British also tried to coax blacks to their side by freeing those who abandoned their rebel owners. In November 1775, Virginia's royal governor, the Earl of Dunmore, issued what came to be called Dunmore's Proclamation freeing any indentured servants and slaves who would join his royal forces. Thousands flocked to British lines, some enlisting with an all-black fighting force known as Dunmore's Ethiopian Regiment. Among the new freedmen was Henry Washington, who had belonged to George Washington.

In June 1779, Sir Henry Clinton, commanding general of Royal forces in America, expanded Dunmore's efforts with his own Philipsburg Proclamation, freeing all rebel-owned slaves in America. Thousands more enslaved people responded to the call, so many that the British could not receive them all. Many hundreds of disappointed refugees were turned away. Even so, slaves refused to return to their owners. Some escaped to the cities. Others fled west to the mountains or south to Florida.

Hoping to gain freedom from the Whigs, some blacks offered their services to the Continental army early in the war, but George

Washington at first resisted efforts to have them as soldiers. In 1779, at the urging of South Carolina's Lieutenant Colonel John Laurens, son of a prominent slaveholder, Congress pushed for a plan to free and arm slaves in South Carolina and Georgia. Though slaveholders ultimately killed the proposal, at least 5,000 blacks eventually served in the Continental army. Some were free. Others were refugees who passed themselves off as free. Still others served as substitutes for their owners, with their families held hostage in slavery. Washington had reservations, but he needed their help.

Having no authority to impose direct conscription, Congress tried to get more men by encouraging the states to conduct militia drafts. Southern state legislatures cooperated but fell far short of their goals. Common folk saw obvious contradictions in being forced to fight a war for "liberty." That wealthy men could avoid the draft by hiring a substitute or paying an exemption fee led many to call the struggle a "rich man's war." In one North Carolina community, a resident informed Whig General Nathanael Greene that "so great was the aversion to military service in this neighborhood that out of fifty-eight persons, fifty-six were found to have artificial hernia." Authorities commonly jailed draft resisters, releasing them only if they promised to enlist. Many complied, then deserted at their earliest opportunity.

From the earliest days of the Revolution, Continental forces faced one defeat after another for lack of soldiers. Unable to get enough help at home, Congress begged for help from Europe, especially France. The French government certainly saw advantages for itself in depriving Britain of its most valuable American colonies. It would open up new possibilities for trade and weaken the British Empire. But France had only recently lost a war with Britain in North America. It was not eager to repeat that humiliation. France would stay out of the conflict until the Continentals could demonstrate some ability to stand against the British army.

That demonstration finally came in October 1777 when a Continental force won America's first major victory at the Battle of Saratoga in New York. American diplomats in Paris played up the win for all it was worth, and in 1778 France entered the war. The decision forced a major change in British strategy. Up to that point, Britain's military efforts had

For all their talk of liberty, South Carolina's John Laurens was virtually alone among planter aristocrats in advocating liberty for the enslaved. He wrote to a friend in 1776: "How can we, whose jealousy has been alarmed more at the name of oppression sometimes than at the reality, reconcile to our spirited assertions of the rights of mankind the galling abject slavery of our negroes?" The young officer, a favorite of George Washington, died at age twenty-seven after being shot off his horse.

Portrait by Charles Wilson Peale, 1780.

focused on the more rebellious Northern colonies. Once they were under control, so the plan went, the Southern colonies, with their larger Loyalist populations, could be easily subdued. Moses Kirkland, a prominent South Carolina Tory who had once been a leading Regulator, seemed to confirm that assumption when he wrote that thousands of Southern Loyalists were ready to form militias as soon as British forces landed on the coast. According to Kirkland, all they needed were arms and a few experienced officers to coordinate with British regulars. Kirkland himself became a colonel and was placed in commanded of a Tory battalion.

As for the Continentals, certainly their forces in the South under General Robert Howe had given the British little cause for concern. Their only major military action had been two attempted invasions of British Florida in 1777 and 1778, both of which had failed miserably. But with France now in the war, British strategists knew that they would have a difficult time coping with a combined force of Continentals and French in the North. So they quickly shifted their efforts to the South.

A Southern Civil War

In December 1778, British troops launched a surprise attack on Savannah and took the city almost unopposed. Fourteen hundred Georgia men rushed to joined the Tory militia. By the end of January British regulars and Loyalists had pushed all the way up to Augusta and Georgia was once more a royal colony.

After fending off an assault of Continental and French forces against Savannah in October 1779, Royal troops were ready to move against Charleston. They began siege operations in late March 1780 and captured Charleston in less than two months. The loss of the city, along with the capture of its 5,000 defenders, was a serious blow to the Continental army. It was the largest surrender of United States soldiers until 1862 when Confederates forced the surrender of Union forces at Harpers Ferry, Virginia.

From Charleston, British forces swept into the South Carolina interior. In late May, Loyalists under Banestre Tarlton massacred Continental troops at the Battle of Waxhaws. Three months later, Lord

Charles Cornwallis led the British to victory at the Battle of Camden, this time destroying Continental forces and securing South Carolina for the Crown.

Over the following months, a bitter partisan war tore the Carolina backcountry apart. Buoyed by British victories, Tory militias increasingly took up arms. Whigs rallied around their militia commanders and harassed British troops and their Tory allies. Ambushes were common, and little mercy was shown on either side. Tory and Whig raiders put each others lives and lands, and those of their less aggressive neighbors, in constant danger. Loyalties shifted frequently depending on which side happened to be locally dominant at any particular time. Most men tried to remain neutral, preferring to stay put and protect their homes from raiders rather than become raiders themselves. But professions of neutrality were nearly always taken as opposition, with both Whig and Tory partisans holding a "with-us-or-against-us" attitude.

Continental fortunes began to change in October 1780 at the Battle of Kings Mountain on the western Carolina border. With British forces threatening the backcountry, Whigs hastily organized a militia composed mainly of Overmountain Men, who had their own reasons for supporting independence. Many were Scots-Irish who had nurtured a hatred for Royal authority ever since their ancestors fled Scotland. More recent trouble with Royal authority had come with their settlement beyond the Proclamation Line of 1763. At Kings Mountain, these Overmountain Men wiped out a Tory militia, killing or capturing nearly the entire force. In January 1781, not far south of Kings Mountain, Continentals inflicted a defeat on Tarleton's men at the Battle of Cowpens. The next month, British forces suffered another setback when Whig militiamen under Colonel Henry "Lighthorse Harry" Lee massacred a Tory militia force at the Battle of Haw River in central North Carolina.

Partisan fighting defined the war in Georgia's upcountry as well. Atrocities were common on both sides. Whig Colonel John Dooly, operating without orders (as most raiders did), wrought havoc in the region until a Tory band murdered him in his bed. In spring 1781, Whig raiders killed around one hundred suspected Loyalists, both government officials and common settlers.

Women were sometimes the victims of guerilla raids, but not always easily victimized. One of the most popular legends to emerge from the period involved Nancy Hart, whose family lived in what would later become Elbert County, Georgia. She and her husband Benjamin were strong Whig supporters. Benjamin served as a lieutenant in the Georgia militia, and Nancy sometimes spied for Whig forces. One day while Benjamin was away, six Tories showed up at the Hart cabin demanding to be fed. After her unwanted guests stacked their arms and helped themselves to dinner, Nancy grabbed one of their guns and threatened to shoot anyone who moved. She killed one man who lunged at her, wounded a second, and held the rest at bay while her young daughter went to find her father. When Benjamin arrived with several Whig friends, they hanged the Tories from a nearby tree. Hart County was later named for Nancy, the only Georgia county to be named for a woman.

Though Continentals and Whig militiamen had achieved some success in the Southern backcountry, General Nathanael Greene, commanding the Southern Continental army, knew that he was in a dangerous position. He was outnumbered by Cornwallis and his men. Lacking sufficient popular support to raise an army large enough to defeat Cornwallis, Greene tried to wear British troops down by forcing them to chase him though the North Carolina backcountry. Only once did he give battle, at Guilford Courthouse in March 1781. Though Greene lost the fight, he inflicted heavy casualties on his opponents. Still, Cornwallis felt that Georgia and the Carolinas had been secured and that Greene's army was no major threat. So he turned north hoping to secure Virginia as well and end the war. It was a strategic blunder from which the British would never recover.

Greene was not as weakened as Cornwallis had thought. When Cornwallis led his men into Virginia, Greene did not follow. Instead, he turned south, driving his forces through the Carolinas and into Georgia. Augusta fell to the Continentals on 5 June, and most of the Southern backcountry was under Whig control. Greene was ruthless in his efforts to maintain that control. He viewed any man who refused to serve with his forces as a Tory, and Toryism would not be tolerated. In a letter to Thomas Jefferson, Greene wrote that during a raid on a presumed

Loyalist settlement, he and his men "made a dreadful carnage of them, upwards of one hundred were killed and most of the rest cut to pieces. It had a very happy effect on those disaffected persons, of which there are too many in this country."

Tories in Retreat

Despite such setbacks Tories, particularly those who had been driven from Augusta, were hardly ready to give up the fight. But their dreams of retaking Augusta and the backcountry proved futile. By fall 1781, the impact of French intervention had made itself felt and things were going badly for the British on all fronts. In fact, had it not been for French forces, the independence movement would likely not have succeeded. That became clear to Cornwallis when he entered Virginia and found that Washington's army outnumbered his own by almost two to one. Nearly half of Washington's troops were Frenchmen.

By September, Washington had trapped Cornwallis at Yorktown and began siege operations. Cornwallis hoped to evacuate his men by sea, but British naval forces were blocked and defeated by the French in September at the Battle of the Chesapeake. In October, Cornwallis finally surrendered, freeing Continental and French troops to pressure the British in their remaining strongholds.

By spring 1782, both sides knew that the war was winding down and took no major military action. But Southern legislatures, like some of their Northern counterparts, did flex their muscles against British Loyalists. Though most remained in their native states unmolested, wealthy land-rich Tories became special targets. In Georgia, for example, the Assembly passed a Confiscation and Banishment Act naming 277 specific individuals as guilty of treason. It ordered them to forfeit their land and leave the state within sixty days. The act also established categories of unnamed persons who at any time might have professed loyalty to the British crown during the course of the Revolution. They too could have their property confiscated by the state.

Such acts essentially gave states license to take nearly any land they wanted since few Southerners had remained steadfastly loyal to either side throughout the conflict. Rather than adhering to abstract notions of liberty on the one hand or fidelity to King George on the other, most followed the more practical course of trying to protect what land they had by acquiescing to whichever government seemed dominant at the time. Most Southerners had little difficulty expressing loyalty to the Whigs from 1775 through 1778 when the British had abandoned the Southern colonies. Loyalties were more fluid, especially in the backcountry, between 1779 and 1781 when the British held much, and sometimes most, of the region.

By the end of 1782, British forces had left and the royal governors were gone. With them went tens of thousands of Tories, many of them blacks who had taken refugee behind British lines. Some went to Britain, but most took land grants in British North America (now Canada) and the Caribbean.

After the war, Britain set up a Loyalist commission to compensate exiled Tories for their lost property. As a percentage of population, the number of claims from former Southerners totaled more than those from any other region. Claims from former Savannah residents totaled more than those from any other American city. Clearly Southerners had been divided in their loyalties during the war and remained considerably so even at its end.

Documents

1. Grievances from the South Carolina Backcountry (1767)

Tensions rose in proportion as coastal elites increasingly shifted financial burdens to backcountry Southerners while ignoring their needs. This petition from representatives of South Carolina's Regulator movement, addressed to the colony's governor and legislature, outlines many of their concerns.

We are *Free-Men*—British Subjects—Not Born *Slaves*—We contribute our proportion in all public taxations, and discharge our duty to the public equally with our fellow provincials, yet we do not participate with them in the rights and benefits which they enjoy, though equally entitled to them....

The trial of small and mean causes by a single magistrate...is now become an intolerable grievance partly through the ignorance of some justices, and the bigotry and partiality of others. Individuals are rather oppressed than relieved by their decisions, for persons are oft times saddled with ten or twelve pounds costs on a debt of as many shillings.... By our birth right as Britons, we ought for to be tried by a jury of our peers....

Sixty thousand pounds public money (of which we must pay the greater part, as being levied on the consumer) hath lately been voted for to build an exchange for the merchants, and a ballroom for the ladies of Charlestown; while near sixty thousand of us back settlers have not a minister or a place of worship to repair to! As if we were not worth even the thought of, or deemed as savages and not Christians!

Oppression will make wise men mad, and many sober persons among us are become almost desperate in seeing the non-attention given to these and other matters.... Can we vote for members of the Assembly, or choose vestry men, or elect parish officers when we have no churches to repair to...? Can our poor be taken charge of when there hath been neither minister, church wardens, or vestry...? The poor and sick, the aged and infirm, must be relieved and supported in some manner, and not left to perish....

Through the non-establishment of public schools, a great multitude of children are now grown up in the greatest ignorance of every thing, save vice, in which they are adept. Consequently they lead idle and immoral lives, for, they having no sort of education, naturally follow hunting, shooting, racing, drinking, gaming, and every species of wickedness....

New settlers greatly repent of their coming out here.... The sober part of them would more willingly return than remain here. They have indeed land given them, and may, with industry, raise a bare subsistence. But they are discouraged from any bold pursuits, or exerting their laudable endeavors to make improvements, through the uncertainty that attends us all, i.e. whether in the end they may reap the fruits of their labor....

The above particulars are, with greatest deference and respect, submitted to the wisdom of the legislature. In the name, by desire, and on behalf of the back inhabitants, and signed in their presence by us, their deputies

Benjamin Hart
John Scott
Moses Kirkland
Thomas Woodward

Fulham Palace Collection, Manuscripts Division, Library of Congress, in Richard J. Hooker, editor, *The Carolina Backcountry on the Eve of the Revolution: The Journal and Other Writings of Charles Woodmason* (Chapel Hill: University of North Carolina Press, 1953) 213–33.

2. The Hillsborough Riot in North Carolina (1770)

In September 1770, North Carolina Regulators numbering about 150 burst into a session of the Orange County superior court and assaulted court officers. Courts in the backcountry had for years been ordering enforcement of tax and rent payments on people who had little or no representation in the legislature. Nor had they had any say regarding who occupied the jury box. Richard

Henderson, who was the court's presiding judge, wrote the following account to Governor William Tryon.

On Monday last being the second day of Hillsborough Superior Court, early in the morning the town was filled with a great number of these people, shouting, hallooing, and making a considerable tumult in the streets. At about 11 o'clock the court was opened, and immediately the house was filled as close as one man could stand by another; some with clubs, others with whips and switches, few or none without some weapon! When the house had become so crowded that none more could well get in, one of them (whose name I think is called Fields) came forward and told me he had something to say before I proceeded to business.... He proceeded to let me know that he spoke for the whole body of the people called Regulators.... They also charged the court with injustice at the preceding term and objected to the jurors appointed by the Inferior Court and said they would have them altered and others appointed....After spending upwards of half and hour in this disagreeable situation the mob cried out "Retire, Retire, and let the Court go on," upon which most of the Regulators went out and seemed to be in consultation in a party by themselves. The little hope of peace derived from this piece of behavior was very transient, for in a few minutes Mr. Williams, an attorney of that court, was coming in and had advanced near the door when they fell on him in a most furious manner with clubs and sticks of enormous size and 'twas with great difficulty he saved his life by taking shelter in a neighboring store house. Mr. Fanning[1] was next the object of their fury. Him they seized and took with a degree of violence not to be described, from off the bench where he had retired for protection and assistance and with hideous shouts of barbarian cruelty dragged him by the heels out of doors while others engaged in dealing out blows with such violence that I made no doubt his life would instantly become a sacrifice to the rage and madness. However Mr. Fanning, by a manly exertion, miraculously broke hold and fortunately

[1]Edmund Fanning, member of the North Carolina legislature and close associate of Governor William Tryon, who had extorted money from backcountry folk but had paid only a nominal fine.

jumped into a door that saved him from immediate dissolution. During this uproar several of them told me with oaths of great bitterness that my turn would be next. I will not deny but in this frightful affair my thoughts were much engaged on my own protection, but it was not long before James Hunter [a Regulator leader] and some others of their chieftains came and told me not to be uneasy for that no man should hurt me on proviso [that] I would set and hold court to the end of the term. I took advantage of this proposal and made no scruple at promising what was not in my intention to perform: for the terms they would admit me to hold a court on were that no lawyer, the Kings Attorney excepted, should be admitted into court, and that they would stay and see justice impartially done.... In about four or five hours their rage seemed to subside a little and they permitted me to adjourn court and conducted me with great parade to my lodgings.... At about ten o'clock that evening, took an opportunity of making my escape by a back way, and left poor Colonel Fanning and the little borough in a wretched situation.

William L. Saunders, editor, *The Colonial Records of North Carolina, Vol. 8, 1769–1771* (Raleigh: Josephus Daniels, 1890) 241–44.

3. An Effort to Bring Backcountry Southerners into the Independence Movement (1775)

In summer 1775, South Carolina's Council of Safety sent a delegation into the backcountry to gain the support of frontier folk for the independence movement, or the "Association" as it was called. One of the delegation members was the Reverend William Tennent, a Presbyterian. His journal makes clear how indifferent, even hostile, many backcountry Southerners were toward supporting colonial elites in their effort to throw off Parliament's authority in America.

[August] 14th.... The pamphlet sent up by the [royal] governor has done much damage here, it is at present their Gospel. It seems as though nothing could be done here, as they have industriously taught the people that no man from Charleston can speak the truth, and that all the papers are full of lies....

20th.... Set off at half after eight for King creek, to a muster of Capt. Robert McAfee's company, after a hard and rough ride of twenty miles, in which crossed King creek at a beautiful rocky ford; found about one hundred people assembled, among whom were some of the most obstinate opposers of the [Continental] Congress. Spoke to the people at large on the state of America. They seemed much affected towards the close, but afterwards aided by two gainsaying Baptist preachers, they all refused to sign the Association except ten.... Parted and crossed the end of King's Mountain about dark, and rode fifteen miles to Col. Polk... having traveled in all thirty-eight miles. This has been a hard day's work.

24th....Went eighteen miles to the general muster, at Mr. Ford's, on Enoree. We found that the captains had dissuaded their people from coming, and met only about 270 men. The gang of [Tory] leaders were there all double-armed with pistols. Mr. Drayton began to harangue them, and was answered in a most scurrilous manner by [Moses?] Kirkland, when Mr. D----- interrupted him, and a terrible riot seemed on the point of happening....I replied to Kirkland, and went at large into the argument; had a most solemn and impressive discourse for an hour and a quarter. Kirkland remained, but the people mostly retired and left only a small circle....a dark design appears to sit upon the brow of the leaders of the party.

[September] 4th....Arose with the early dawn, took a guide and crossed Savannah river, at Cawan's ferry....Met with one of the *King's men,* as they are absurdly called, from whom I learned, that they expected a meeting on Wednesday of all their comrades on the banks of the Savannah, about twenty miles above Augusta, from which, from sundry circumstances, it appears that they mean some stroke.... Consulted with Mr. Drayton and found that on a discovery of the intention of Kirkland and the others to embody on Wednesday and go upon some enterprise, he had ordered the Regiment of horse to march, and the militia....I consented to make the best of my way to Charleston, to lay a state of the whole matter before the Council of Safety.

Robert W. Gibbes, editor, *Documentary History of the American Revolution, 1764-1776* (New York: D. Appleton, 1855) 228–30, 234–35.

4. Lord Dunmore's Freedom Proclamation (1775)

On November 7, 1775, Virginia's royal governor, John Murray, the fourth Earl of Dunmore, issued a proclamation freeing any slaves or indentured servants who would take up arms for the Loyalist cause. Though he had been accepting their services for months, this document publicly advertised the practice and invited more escapees to come.

A Proclamation.

As I have ever entertained hopes that an accommodation might have taken place between Great Britain and this colony, without being compelled by my duty to this most disagreeable but now absolutely necessary step, rendered so by a body of armed men, unlawfully assembled, firing on His Majesty's tenders, and the formation of an army, and that army now on their march to attack His Majesty's troops, and destroy the well disposed subjects of this colony: To defeat such treasonable purposes, and that all such traitors, and their abetters, may be brought to justice, and that the peace and good order of this colony may be again restored, which the ordinary course of the civil law is unable to effect, I have thought fit to issue this my Proclamation, hereby declaring, that until the aforesaid good purposes can be obtained, I do in virtue of the power and authority to me given by His Majesty, determine to execute martial law, and cause the same to be executed throughout this colony.... And I do hereby further declare all indented Servants, Negroes, or others (appertaining to Rebels) free that are able and willing to bear arms, they joining His Majesty's troops as soon as may be, for the more speedily reducing this colony to a proper sense of their duty to His Majesty's Crown and Dignity....

Printed Ephemera Collection, Rare Book and Special Collections Division, Library of Congress, Washington DC.

5. Virginia Slaves Claim Their Liberty (1775)

Within days of Dunmore's Proclamation, Robert Brent of Stafford County lost one slave and two mares (document A). Brent seemed puzzled that his slave, apparently better treated than most, would try to claim liberty. He seemed reluctant to acknowledge, perhaps even to himself, that enslavement might in itself be ill treatment. Edmund Ruffin of Prince George County lost four slaves, also presumed to have escaped to Dunmore's forces (document B).

A.

RAN away last night from the subscriber, a Negro Man named CHARLES, who is a very shrewd sensible fellow and can both read and write; and as he always waited upon me, he must be well known through most of Virginia and Maryland. He is very black, has a large nose, and is about 5 feet 8 or 10 inches high. He took a variety of clothes...stole several of shirts, a pair of saddle bags, and two mares.... From many circumstances, there is reason to believe he intends an attempt to get to Lord Dunmore; and as I have reason to believe his design of going off was long premeditated, and that he has gone with some accomplices, I am apprehensive he may prove daring and resolute, if endeavored to be taken. His elopement was from no cause of complaint, or dread of a whipping (for he has always been remarkably indulged, and indeed too much so) but from a determined resolution to get Liberty, as he conceived, by flying to Lord Dunmore.

Virginia Gazette (Williamsburg), 18 November 1775.

B.

RUN away from the subscriber, the 26th of November last, 4 negro men, viz. HARRY, Virginia born, 5 feet 8 or 9 inches high, 30 years of age, a dark mulatto, with long bushy hair.... He has worked several years at the carpenter's and wheelwright's trade, and can glaze and paint. LEWIS, an outlandish, short, thick fellow, remarkably bow-legged, and excellent wheelwright and wagon maker, and very good blacksmith.

He carried with him, amongst other clothes, a blue suit. AARON, a likely Virginia born fellow, of the middle size, stoops a little, has a hoarse voice, and had on the usual clothing of negroes. MATTHEW, a Virginia born, dark mulatto, 18 years of age, 5 feet 8 or 9 inches high, stammers a little, and speaks quick, when surprised, and is close kneed. These 4 went off in a yawl with two others, who have been since committed to the public jail.... I conclude the other 4 are in Lord Dunmore's service.

Virginia Gazette (Williamsburg), 13 January 1776.

6. John Laurens Proposes Freeing Slaves (1778)

Most men from slaveholding families supported the independence movement but objected to blacks serving in the Continental army. One who did not was John Laurens, son of a rice planter with holdings along the South Carolina and Georgia coasts. Educated in London, John was drawn to antislavery ideas. During the Revolution, John became one of the most dashing officers in the Continental army, a favorite aide-de-camp of Washington's and best friends with Alexander Hamilton. In January 1778, after receiving a letter from his father, then president of the Continental Congress, in which the elder Laurens expressed some discomfort with slavery, John wrote back with a bold proposal.

Headquarters, Valley Forge,
January 14, 1778

I barely hinted to you my dearest Father my desire to augment the Continental Forces from an untried source. I wish I had any foundation to ask for an extraordinary addition to those favors which I have already received from you. I would solicit you to cede me a number of your able bodied men slaves, instead of leaving me a fortune. It would bring about a twofold good, first it would advance those who are unjustly deprived of the rights of mankind to a state which would be a proper gradation between abject slavery and perfect liberty, and besides it would reinforce the defenders of liberty with a number of gallant soldiers. Men who have the habit of subordination almost indelibly impressed on them, would have one very essential qualification of soldiers. I am persuaded that if I could obtain authority for the purpose I would have a corps of such men trained, uniformly clad, equipped, and ready in every respect to act at the opening of the next campaign. The ridicule that may be thrown on the colour I despise, because I am sure of rendering essential service to my country. I am tired of the languor with which so sacred a war as this is carried on. My circumstances prevent me from writing so long a letter as I expected and wished to have done on a subject which I have much at heart. I entreat you to give a favorable answer to

Your most affectionate
John Laurens.

David R. Chesnutt, et al., editors, *The Papers of Henry Laurens, Vol. 12* (Columbia: University of South Carolina Press, 1990) 305–306.

7. Eliza Wilkinson Demands Liberty of Thought for Women (1780)

To gain domestic support, leaders of the independence movement used the language of liberty and equality with little practical commitment to either one. Though member of a South Carolina slaveholding family herself, Eliza Wilkinson wrote that the word "liberty...carries every idea of happiness in it." As a supporter of American independence, she claimed that liberty for herself and for women generally.

I do not love to meddle with political matters; the men say we have no business with them, it is not in our sphere! and Homer...gives us two or three broad hints to mind our domestic concerns, spinning, weaving, &c. and leave affairs of higher nature to the men; but I must beg his pardon—I won't have it thought, that because we are the weaker sex as to *bodily* strength...we are capable of nothing more than minding the dairy, visiting the poultry-house, and all such domestic concerns; our thoughts can soar aloft, we can form conceptions of things of higher nature; and have as just a sense of honor, glory, and great actions, as these "Lords of the Creation." What contemptible *earth worms* these authors make us! They won't even allow us the liberty of thought, and that is all I want. I would not wish that we should meddle in what is unbecoming female delicacy, but surely we may have sense enough to give our opinions to commend or discommend such actions as we may approve or disapprove; without being reminded of our spinning and household affairs as the only matters we are capable of thinking or speaking of with justness or propriety. I won't allow it, positively won't.

Caroline Gilman, editor, *Letters of Eliza Wilkinson* (New York: Samuel Colman, 1839) 60–61.

8. David Fanning Recounts the South's Civil War (ca. 1780)

Colonel David Fanning was a North Carolina Loyalist who, at the age of nineteen, joined the Tory militia. After the war he was "forced to leave the place of my nativity." He fled to New Brunswick, Canada, where he "enjoyed the sweets of peace and freedom under the benevolent auspices of the British Government." His account gives us a vivid portrait of the brutal nature of partisan civil war in the South.

After a little while some of us had assembled at a friend's house, where we were surrounded by a party of 14 Rebels under the command of Capt. John Hinds; we perceived their approach and prepared for to receive them; when they got quite near us, we run out of the doors of the house, fired upon them, and killed one of them; on which we took three of their horses, and some firelocks. We then took to the woods and unfortunately had two of our little company taken, one of which the Rebels shot in cold blood, and the other they hung on the spot where we killed the man a few days before. We were exasperated at this, that we determined to have satisfaction, and in a few days I collected 17 men well armed, and formed an ambuscade on Deep River at Coxe's Mills, and sent out my spies. In the course of two hours, one of my spies gave me information of a party of Rebels plundering his house, which was about three miles off. I instantly marched to the place and discovered them in a field near the house. I attacked them immediately, and kept up a smart fire for half an hour, during which time we killed their Captain, and one private, on the spot—wounded three of them, and took two prisoners besides eight of their horses well appointed, and several swords. This happened on the 11th of May, 1781....

About the 7th March 1782 Capt. Walker and Currie, of the Loyal Militia fell in with a party of Rebels and came to an engagement and fired for some time 'till the rebels had fired all their ammunition; and then wished to come to terms of peace between each party; and no plundering, killing or murdering should be committed by either party or side; which was concluded upon by each Colonel, for such certain limited bounds; which was to be agreed upon by each col.; and if they could not agree, each party was to be neutral until matters was made known respecting the terms which they had to agree upon. Soon after my men came to me and informed what they had done; we received the rebel Col. Balfour's answer; that "there was [no] resting place for a tory's foot upon the Earth." He also immediately sent out his party, and on the 10th, I saw the same company coming to a certain house where we were fiddling and dancing. We immediately prepared ourselves in readiness to receive them, their number being 27 and our number only seven. We immediately mounted our horses, and went some little distance from the house, and commenced a fire for some considerable time; night coming on they retreated, and left the ground.... I had ordered and collected twenty-five men.... On Balfour's plantation, when we came upon him, he endeavored to make his escape; but we soon prevented him, fired at him, and wounded him. The first ball received was through one of his arms, and ranged through his body; the other through his neck; which put an end to his committing any more ill deeds.

The Narrative of Colonel David Fanning (New York: Alvord, 1865) xxiv, 15–16, 50–51.

9. The Humble Memorial of Ann Glover, widow of Samuel Glover (1780)

Desertion rates were high and mutiny not uncommon in the Continental army, especially in the South. This petition from Ann Glover of North Carolina, widow of an executed mutineer, gives us a sense of conditions for soldiers' families and why even the most dedicated soldiers sometimes refused to serve.

To the Honorable the General Assembly of the said State now sitting.

The Humble Memorial of Ann Glover, widow of Samuel Glover, late a soldier in this State, who enlisted himself some time in the year 1775, in the Continental Service in the Second Regiment raised here,

Humbly Sheweth,

That your petitioner's late husband well and faithfully discharged his duty as a soldier and friend to the cause of American freedom and independence, and marched to the northward under the command of Col. Robert Howe, who, if he was here, would bear honest and honorable testimony that your memorialist's deceased husband was deemed by him and every other officer in that battalion a good soldier, and never was accused of being intentionally guilty of a breach of the laws, martial or civil. Your petitioner begs leave to inform your honors that her late husband continued in the service of the United States of America upwards of three years, and then returned, by orders of his commanding officers, to the southward, at which time he had above twelve months' pay due for his services as a soldier, and which he ought to have received, and would have applied for the sole support of himself, his wife, your petitioner, and two helpless orphan children. That many of the poor soldiers then on their march under Command of Gen. Hogun, possessed of the same attachment and affection to their families as those in command, but willing to endure all the dangers and hardships of war, began their march for the defense of the state of South Carolina, could they have obtained their promised but small allowance dearly earned for the support of their distressed families in their absence;

but as they were sure of suffering for want of that subsistence which at that time and unjustly was cruelly withheld from them, a general clamor arose among the common soldiery, and they called for their stipend allowed by Congress, but it was not given them, although their just due. Give your poor petitioner leave to apologize for her unhappy husband's conduct, and in behalf of her helpless self, as well as in favor of his poor children on this occasion, and ask you what must the feeling of the man be who fought at Brandywine, at Germantown, and at Stony Point and did his duty, and when on another march in defense of his country, with poverty staring him full in the face, he was denied his pay? His brother soldiers, incensed by the same injuries and had gone through the same services, and would have again bled with him for his country whenever called forth in the service, looked up to him as an older soldier, who then was a sergeant, raised by his merit from the common rank, and stood forth in his own and their behalf, and unhappily for him demanded their pay, and refused to obey the command of his superior officer, and would not march till they had justice done them. The honest laborer is worthy of his hire. Allegiance to our country and obedience to those in authority, but the spirit of a man will shrink from his duty when his services are not paid and injustice oppresses him and his family. For this he fell an unhappy victim to the hard but perhaps necessary law of his country. The letter penned by himself the day before he was shot doth not breathe forth a word of complaint against his cruel sentence, although he had not received any pay for upwards of fifteen months. He writes to your humble petitioner with the spirit of a Christian. This letter is the last adieu he bid to his now suffering widow, and she wishes it may be read in public Assembly, and then returned her by some of the members, who will take it with them when they return to Newbern, and leave it in the care of Major Pasteur. Your humble petitioner, distressed with the recollection of the fatal catastrophe, will not trouble your honors any longer upon the subject, but humbly request that you will extend your usual benevolence and charity to her and her two children, and make her some yearly allowance for their support.

I am, &c.,
Ann Glover.

Walter Clark, editor, *The State Records of North Carolina, Vol. 15* (Goldsboro: Nash Bros., 1898) 187–88.

10. Land Grants to Discourage Desertion (1781)

In an effort to stem the tide of desertion from state militia forces, in August 1781 the Georgia General Assembly, which had already promised 100 acres of land to veterans, offered even more land to those who would stay.

Whereas numbers of persons are daily absenting themselves and leaving their fellow citizens to encounter the difficulties of the present crisis, *Be it enacted by the authority aforesaid,* That any person or persons who shall produce a certificate from the commanding officer of the district to which he belongs, to the legislature of this State (on the total expulsion of the enemy from it) of his having steadfastly done his duty from the time of passing of this act, shall be entitled to two hundred and fifty acres of good land (which shall be exempt from taxes for the space of ten years thereafter;) *Provided* such person or persons cannot be convicted of plundering or distressing the country.

Robert and George Watkins, *A Digest of the Laws of the State of Georgia* (Philadelphia: R. Aitken, 1800) 238.

11. "The Volunteers of Augusta" (1781)

Despite their setbacks in 1781, especially the loss of Augusta, many Tories did not want to give up the fight. Their mood was reflected in a popular song called "The Volunteers of Augusta" set to the tune "The Lilies of France."

Come join, my brave lads, come all from afar,
We're all Volunteers, all ready for war;
Our service is free, for honour we fight,
Regardless of hardships by day or by night.
Then all draw your swords, and constantly sing,
Success to our Troop, our Country, and King.

The Rebels they murder, Revenge is the word,
Let each lad return with blood on his sword;
See Grierson's pale ghost point afresh to his wound,
We'll conquer, my boys, or fall dead on the ground.
Then brandish your swords, and constantly sing,
Success to our Troop, our Country, and King.

They've plundered our houses, attempted our lives,
Drove off from their homes our children and wives;
Such plundering miscreants no mercy can crave,
Such murdering villains no mercy shall have.
Then chop with your swords, and constantly sing,
Success to our Troop, our Country, and King.

Then think not of plunder, but rush on the foe,
Pursue them, my boys, with blow after blow;
Till in their own blood we see them all welter,
Or behind the Blue Mountains retreat for a shelter.
Then chop with your swords, and constantly sing,
Success to our Troop, our Country, and King.

There the Indians to them that mercy will owe,
Which they, when victorious, to others did show;
But we will return our estates to enjoy,
In rooting out Rebels our time we'll employ.
Then sheath, boys, your swords, and constantly sing,
Success to our Troop, our Country, and King.

When back through Augusta our horses shall prance,
We'll dismount at the Captain's, and there have a dance,
We'll toss off full bumpers of favorite grog,
Be merry all night, in the morning drink knog.
Then rest on your swords, and constantly sing,
Success to our Troop, our Country, and King.

Here's a health to our Governor, Peace at our homes,
Honour to Ingram, to Douglass, and Holmes,
A wife to each soldier, and other good chear,
And victory for ever to each Volunteer.
Then lay by your swords, and constantly sing,
Success to our Troop, our Country, and King.

Royal Georgia Gazette (Savannah), 4 October 1781.

12. Ned Griffin, Enslaved Veteran of the Revolution, Petitions for Freedom (1784)

Ned Griffin agreed to serve as a Continental soldier, substitute for a deserter, in exchange for a promise of freedom. That promise was broken, as the following petition attests.

To the General Assembly of the State of North Carolina

The petitioner of Ned Griffin, a man of mixed blood, humbly saieth that a small space of time before the Battle of Gilford [Guilford Courthouse, North Carolina, 15 March 1781] a certain William Kitchen then in the service of his country as a soldier deserted from his line, for which he was turned in to the Continental service to serve as the law directs. Your petitioner was then a servant to William Griffin and was purchased by the said Kitchen for the purpose of serving in his place, with a solemn assurance that if he, your petitioner, would faithfully serve the term of time that the said Kitchen was returned for, he should be a free man—Upon which promise and assurance your petitioner consented to enter in to the Continental service in said Kitchen's behalf and was received by Colonel James Armstrong at Martinborough as a free man. Your petitioner further saieth that at that time no person could have been hired to have served in said Kitchen's behalf for so small a sum as what I was purchased for, and that at the time that I was received into service by said Colonel Armstrong, said Kitchen openly declared me to be a free man. The faithful performance of the above agreement will appear from my discharge. Some time after your petitioner's return he was seized upon by said Kitchen and sold to a certain Abner Roberson who now holds me as a servant. Your petitioner therefore thinks that by contract and merit he is entitled to his freedom. I therefore submit my case to your honorable body hoping that I shall have that justice done me as in your wisdom shall think I am entitled to and deserving of and your petitioner as in duty bound will pray.

N Carolina
Edgecomb County
April 4th 1784

his
Ned X Griffin
mark

Herbert Aptheker, editor, *A Documentary History of the Negro People in the United States, Vol. 1* (Secaucus NJ: The Citadel Press, 1951) 13–14.

13. Benjamin Banneker, a Free Black, Chides Thomas Jefferson for his Hypocrisy (1791)

Benjamin Banneker (or Bannaker), born in Baltimore, Maryland, the son of a former slave, was a mathematician, astronomer, surveyor, farmer, and author of Banneker's Almanac. *On 19 August 1791, he sent a copy of his almanac to Secretary of State Thomas Jefferson, author of the Declaration of Independence, along with a letter urging Jefferson to renounce slavery and hold true to the principles he outlined in the nation's founding document.*

Sir,

I am fully sensible of the greatness of that freedom, which I take with you on the present occasion; a liberty which seemed to me scarcely allowable, when I reflected on that distinguished and dignified station in which you stand, and the almost general prejudice and prepossession, which is so prevalent in the world against those of my complexion....

Sir, I have long been convinced, that if your love for yourselves, and for those inestimable laws, which preserved to you the rights of human nature, was founded on sincerity, you could not but be solicitous, that every individual, of whatever rank or distinction, might with you equally enjoy the blessings thereof; neither could you rest satisfied short

Benjamin Banneker, who publicly criticized Thomas Jefferson for holding slaves while proclaiming "all men are created equal," has been called the first African American man of science. If Jefferson's words had been sincere, wrote Banneker, he could hardly participate in the cruel oppression of slavery.

Engraving from *Benjamin Bannaker's Almanac for the Year of Our Lord 1795.*

of the most active effusion of your exertions, in order to their promotion from any state of degradation, to which the unjustifiable cruelty and barbarism of men may have reduced them....

You publicly held forth this true and invaluable doctrine, which is worthy to be recorded and remembered in all succeeding ages: "We hold these truths to be self-evident, that all men are created equal; that they are endowed by their Creator with certain unalienable rights, and that among these are, life, liberty, and the pursuit of happiness." Here was a time, in which your tender feelings for yourselves had engaged you thus to declare, you were then impressed with proper ideas of the great violation of liberty, and the free possession of those blessings, to which you were entitled by nature; but, Sir, how pitiable is it to reflect, that although you were so fully convinced of the benevolence of the Father of Mankind, and of his equal and impartial distribution of these rights and privileges, which he hath conferred upon them, that you should at the same time counteract his mercies, in detaining by fraud and violence so numerous a part of my brethren, under groaning captivity and cruel oppression, that you should at the same time be found guilty of that most criminal act, which you professedly detested in others....

Letter from Benjamin Banneker to the Secretary of State (Philadelphia: Daniel Lawrence, 1792), Early American Imprints, University of Virginia, Charlottesville.

3

The South Moves West: Expansion and the Tragedy of Indian Removal

Launching the Westward Invasion

With the Treaty of Paris of 1783, the United States became internationally recognized as an independent nation. The US South stretched from the Atlantic west to the Mississippi and from Maryland and the Ohio River southward to Florida, now back in Spanish hands. Southern state governments controlled roughly the eastern third of that region. Beyond the Appalachians and Georgia's Ogeechee River, the land was still held by native Cherokees, Creeks, Choctaws, and Chickasaws. Over the next half-century nearly all these peoples would be driven west by whites, or as the Creeks called them, *Ecunnaunuxulgee*, meaning "greedy people grasping for Indian lands."

Even before the Revolution some Southerners pressed white-occupied territory well into the backcountry, past the Proclamation Line of 1763. Watauga settlers had done so as early as 1772. Two years later, in 1774, Virginia pushed the Shawnee and Mingo peoples west to the Kentucky River during Lord Dunmore's War. In 1775, a land-speculating venture from North Carolina called the Transylvania Company purchased 20 million acres from Cherokees west of the Kentucky River between the Ohio and Cumberland rivers under the Treaty of Sycamore Shoals. That same year Daniel Boone and others led parties of whites into the area, which met stiff resistance from the Shawnees. Much of the region had long been disputed between the Cherokees and Shawnees. Now the dispute was between Shawnees and white settlers. The Shawnees became eager allies of the British during the Revolution, but capitulated when the British withdrew. From 1776, the United States officially recognized the region as Virginia's western county of Kentucky. In 1792 it became the fifteenth state.

A movement for independent statehood was brewing to the south as well. In 1784, settlers in the old Watauga Association region seceded from North Carolina, called themselves the State of Franklin, and made John Sevier their governor. Congress rejected Franklin's application for statehood, so it declared itself an independent republic. At the same time Franklin pressured local Cherokees for more land. Koatohee, or Corn Tassel, one of the Cherokees' most respected chiefs, at first opposed any further land cession but finally gave in hoping it would bring peace with the whites. In 1785, he and other Cherokee leaders met with US agents and signed the Treaty of Hopewell, establishing what they were promised would be a permanent boundary.

Not all Cherokees went along with the deal. In the late 1780s, a large faction of Cherokees led by Dragging Canoe raided white settlements along the Holston, Watauga, Nolichuky, and Cumberland rivers. With little funds to raise and supply a militia, Governor Sevier sought aid from the Spanish. That was too much for North Carolina. In 1788, North Carolina militiamen entered Franklin to arrest Sevier, who gave up after a brief resistance, and to stop Cherokee attacks.

In 1790, North Carolina ceded to the United States all of its lands beyond the Appalachians. The entire region west to the Mississippi was declared the Southwest Territory. Federal agents set about coaxing more land from the Cherokees with the Treaty of Holston (1791), though both they and the Chickasaws retained much of their traditional holdings. Still, Dragging Canoe refused to sign the treaty. Instead he tried to build a confederation of resistant Cherokees, Creeks, Choctaws, and Chickasaws, but died of natural causes in 1792 before he could form his alliance. Four years later, in 1796, the territory became the state of Tennessee and elected John Sevier its first governor.

In Georgia, whose claims stretched to the Mississippi River, some Cherokees and Creeks tried to satisfy white greed for land by giving up areas along their eastern borders. Many natives had fled these lands during the Revolution, seeking safety farther west. In May 1783, Cherokees sold off more than 1 million acres north and west of Georgia's holdings to that time. Later that year, two Creek chiefs released a much larger tract of land between the Ogeechee and Oconee rivers. Whites began moving into the area before it was surveyed, some even beyond the Oconee River boundary. This aggravated an already tense situation in that many Creeks had opposed giving up any land at all. These Creeks were led by Chief Alexander McGillivray, son of a Creek woman and a Scottish trader. McGillivray and his followers threatened war if the ceded lands were not returned, but whites continued to settle in what Georgia was now calling Washington County. Finally, McGillivray's Creeks mounted a series of raids from 1787 to 1789 known as the Oconee War. Whites made raids of their own, burning Creek towns and crops. Over eighty whites were killed along with an unknown number of Creeks.

The issue was settled only after President George Washington invited McGillivray and other Creek chiefs to New York, then serving as temporary capital of the United States. In the resulting Treaty of New York (1790), Creek leaders, including McGillivray, agreed to give up their lands east of the Oconee in exchange for a $1500 annual payment and a promise that no whites could legally settle west of the river. Elijah Clarke, a former Revolutionary War general, tested that promise in 1794 when he and hundreds of adventurers and land speculators tried to establish their own country beyond the Oconee, independent of the US and loosely allied with France. They built several fortified towns in what they called their Trans-Oconee Republic. But when the Georgia militia moved against them almost all of Clarke's men deserted.

Speculation and Land Frauds

The Georgia General Assembly initially tried to discourage land speculation, so common in the expansion states of Kentucky and Tennessee. Speculation led to heavy concentrations of land and low rates of land ownership. In a study of land distribution in eastern Tennessee around 1800, historian Lee Soltow notes that "the top 1 percent of the 2701 residents had 13 percent of the land, while the top 10 percent had 37 percent of the acreage. Half the taxable area was reported by but one-sixth of the people. In this sense we can say that Tennessee was far from a land of equality."

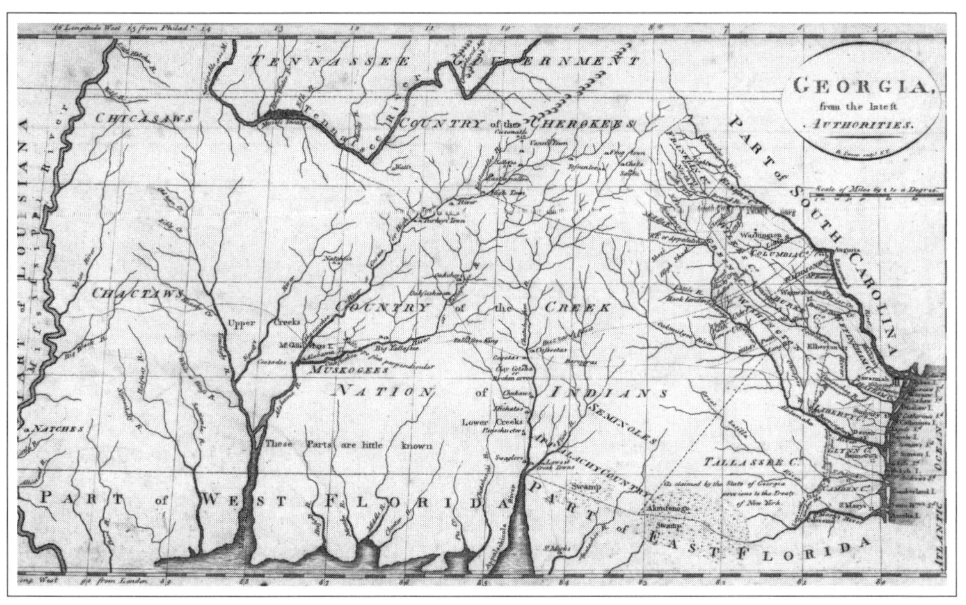

Though Georgia's organized counties extend barely fifty miles west of the Savannah River and inland from the Atlantic Ocean, its land claims are shown stretching all the way to the Mississippi River and engulfing the Cherokees, Creeks, Seminoles, Chickasaws, and Choctaws.

Engraving from *Carey's American Atlas* (1795).

Rather than distributing land by large grants to individuals or land speculation companies, Georgia gave land to small farmers under the headright system. The idea was to get land into the hands of settlers who would cultivate it rather than hold it waiting for higher prices, thus promoting economic growth. Every head of household had a right to 200 acres of land, plus 50 more for each additional family member or slave held, but with a maximum allotment of 1000 acres. Still, wealthy or well-connected men, even land speculators, could get much more with legislative approval and the governor's backing. Governor George Walton, a signer of the Declaration of Independence, approved grants of up to 50,000 acres. His successor, Edward Telfair, signed off on grants for twice that amount. Governor George Mathews approved even larger grants.

The headright system worked well to draw settlers to Georgia, mostly from Virginia and the Carolinas. Though the headright system encouraged settlement, as a deterrent to land speculation, legal and otherwise, it was a dismal failure. Legislators frequently took bribes in exchange for approving large land grants to speculators. The problem became even worse after 1789 when headright land granting was placed in the hands of county officials. They regularly drew up title deeds, or warrants, to fictitious land lots, listing nonexistent creeks and trees as boundary markers. They advertised these warrants for sale in newspapers up and down the eastern seaboard, lining their pockets with cash from individual buyers or, more often, land speculation companies. Company managers, often located hundreds of miles away, would rarely survey their purchases. Their only interest was to resale the land at a profit to the next unsuspecting buyer.

These headright land frauds created enormous tracts of land that existed only on paper. Effingham County contained only 310,440 acres. Yet it distributed lands totaling 1,149,791 acres. The worst offender was Montgomery County, which contained 407,680 acres. Its officials put 7,436,995 acres worth of deeds in circulation, representing nearly twenty times more land than actually existed in the county. In total, although Georgia's twenty-four counties as of 1796 contained only 9 million acres, county officials issued deeds for 29 million acres.

Corruption was rampant in the General Assembly as well. Far from trying to rein in fraud at the county level, state legislators jumped on the speculation bandwagon to enrich themselves using Georgia's vast claims between the Oconee and Mississippi rivers. Those lands were still occupied by Native Americans, though that was of little concern to the Assembly. Of greater concern was that the southern part of the territory was claimed as part of West Florida by Spain. That claim was settled at the thirty-first parallel with the 1795 Treaty of San Lorenzo, or Pinckney's Treaty after minister to Great Britain Thomas Pinckney, who represented the United States in the negotiations.

Even before the treaty went into effect, legislators plotted to sell up to 50 million acres of Native American land to four land speculation companies for $500,000, or about one penny per acre, a ridiculously low price even for the time. In return for their votes approving the sale, called the Yazoo Act after the Yazoo River in the far west of Georgia's claim, legislators received bribes in the form of land, slaves, rice, and money. Those few assemblymen who refused to cooperate were encouraged to leave Augusta, Georgia's then-capital city, under threats to their lives. In January 1795, Georgia's General Assembly passed the Yazoo Act. Governor Mathews, himself known for shady land deals, signed the bill into law.

Those who opposed the act began an intense and very public campaign to have it overturned. As word spread that Georgians had been cheated out of any future hope of land grants in areas covered by the Yazoo Act, public outrage built to a fever pitch. Local grand juries allied with Yazoo opponents brought charges against pro-Yazoo legislators. Threats against corrupt legislators became so serious that some fled the state.

Not surprisingly, nearly every member of the old Assembly was turned out. The new Assembly quickly moved not only to overturn Yazoo with the Rescinding Act of 1796 but also to wipe every vestige of it from state records. In 1796, on the grounds of the new state capitol at Louisville, members of the Assembly gathered to burn all records associated with Yazoo. As far as Georgia was concerned, the Yazoo sales were now void.

The Foundations of Removal

During the year-long process of electing new legislators and rescinding Yazoo, much of the land involved had been sold and re-sold. Though Georgia offered purchasers their money back, many insisted on making a profit and refused the deal. Litigation followed in which buyers argued that Georgia had no right to take back the Yazoo lands. The situation became so troublesome to Georgia that it finally turned the problem over to Washington. Under the Compact of 1802, Georgia sold what are today Alabama and Mississippi to the federal government for $1,250,000. At the time, the entire region was called the Territory of Mississippi.

Like Georgia's General Assembly, Congress continued to deny the Yazoo deal's legitimacy. Buyers continued to press their claim to ownership through the courts. Their position was finally heard by the Supreme Court in *Fletcher v. Peck* (1810). Land speculator John Peck held title to Yazoo lands and sold parts of his land to Robert Fletcher, also a speculator. In a deal worked out between the two, Fletcher brought suit against Peck, charging that Peck did not have title to the land when he sold it. Fletcher hoped to lose the case, and thus secure both for himself and Peck, as well as other Yazoo claimants, clear title to their lands or a profitable buyout from Congress.

A unanimous court obliged by ruling that Georgia's Rescinding Act was unconstitutional. The decision authored by Chief Justice John Marshall stated that even though corruption was at its heart, the Yazoo Act was a binding contract under Article I, section 10, clause I of the Constitution (the Contract Clause) and that neither party to a contract could alter it without consent from the other. This case was one of the earliest in which the Supreme Court declared a state law unconstitutional, thus upholding Article VI's Supremacy Clause making the Constitution the "supreme law of the land." With this decision in hand, Yazoo claimants pressured Congress into a buyout that totaled $4.25 million. Added to monies paid under the Compact of 1802, it had cost the nation's taxpayers roughly $5.5 million to settle Georgia's corrupt land deal.

In addition to cash received under the Compact of 1802, Georgia demanded from Washington a promise to remove all the Creeks and Cherokees remaining on state land claims. Even though lands west of the Oconee had been guaranteed to the Native Americans under the 1790 Treaty of New York, federal representatives agreed to insert into the compact that "the United States shall, at their own expense, extinguish for the use of Georgia, as early as the same can be peacefully obtained on reasonable terms...Indian title to all the other lands within the state of Georgia." The phrase "peacefully obtained on reasonable terms" implied that Native Americans must freely agree to give up their lands. Congress further stressed the point in its Indian Trade and Intercourse Act, also passed in 1802, under which no Native American land could be taken without a treaty. Nevertheless, Georgia took the Compact of 1802 to mean that the Creeks and Cherokees would soon be gone one way or another.

As to where they might go, in 1803 the United State purchased from France a huge tract of land west of the Mississippi River called Louisiana. The deal roughly doubled the nation's land mass. As part of his effort to have the treaty ratified in the Senate, President Thomas Jefferson pointed out that a portion of the purchase area could be set aside as a reserve for Native Americans being pushed out of the East. For that reason, Jefferson is sometimes called the father of Indian Removal.

Soon after the Compact of 1802 was signed, in a vain effort to satisfy the *Ecunnaunuxulgee*, the Creeks agreed to sell lands that Georgia had long sought between the Oconee and Ocmulgee rivers. In exchange, the Creeks got $25,000 in goods, merchandise, and debt relief. Additionally, each chief would receive $1,000 for ten years, and the Creek Nation would be paid $3,000 in annual payments, or annuities, indefinitely.

Once those lands were state property, rather than distribute them using the discredited headright system, Georgia tried to end both corruption and speculation by instituting land lotteries, a practice that was unique to Georgia. Under the new lottery system, former Native American lands were organized into counties and surveyed into land lots of usually between 160 and 490 acres depending on the estimated land values in each new county. Citizens could then register for a lottery in which these lands would be raffled off. Veterans, widows, and heads of household received additional chances.

Tickets bearing the names of those registering for the lottery were sent to the state capital at Milledgeville where they were placed in a large rotating wooden drum. Tickets with land lot numbers were deposited in a second drum. Both drums were spun and one ticket from each was drawn. Since there were always several times more people registered than land lots available, most participants won no land. But for those who did, on payment of a nominal fee of $4.00 per 100 acres, they became the new owner of a land lot.

Though the system remained in place until the last lottery in 1832-33, it ended neither speculation nor corruption completely. Land companies sometimes cheated winners out of their land by offering them undervalued prices before they knew their land's true worth. Many people registered who were not citizens of Georgia. Some claimed to be heads of households that were in fact nonexistent. Others who never served in the military passed themselves off as veterans. State officials were sometimes caught trying to rig the lottery's outcome. Despite its flaws, the lottery never approached levels of corruption seen when the headright system was in effect.

Fracturing the Creek Nation

Native Americans tended to have a different view of the land lottery. To them it only encouraged the greed that they had long observed among whites–a greed that had already begun to infect and divide the Native Americans themselves. Several generations of intermarriage between white traders and native women had produced a class of well-to-do mixed bloods. Because of their families' trade ties and wealth, these men exercised great influence and rose to positions of leadership in the Cherokee and Creek nations, especially among the Lower Creeks. They became the conduit by which white customs were introduced—customs such as a monetary system, slavery, and private as opposed to communal land ownership. They also introduced a growing economic dependence on, and indebtedness to, the whites that would make it increasingly difficult to resist their demands for land.

The Upper Creeks of central and northern Alabama were less directly affected since they were more geographically isolated. Upper Creek chiefs and full-bloods tended to be more resistant to these changing customs. But such was the mixed-blood influence among Lower Creeks and on the national council that resistance became increasingly futile.

It became more so after Benjamin Hawkins was made US agent to the Creek Nation in 1796. Hawkins encouraged the Creeks to view landholding and farming rather than commercial hunting as the path to economic prosperity. It was a radical change from what whites of a century earlier had done. For nearly 3000 years, Southeastern natives had been communal farmers, developing some of the most productive crop varieties in the world. When the British arrived in Charleston, their demand for deerskins and beaver pelts transformed Native Americans largely into commercial hunters. Now Hawkins sought to reverse that trend, hoping to open huge tracts of hunting grounds for land cessions to whites. Lower Creeks, desperate to pay off debts to white traders, more readily acquiesced to white notions of privately owned farms. Upper Creeks, more economically independent of whites, tended to adhere to the old communal ways.

Though becoming more and more divided along geographic, economic, and ethnic lines, the Creeks remained united in their opposition to giving up land. But underlying tensions festered and finally came to a head in 1811 after the United States widened an old horse path through the Creek Nation, making it a major roadway running from Macon, Georgia, to New Orleans. Some Lower Creeks agreed to the construction of what was called the Federal Road, seeing in it new opportunities for trade together with road, bridge, and ferry tolls. Most Upper Creeks strongly opposed the road. They saw it as little more than a route to bring more whites and their ways into Creek country. Even Creeks who had supported the Federal Road were soon dismayed to find that whites refused to pay access tolls. Even more disturbing was the string of forts that federal troops were building along the road. What began as a trade route was starting to look like preparation for an invasion.

Tensions among the Creeks were further strained when a Shawnee chief named Tecumseh spoke to a tribal council in late 1811. In an effort to halt white expansion, Tecumseh hoped to create a vast Native American confederacy stretching from the Great Lakes to the Gulf of Mexico. Already many natives of the Ohio River Valley were on board. Now Tecumseh, whose mother was Upper Creek, invited the Creek Nation to join him. Most Lower Creeks objected, but Upper Creeks largely backed the plan. They were ready to drive the whites from their land with or without support from their Lower Creek cousins.

In early 1812, Tecumseh's supporters, mostly Upper Creeks called "Red Sticks," killed several whites traveling along the Federal Road. Hawkins demanded that the killers be executed or Creek trading posts would be shut down and annuity payments cut off. Mixed-blood Lower Creek Chief William McIntosh of Coweta sent a detachment of "Friendlies," as whites called the more compliant Creeks, to hunt down suspected Red Stick killers and executed eleven of their number on sight. Red Sticks retaliated by killing several of the executioners. Reprisals followed reprisals until a civil war was raging in the Creek Nation.

Early 1812 also found expansionists in Congress persuading their colleagues that British Canada, or parts of it, might easily be annexed to the United States. Already the US had seized West Florida from Britain's ally Spain. Two years earlier, in a bloodless coup, American "filibusters" occupied Baton Rouge, declared West Florida independent eastward to the Perdido River (just west of Pensacola), and had themselves annexed to the United States as the Territory of Orleans. In 1812, the region was admitted to the Union as the state of Louisiana eastward to the Pearl River. The area between the Pearl and Perdido rivers, dominated by Mobile Bay, was adjoined to the Mississippi Territory.

In June 1812, with a taste for more territory, Congress declared war on Britain. Tecumseh quickly allied with the British. In January 1813, hundreds of British troops and Native Americans, including Creek Red Sticks, defeated an American detachment in Michigan. Whites feared a similar alliance in the South. That spring and summer Red Stick attacks along the Federal Road increased, and both Georgia and Tennessee called up their militias.

In August, Red Sticks led by Red Eagle, also known as William Weatherford, attacked Fort Mims, an outpost near the Federal Road in southern Alabama. They were chasing a party of Lower Creeks who had taken refuge in the fort. The Lower Creeks, along with about 400 whites, including some women and children, were killed in the massacre, though Red Eagle was later said to have tried to restrain his warriors. There were about 100 survivors, whom the Red Sticks took captive. In response, an army of US troops, together with Georgia militia, Tennessee militia, and Lower Creeks, all led by General Andrew Jackson, entered the Creek Nation to subdue the Red Sticks. They were joined by a regiment of Cherokees that included Major Ridge and John Ross, who hoped that an alliance with the whites would help secure Cherokee lands.

In March 1814 the last Red Stick stronghold was wiped out at the Battle of Horseshoe Bend, located in what would soon be eastern Alabama. That August, Creeks as a whole, Lower Creeks included, were forced to sign the Treaty of Fort Jackson. Under its terms, the Creeks lost 23 million acres, well over half their nation, in northwestern, west-central, and southern Alabama and south Georgia. Now all they had left were lands between the Ocmulgee and Chattahoochee rivers in west-central Georgia, along with the area of east-central Alabama between the Chattahoochee and Coosa rivers–lands that the Fort Jackson Treaty promised would be theirs as long as they wished.

Seminoles and Creeks Pressed to the Margins

Over the next few years Jackson's army rounded up thousands of destitute Creeks, both Red Stick and Friendlies, and drove them onto their remaining lands. Some wanted no more to do with the US and sought refuge in Spanish Florida among the Seminoles, most of whom were themselves Creek refugees or their descendants from earlier days (the term *seminole* comes from the Spanish word *cimarron* meaning refugee). Living among the Seminoles were a handful of remaining Appalachee and Timucua natives, descendants the few Appalachee Massacre survivors of more than a century earlier. There were also hundreds of African American Seminoles, most of whom were refugees from slavery or their descendants. By the early nineteenth century, blacks made up roughly a fourth of Florida's Seminoles and a few were Seminole chiefs.

For years the United States had pressed Spain to give up Florida with no result. Now President James Monroe and Andrew Jackson concocted a scheme to test Spanish resolve. In what came to be called the First Seminole War (1817–1818) Jackson's army ranged across northern Florida, attacking Seminole towns and Spanish forts, daring Spain to stop him. Instead, Spain offered to sell Florida to the US. The two governments worked out an arrangement under the Adams-Onis Treaty (1819), named for Secretary of State John Quincy Adams and Spanish Minister Luis de Onis, and Florida became a US territory in 1821. As a reward for Jackson's service, Monroe appointed him governor of Florida. Jackson's subsequent land deals in Florida made him a wealthy man.

Those Creeks who could not escape into the Florida interior were herded on lands left to them under the 1814 Fort Jackson treaty. With so much land gone, the Creeks were even more dependent not only on trade with the whites but also on government annuities that were supposed to come in payment for their land. But US agent David B. Mitchell, a former governor of Georgia, partnered with Chief William McIntosh to siphon off more than a third of those annuities for an illegal slave-smuggling operation. What money did get through went mostly into the pockets of white traders who were cheating the Creeks and running up their debts. In 1821 the US offered to pay off those debts for more land. McIntosh brokered the deal, receiving a kickback of 1,000 acres and $12,000 for his trouble. Under this Treaty of Indian Springs, the Creeks lost another 5 million acres in Georgia between the Ocmulgee and Flint rivers. With only 10 million acres left, the Creek National Council reaffirmed an earlier edict widely known as the Blood Law. If any Creek should sign land over to the whites without permission from the council, he would be subject to execution on sight.

William McIntosh, robbed of his status as a chief for his secret dealings with the whites, tested that law in 1825. Offered bribes from Georgia's new governor, McIntosh's own first cousin, George M. Troup, he and several headmen signed a second Treaty of Indian Springs without council approval. It relinquished Creek lands between the Flint and Chattahoochee rivers. McIntosh's pay-off for the deal amounted to $35,000. Troup had become Georgia's first popularly elected governor the year before, campaigning on a promise to get more Native American land for another lottery. He kept that promise to the voters of Georgia. Now the Creek National Council would keep its promise too. In April 1825 it sent a party of Creek warriors to enforce the Blood Law against McIntosh.

The council also declared McIntosh's treaty void and sent word of that decision to Governor Troup. Nevertheless, Troup sent Georgia militiamen to secure the disputed area. The Creeks appealed for protection to President John Quincy Adams, reminding him of the Fort Jackson Treaty's promise of their right to the land. Adams refused to intervene, but did agree to pay the Creeks for their lost land. Under the Treaty of Washington (1826), the Creeks would get an up-front sum of $217,600 plus a perpetual annuity of $20,000. Now all the Creeks had left to them was 5 million acres in the eastern part of what since 1819 had been the state of Alabama.

By the late 1820s, other tribal lands had been whittled away as well. The Choctaws and Chickasaws, whose lands once stretched from the Ohio to the Gulf of Mexico, were now confined to upper Mississippi, which became a state in 1817. The Seminoles were confined to a reservation that occupied most of central Florida. And the Cherokees held barely a tenth of their original lands. What they had left lay mostly in northwestern Georgia. The final chapter for Native American nations in the Southeast began with Andrew Jackson's election to the presidency in 1828. Within a decade, nearly all the South's native peoples would be gone.

Choctaws and Chickasaws Forced Out

One of Jackson's first legislative initiatives was the Indian Removal Act (1830) "to provide for an exchange of lands with the Indians residing in any of the states or territories, and for their removal west of the river Mississippi." The act was by no means a forgone conclusion. It was opposed by most Northeastern congressmen, whose states had already banished most of their Native American populations and who feared the rising power of the South and West. Native removal in those regions would mean more congressional districts for them. There were even a few congressmen from the South and West who opposed removal,

David Crockett of western Tennessee included. Such were the economic and kinship ties between the Native Americans and whites living adjacent to and among them that removal would mean a severe disruption of business and family relationships. The push for removal came mainly from land speculators who had a great deal of influence in Congress and the White House. Jackson himself had made his fortune as a land speculator during his tenure as Florida's first territorial governor.

With passage of the Indian Removal Act, by only a narrow margin, a large swath of land west of the Mississippi was designated Indian Territory. Congress described the region as "all that part of the United States west of the Mississippi and not within the states of Missouri and Louisiana, or the territory of Arkansas," which became a state itself in 1836. Jackson promised Native Americans that the land would be theirs "as long as the grass grows, or water runs." It would later become the state Oklahoma, so called from two Choctaw words meaning "red people."

The government first moved against the Choctaws of central Mississippi. In September 1830, US agents met at Dancing Rabbit Creek with a council of several thousand Choctaws, who soundly rejected signing a removal treaty. When the gathering broke up, the agents convinced three chiefs to remain behind. With bribes of land and cash to these chiefs and more bribes going to fifty other influential members of the tribe, the chiefs signed over all Choctaw lands in Mississippi with the Treaty of Dancing Rabbit Creek.

Most Choctaws were infuriated when they learned of the treaty. The chiefs had not been authorized to sign such a document. At least two chiefs were removed from office. The men who replaced them tried to rescind the treaty, but Jackson refused to recognize them as legitimate chiefs. Only those who had signed the treaty had any standing in Jackson's eyes.

By the treaty terms, Choctaws might choose to remain on restricted lands subject to the laws of Mississippi. A few thousand did remain. But most, about 13,000, chose to keep their nation intact and emigrate. Of those, at least 4,000 died on the way from cold, hunger, and a cholera epidemic. One Choctaw chief called the journey "a trail of tears and death." Over the next several years, those Choctaws remaining in

Mississippi were so badly treated, their lands overrun and their families abused, that most of them finally left as well.

By 1832, Chickasaw land in northern Mississippi was being overrun too. Early that year the chiefs met in council and decided that removal was the only option for their survival as a nation. In October they signed the Treaty of Pontotoc Creek, ceded their lands to the United States, and encouraged their people to begin preparations for the move west.

Not all Chickasaws were willing to go along. One chief led a delegation to Washington to prevent the treaty's ratification by the Senate, but the mission was turned away. Most of 1833 passed with no effort on the part of most Chickasaws to move. But whites were still squatting on their lands and there was little they could do about it. Over the next several years, in groups of a few hundred at a time, nearly the entire Chickasaw Nation, about 4,000 of them, made the journey to Indian Territory. As many as 800 perished along the way.

Creeks Robbed; Seminoles Resist

Like the Choctaws and Chickasaws, the Creeks of eastern Alabama were suffering with squatters as well. They raided Creek farms, stealing their cattle and corn, and Alabama authorities refused to bring the intruders to justice. In 1832 a Creek delegation met with Secretary of War Lewis Cass, who was charged with enforcing treaties that protected Native Americans on their lands. They explained that their lands were being overrun by whites who "daily rob us of our property." Cass refused to help unless the Creeks agreed to give up their lands and go west. They responded by telling Cass that "our aged fathers and mothers beseech us to remain upon the land that gave us birth, where the bones of their kindred are buried, so that when they die they may mingle their ashes together."

One party of Creek warriors became so enraged at the lack of protection that they attacked and burned the Chattahoochee River town of Roanoke, Georgia. Whites had been using Roanoke as a staging post for raids into the Creek Nation. Soon after, in March 1832, federal agents met with Creek chiefs at Cusseta and threatened war unless the Creeks gave in and moved west. Left with no choice, Creek leaders signed the

Osceola was one of the Seminoles' foremost leaders in their fight against removal. Unable to defeat Osceola in battle, General Thomas Jesup coaxed him out for peace talks under a flag of truce. Jesup then violated the truce by taking Osceola prisoner. Three months later, the chief died of malaria at Fort Moultrie in Charleston, South Carolina.

Illustration from *Francis Drake, Indian History for Young Folks* (1912). Based on a bust portrait by George Catlin, 1838.

Treaty of Cusseta, also known as the Treaty of Washington (1832). It dissolved the Creek Nation and turned their lands over to Alabama, but promised to protect the Creeks on small land plots for five years or until they were removed.

Most Creeks began making preparations, but organizing the emigration of around 20,000 people took time. Even as they prepared to move, invaders continued to harass them, backed by the state of Alabama. Whites frequently made claims on lands that were not theirs, were granted title to it by the state, and had the natives evicted from their homes by local law enforcement. Rushed into leaving before most were ready, nearly 4,000 lost their lives from hunger and disease. In 1836, in what became known as the Second Creek War, soldiers hunted down the starving Creeks, most of whom were hiding in the woods and living only by raiding farms that had until recently been their own. Once captured, they were deported to Indian Territory.

Capturing the Seminoles in Florida would be much more difficult. Though some of their chiefs had signed the 1832 Treaty of Paynes Landing agreeing to move, army officers admitted that the chiefs had been "wheedled and bullied into signing." The treaty gave Florida's nearly 4,000 Seminoles three years to move voluntarily. A few did, but 1835 found most Seminoles refusing to budge. Jackson sent the army in to move them by force, touching off the Second Seminole War.

The Seminoles struck back, raiding white farms and settlements at will. One war party led by the young Chief Osceola destroyed sugar plantations south of St. Augustine, adding to his strength when enslaved blacks joined the Seminoles. On Florida's west coast near Tampa, Seminoles ambushed an army detachment totaling 110 men in December 1835. All but two were killed. One later died of his wounds.

The Seminoles' guerrilla war and ambush tactics were beyond the army's ability to effectively counter. In 1837, the army resorted to trickery, calling Seminole leaders to peace talks, then capturing them when they arrived. Several chiefs and their escorts were seized in this way, including Osceola, who died of malaria after three months in prison. Congress next authorized $55,000 to bribe Seminole leaders into surrendering their people. Some took the bribes, but most did not.

By 1842, Congress had devoted tens of millions of dollars and tens of thousands of men to rooting the Seminoles out of Florida. Nearly 1,500 of those men had lost their lives in the effort. Still, almost a thousand Seminoles, about one-fourth the Seminole Nation, remained. Early that year, the commander of US forces in Florida recommended to Congress that the Seminoles be left in peace. Tired of the war's high cost in money and men, Congress agreed. It declared the war over and withdrew its troops. Though there was no treaty agreement, Congress recognized a vast region in southern Florida west of Lake Okeechobee as Seminole land.

Had there been a treaty, as with nearly all promises made to the Native Americans, their lands would still have been subject to confiscation. Even when the lands Native Americans held was legally theirs—even if the nation's highest judicial body, the Supreme Court, backed them up—they could still lose their land, as the Cherokees discovered through bitter experience.

The Cherokees and Worcester v. Georgia

In December of 1828, the Georgia Assembly passed an act declaring that on the first day of June 1830, those portions of the Cherokee Nation lying within what the state claimed as its boundary would be subject to the laws of Georgia. All Cherokee laws and customs were to be rendered null and void on that date.

Regardless of Georgia's claim, the Cherokees had no intention of giving up their land. In fact, they had long since adopted many ways of the white man in an attempt at assimilation and as a means of avoiding removal. By the 1820s, the Cherokees were no longer communal farmers or commercial hunters. They were land-owning farmers, merchants, blacksmiths, and carpenters. They had built towns and established networks of trade and commerce within their nation and far beyond its borders. Sequoyah, or George Guess by his Anglo name, developed a written form of the Cherokee language, and in 1828, the first issue of the *Cherokee Phoenix* went to press. This newspaper was printed in both English and Cherokee.

John Ross, principal chief of the Cherokees, tried to fight Georgia's annexation of his people's land through the judicial system. Though the Supreme Court found that the Constitution protected Cherokee land rights, President Andrew Jackson refused to enforce the ruling. In the winter of 1838-39, four thousand people died on the Cherokee Trail of Tears, including John Ross's wife Quatie.

Portrait by Charles Bird King from *History of the Indian Tribes of North America* (1843).

Many Cherokees had adopted the religion of the white man through the efforts of Christian missionaries who helped establish churches and schools in the Cherokee Nation. In 1827, the Cherokees established a tribal government modeled after the US Constitution, and made New Echota their capital. Under that constitution, there would be no question that only the pirncipal chief and council spoke for the Cherokees in treaty matters. Elias Boudinot, editor of the *Cherokee Phoenix,* pointed to the success of assimilation by quoting from an 1826 census that showed the 16,000 people of the Cherokee Nation holding 22,000 cattle; 7,600 horses; 46,000 swine; 2,500 sheep; 762 looms; 2,488 spinning wheels; 172 wagons; 2,943 ploughs; 10 saw-mills; 31 gristmills; 62 blacksmith shops; 8 large cotton gins; 18 schools; 18 ferries; and a number of public roads.

For all this, most whites continued to view Cherokees as little more than ignorant savages. Georgia's Governor George Gilmer went so far as to question "whether they are the descendants of Adam and Eve." In early nineteenth-century terms, this was to doubt the very humanity of the Cherokees. Faced with such attitudes on the part of most whites, the Cherokees knew that their position was precarious. It would shortly become even more so.

In August 1829, a Milledgeville newspaper, the *Georgia Journal,* announced that gold had been discovered in northern Georgia. By autumn a flood of gold-fevered miners were pouring into Cherokee country. Principal Chief John Ross appealed to the federal government to honor its treaty obligations and expel the intruders. But Governor Gilmer objected, and President Andrew Jackson left the Cherokees at the mercy of Georgia.

With thousands of intruders swarming over their lands and no assistance to be had from Jackson, the Cherokees realized that the only remaining way to challenge Georgia's action was through the judicial system. They employed William Wirt, a Baltimore lawyer, who began to search for a case that might bring the Cherokee cause to the Supreme Court. Georgia itself provided the opportunity when state officials arrested eleven missionaries among the Cherokees for refusing to pledge an oath of allegiance to the state. Nine of the eleven relented, but Samuel A. Worcester and Dr. Elizur Butler refused and were sentenced to four years at hard labor. Their only recourse was an appeal to the United States Supreme Court.

In 1832, in the case of *Worcester v. Georgia,* Chief Justice John Marshall handed down the court's decision.

> The Cherokee Nation, then, is a distinct community, occupying its own territory, with boundaries accurately described, in which the laws of Georgia can have no force, and which the citizens of Georgia have no right to enter but with the assent of the Cherokees themselves or in conformity with treaties and with the acts of Congress.... The whole intercourse between the United States and this nation is, by our Constitution and laws, vested in the government of the United States... The act of the State of Georgia under which the plaintiff in error was prosecuted is consequently void.

John Ross and the rest of the Cherokee Nation received the news with overwhelming relief. Under treaty, Congressional law, and the US Constitution itself, their ancestral homeland was safe from the grasping hands of Georgia. Elias Boudinot, in the *Cherokee Phoenix*, proclaimed the decision "a great triumph on the part of the Cherokees so far as the question of their rights [is] concerned. The question is forever settled as to who is right and who is wrong." Two days after announcing the Court's ruling, Marshall issued a formal mandate ordering Georgia to release Worcester and Butler.

Treaty of New Echota and the Trail of Tears

The Cherokees' victory was short-lived, for it quickly became clear that Georgia would not abide by the Supreme Court's ruling. Georgia refused to recognize the Court's authority in the case, the missionaries remained in the state penitentiary, and Georgia continued to claim authority over Cherokee lands.

Infuriated and distraught that all their efforts might come to nothing, the Cherokees sent a delegation to Washington in a last-ditch effort to obtain President Jackson's cooperation. John Ridge, leader of the delegation, asked Jackson directly whether he intended to carry out his constitutional obligation to enforce the Supreme Court's decision in the *Worcester* case. Jackson replied pointedly that he had no such intention.

Instead, he advised Ridge to return home and tell his people that their only hope for survival as a nation was to abandon their homes and move beyond the Mississippi River.

With a promise of non-interference from Jackson, Georgia had a free hand in what was now solidly its northern territory. In late 1831, surveyors began partitioning Cherokee lands. Teams consisting of a surveyor, a chain carrier, a pack carrier, two axe men, and a cook roamed the hills and valleys of north Georgia for months preparing the region to be raffled off in the state's final land lottery.

Most Cherokees continued to resist, but by 1835 a small Cherokee faction led by Major Ridge and his son John was ready to relent. Together with *Cherokee Phoenix* editor Elias Boudinot and others, they signed the Treaty of New Echota in December. To Major Ridge, it seemed clear that there was "but one path to safety, one road to future existence as a Nation." That road lay west.

The Treaty of New Echota was a fraud. No more than a few hundred Cherokees supported the treaty's terms. Neither was it authorized by Principal Chief John Ross nor the Cherokee National Council. Even so, the United States Senate ratified the treaty in early 1836, insisting that the entire Cherokee Nation move west within two years or be forced to do so. Still they refused to leave.

In May 1838, General Winfield Scott arrived with 5,000 troops and began rounding up the Cherokees like cattle. By autumn of that year, almost the entire Cherokee Nation had been rounded up and the long journey began toward Indian Territory. The journey lasted through the winter, which was one of the coldest on record. Of nearly 16,000 people who set out on the march, forever to be known as the Trail of Tears, over 4,000 died on the journey. Among them was John Ross's wife Quatie. She gave up her blanket to a sick child and contracted pneumonia. The child lived, but Quatie died shortly after and was buried near Little Rock, Arkansas.

For some, the emotional wounds they suffered that winter never healed. In later life one old Cherokee remembered how his father collapsed in the snow and died. He was buried by the trail and the family continued on. Then his mother sank down. "She speak no more," he recalled. "We bury her and go on." Finally his five brothers and sisters all became ill and died. "One each day," he said, "and all are gone." Even after the passage of decades, the old man could still hear the cries of his dying family. "People sometimes say I look like I never smile, never laugh in lifetime."

Documents

1. Corn Tassel Defends Indian Land Rights (1785)

In 1785, whites pressed Cherokees in Tennessee to give up more land. Corn Tassel, who, like most Cherokees, had sided with the Tories and fought against white encroachment during the Revolution, defended Native American land rights. He finally relented and signed the Treaty of Hopewell, attempting to make a permanent peace with the whites.

It is a little surprising that when we entered into treaties with our brothers, the whites, their whole cry is *more land!* Indeed, formerly it seemed to be a matter of formality with them to demand what they knew we durst not refuse. But on the principles of fairness, of which we have received assurances during the conducting of the present treaty, and in the name of free will and equality, I must reject your demand....

Let us examine the facts of your present eruption into our country.... You marched into our territories with a superior force; our vigilance gave us no timely notice of your maneuvers; your numbers far exceeded us, and we fled to the stronghold or our extensive woods, there to secure our women and children.

Thus, you marched into our towns; they were left to your mercy; you killed a few scattered and defenseless individuals, spread fire and desolation wherever you pleased.... Again, were we to inquire by what law or authority you set up a claim, I answer, *none!* Your laws extend not into our country, nor ever did. You talk of the law of nature and the law of nations, and they are both against you.

Indeed, much has been advanced on the want of what you term civilization among the Indians; and many proposals have been made to us to adopt your laws, your religion, your manners and your customs. But we confess that we do not yet see the propriety or practicability of such a reformation, and should be better pleased with beholding the good effect of these doctrines in your own practices than with hearing you talk about them, or reading your papers to us upon such subjects....

We wish, however, to be at peace with you, and to do as we would be done by....

The great God of Nature has placed us in different situations. It is true that he has endowed you with many superior advantages; but he has not created us to be your slaves.

Samuel C. Williams, editor, "William Tatham, Wataugan," *Tennessee Historical Magazine* 7,3 (October 1921): 176–78.

2. Alexander McGillivray Repudiates the 1783 Treaty of Paris (1785)

Like Corn Tassel, Chief Alexander McGillivray of the Creeks sided with Britain during the Revolution, hoping to preserve the Proclamation Line of 1763 and hold back the tide of white encroachment. Here, in a 1785 letter representing most of the Southeastern Native Americans, he warns the Spanish in Florida against recognizing postwar US land claims stretching to the Mississippi River.

We, the chiefs and warriors of the said nations of Creek, Chickasaw, and Cherokee Indian nations...do hereby, in the most solemn manner, protest against any title, claim, or demand the American Congress may set up for or against our lands, settlements, and hunting grounds in consequence of the said treaty of peace between the King of Great Britain and the States of America, declaring that, as we were not parties, so we are determined to pay no attention to the manner in which the British negotiator has drawn out the lines of the lands in question, ceded to the American States. It being a notorious fact, known to the Americans—known to every person who is any ways conversant in, or acquainted with, American affairs—that his Britannic Majesty was never possessed, either by cession, purchase, or by right of conquest, of our territories, and which the said treaty gives away. On the contrary, it is well known that from the first settlement of the English colonies of Carolina and Georgia, up to the date of the said treaty, no title has ever been pretended to be made by his Britannic Majesty to our lands, except what was obtained by free gift, or by purchase for good and valuable considerations.... Nor did we the nations of Creeks, Chickasaws, and Cherokees do any act to forfeit our independence and natural rights to the said King of Great Britain, that could invest him with the power of giving our property away, unless fighting by the side of his soldiers in the day of battle, and spilling our best blood in the service of his nation, can be deemed so. The Americans, although sensible of the injustice done to us on this occasion, in consequence of this pretended claim, have divided our territory into counties, and set themselves down on our lands as if they were their own.... We have repeatedly warned the states of Carolina and Georgia to desist from these encroachments.... To these remonstrances we have received friendly talks, or replies, it is true; but while they are addressing us by the flattering appellations of friends and brothers, they are stripping us of our natural rights by depriving us of that inheritance which belonged to our ancestors, and has descended from them to us since the beginning of time.

Record in the Case of Colin Mitchell and Others, versus the United States, Supreme Court of the United States, January Term, 1831 (Washington DC: Duff Green, 1831) 293–95.

3. Committee Report on the Yazoo Land Fraud (1796)

In 1795, Georgia's legislators accepted bribes to sell vast tracts of land west of the Chattahoochee River to speculators at the ridiculously low price of a penny an acre. It made little difference that those lands were still occupied by Cherokees, Creeks, Choctaws, and Chickasaws. Nor did it matter that common folk would see little benefit from those sales. But after a firestorm of public protest and the ousting of nearly all members of Georgia's old Assembly, an investigative committee of the new Assembly laid out its findings and recommendations.

The committee to whom the consideration of the constitutionality and validity of a certain act of the last session of the Legislature passed at Augusta on the 7th day of January 1795...report that they have had the same under their serious consideration, and lament that they are compelled to declare that the Fraud, corruption and collusion by which the said Act was obtained, and the unconstitutionality of the same, evinces the utmost depravity in the majority of the late Legislature. It appears to your committee that public good was placed entirely out of view, and private interest alone consulted, and the rights of the present generation were violated and the rights of Posterity bartered by the said act.... The committee, whilst they thus with shame and confusion acknowledge that such a Legislature entrusted with the rights of their constituents should have existed in Georgia, cannot however forbear to congratulate the present Legislature and the community at large that there are sufficient grounds as well with respect to the unconstitutionality of the Act as from the testimony before the committee of the Fraud, practiced to obtain it, to pronounce that the same is a nullity of itself and not binding or obligatory on the people of this State, and they flatter themselves that a declaration to that purport, by a Legislative Act will check that rapacious and avaricious spirit of speculation which has in this State over leaped all decent bounds, and which if it were to continue would totally annihilate morality and good faith from among the citizens of this State. The committee for this purpose beg leave to report "An Act for declaring the said usurped Act void and for expunging the same from the face of the public records."

Christopher C. Meyers, editor, *Empire State of the South: Georgia History in Documents and Essays* (Macon GA: Mercer University Press, 2008) 53–54.

4. Tecumseh on Plans for an Indian Confederation (1810)

In 1810, Chief Tecumseh, son of a Shawnee father and Upper Creek mother, told William Henry Harrison, governor of Indiana Territory and future US president, that Native Americans had a right to their land and that he intended to unite them in defending that right.

My forefathers were warriors. Their son is a warrior. From them I only take my existence; from my tribe I take nothing.... The being within, communing with past ages, tells me that once, nor until lately, there was no white man on this continent. That it then all belonged to red men, children of the same parents, placed on it by the Great Spirit that made them, to keep it, to traverse it, to enjoy its productions, and to fill it with the same race. Once a happy race. Since made miserable by the white people, who are never contented, but always encroaching. The way, and the only way to check and stop this evil is for all the red men to unite in claiming a common and equal right in the land, as it was at first, and should be yet; for it never was divided, but belongs to all, for the use of each. That no part has a right to sell, even to each other, much less to strangers; those who want all, and will not do with less. The white people have no right to take the land from the Indians, because they had it first; it is theirs.... There cannot be two occupations in the same place. The first excludes all others. It is not so in hunting or traveling; for there the same ground will serve many, as they may follow each other all day; but the camp is stationary, and that is occupancy. It belongs to the first who sits down on his blanket or skins, which he has thrown upon the ground, and till he leaves it no other has a right.

Samuel G. Drake, *The Aboriginal Races of North America* (Philadelphia: Charles Desilver, 1859) 617–18.

5. Red Eagle's Surrender (1814)

Soon after the last defeat of Red Sticks at Horseshoe Bend, Chief Red Eagle entered Andrew Jackson's camp at Fort Jackson, near the future site of Montgomery, Alabama, and asked for peace. Jackson declined to take Red Eagle's life, but took half the Creek Nation with the Treaty of Fort Jackson.

General Jackson, I am not afraid of you. I fear no man, for I am a Creek warrior. I have nothing to request in behalf of myself; you can kill me, if you desire. But I come to beg you to send for the women and children of the war party, who are now starving in the woods. Their fields and cribs have been destroyed by your people, who have driven them to the woods without an ear of corn. I hope that you will send out parties who will safely conduct them here in order that they may be fed. I exerted myself in vain to prevent the massacre of the women and children at Fort Mims. I am now done fighting. The Red Sticks are nearly all killed. If I could fight you any longer I would most heartily do so. Send for the women and children. They have done you no harm. But kill me, if the white people want it done.

Albert James Pickett, *History of Alabama, and Incidentally of Georgia and Mississippi from the Earliest Period, Vol. 1* (Charleston: Walker and James, 1851) 349.

6. Speckled Snake Warns against Trusting the Whites (1829)

In reflecting on a century of white encroachment and Jackson's new offer of land west of the Mississippi, an elderly Creek man named Speckled Snake, "whose head was whitened with the frost of more than a hundred winters," expressed skepticism in an address to his fellow Creeks.

Brothers! We have heard the talk of our great father; it is very kind. He says he loves his red children.

Brothers! I have listened to many talks from our great father. When he first came over the wide waters, he was but a little man, and wore a red coat.—Our chiefs met him on the banks of the Savannah, and smoked with him the pipe of peace. He was then very little. His legs were cramped by sitting long in his big boat, and he begged for a little land to light his fire on. He said he had come over the wide waters to teach Indians new things, and to make them happy. He said he loved his red brothers, he was very kind.

The Muscogees gave him land, and kindled him a fire, that he might warm himself; and when his enemies, the pale faces of the south [the Spanish in Florida], made war on him, their young men drew the tomahawk, and protected his head from the scalping knife. But when the white man had warmed himself before the Indian's fire, and filled himself with their hominy, he became very large. With a step he bestrode the mountains, and his feet covered the plains and the valleys. His hands grasped the eastern and western sea, and his head rested on the moon. Then he became our Great Father. He loved his red children, and he said,

"Get a little further, lest I tread on thee." With one foot he pushed the red man over the Oconee, and with the other he trampled down the graves of his fathers, and the forests where he had so long hunted the deer.—But our Great Father still loved his red children, and he soon made them another talk. He said, "Get a little further; you are too near me." But there were some bad men among the Muscogees then, as there are now. They lingered around the graves of their ancestors, till they were crushed beneath the heavy tread of our Great Father. Their teeth pierced his feet, they made him angry. Yet he continued to love his red children; and when he found them too slow in moving, he sent his great guns before him to sweep his path.

Brothers! I have listened to a great many talks from our great father. But they always began and ended in this—"Get a little further; you are too near me."...

Brothers! When our Great Father made us a talk on a former occasion, he said, "Get a little farther; go beyond the Oconee, the Ocmulgee; there is a pleasant country," he also said, *"It shall be yours forever."* I have listened to his present talk. He says the land where you now live is not yours. Go beyond the Mississippi; there is game; and you may remain while the grass grows or the water runs. *Brothers!* Will not our Great Father come there also? He loves his red children... Yet where are the red children which he loves, once as numerous as the leaves of the forest? How many have been murdered by his warriors? How many have been crushed beneath his own footsteps.

Savannah Mercury in *Niles' Weekly Register* (Baltimore), 20 June 1829.

7. Squatters and Speculators Steal Indian Lands (1832)

White squatters moving onto Native American lands had been a problem since colonial times. In the 1830s as removal treaties were being forced on the Native Americans, despite Jackson's promise to protect them prior to their removal, the problem was compounded by land speculators as well. In document A, federal agent John Crowell reported in August 1832 to his superiors that Creek farms in Alabama, which Crowell calls "improvements," were being occupied by whites with the help of local authorities even as the federal marshal was trying to drive off the whites. Document B, from two letters by a federal agent, tells of similar hardships suffered by Mississippi's Choctaws in April and May 1832.

A.

Sir: the marshal of Alabama has commenced removing intruders from Indian improvements. The first he removed have returned with a reinforcement armed, and threaten to defend themselves. I understand they have brought the sheriff of the county, with writs to serve on the marshal and the officer commanding the troops, and such Indians as should be found in possession of the places from which they had been removed; but the marshal and officer having left the neighborhood, they run the Indians off and are again in peaceable possession of the improvements from which they had been removed.

The principal chief of that town was with me yesterday, and gives a distressing account of the situation of the Indians; the most of them in the woods, without means of subsistence, hiding from the intruders, who treat them cruelly when they meet them. This chief expressed much regret that the late treaty [of Cusseta] stipulation, in relation to the removal of intruders, could not have been executed by the Government.

B.

Owing to the law of the State of Mississippi passed at the last session granting permission to whites to settle in the Choctaw Nation, hundreds have come in and are squatting on the lands in all directions. Some of the settlers have brought reserves, and are very rich, and a town has already been laid out on the Tombigbee, at Young's bluff, called Gainsville.... A great many complaints from the Indians are made at the agency against the whites, who are rapidly settling in every direction. I send you herewith enclosed, the copy of a communication addressed to Colonel Ward, the agent, to show the difficulties the Indians have to encounter in their intercourse with the worthless population squatted in the nation, particularly from Alabama. There are many exceptions, but, for the most part, every purchaser of cultivation reservations have made small advances to the Indians, with a promise to pay the balance when the Indian makes a good title; which can hardly ever be effected, owing to the remote residence of the Indians when they remove to the West.

US Senate, *Correspondence on the Subject of the Emigration of Indians, 1833–35*, 23rd Congress, 1st Session, 1833, 5 vols. (Washington DC: Duff Green, 1834) 3:413, 1:605–606, 607–608.

8. Suffering Among Exiled Choctaws (1832)

Some whites were appalled at the suffering they witnessed among the Choctaws on their forced march to Indian Territory. One was Joseph Kerr, a Louisiana farmer who allowed a party of Choctaws access to his pumpkin patch in fall 1831. When he read that a similar fate befell the Creeks, he wrote to the secretary of war and former governor of Michigan Territory, Lewis Cass, who was in charge of Indian affairs.

Dear Sir: ...I live now on the side of, and within forty feet of, the road, and the only one by which the Choctaw Indians have passed, and must pass, that go by land. Their extreme poverty and consequent suffering in passing last fall, attracted my particular notice.... I do not yet know who is the contractor for furnishing them rations. But be him or them who they may, their object is to make money without the least feeling for the suffering of this unfortunate people. From Vicksburg to this place is sixty-eight miles. On this route they received a *scanty* supply...through an uninhabited country, fifty miles of which is an overflowed swamp, and in which distance are two large deep streams that must be crossed in a boat or raft, and one other nearly impassable in any way. This, they had to perform or perish, there being no provision made for them on the way. This, too, was to be done during the worst time of weather I have ever seen in any country—a heavy sleet having broken and bowed down all the small and much of the larger timber. And this was to be performed under the pressure of hunger by *old* women and young children, without any covering for their feet, legs, or body, except a cotton under-dress generally. In passing, before they reached the place of getting rations here, I gave a party leave to enter a small field in which pumpkins were. They would not enter without leave, though starving. Those they ate *raw* with greatest avidity....

I have seen poverty amongst the Northern Indians, but theirs is nothing compared to that of those of the South. Friendship for the whites never can exist in the bosom of any of those that passed here last fall. The least sensible of them has been touched too deeply in the tender part ever to become reconciled.

Report says, and I have no doubt of the truth of it, that the Choctaws have been greatly defrauded in the sale of their stock cattle. Indeed, it appears to us, who are near enough to almost see the whole, that few, if any, are sent amongst them, or entrusted to act for or with them, that are not the most unprincipled of the human family. How this should so invariably happen is difficult to suppose. Blame is due somewhere, and to a great extent....

US Senate Document 512, *Correspondence on the Subject of the Emigration of Indians, 1833–35*, 23rd Congress, 1st Session, 1833, 5 vols. (Washington DC: Duff Green, 1834) 1:719–20.

9. The Second Creek War a "Humbug" (1836)

In May 1836, as land speculators called for a final war of extermination against Alabama's few remaining Creeks, the Montgomery Advertiser *saw the effort for what it was.*

Is this community never to enjoy a season of repose? Are interested land speculators from Alabama and Georgia longer to palm off their deception on the public? Who believes that the Creeks are about to assume a hostile attitude towards the whites? We answer, no one.

The idea of a war with the Creeks is all a *humbug*. It is a base and diabolical scheme devised by interested men to keep an ignorant race of people from maintaining their just rights, and to deprive them of the small remaining pittance placed under their control, through the munificence of the government. We do trust, for the credit of those concerned, that these blood suckers may be ferreted out, and their shameful misrepresentations exposed.

We have lately conversed with many of the settlers of the nation, and also the Superintendent of Indian Affairs, and the unanimous opinion is that there is nothing like a system of hostility meditated by the Creeks; that the chiefs are utterly averse to a warfare with the whites; that it is foreign from their intention to resist the Treaty; that they are preparing to remove, and will, in a short time, commence emigrating west of the Mississippi.

The red men must soon leave. They have nothing left on which to subsist. Their property has been taken from them—their stock killed up, their farms pillaged—and by whom? By white men. By individuals who should have scorned to take such mean advantages of those who were unprotected and defenseless. Such villainy may go unpunished in this world, but the day of retribution will most certainly arrive.

Montgomery Advertiser in *The Southern Advocate* (Huntsville AL), 17 May 1836.

10. Suffering and Death on the Creek Road West (1836)

The following letter written on Christmas Day 1836 by a witness at Fort Gibson, Indian Territory, makes clear why removal amounted to a death sentence for many thousands of Southeastern Native Americans.

There is now arriving at Fort Gibson, and on the road between that place and the Mississippi River, near 14,000 Creek Indians.... The removal is made by a company of contractors, who receive a stated sum per head.... The removal of the Indians is, to them, a matter of speculation.... No portion of American history can furnish a parallel of the misery and suffering at present endured by the emigrating Creeks.... Thousands of them are entirely destitute of shoes or covering of any kind for their feet; many of them are almost naked, and but few of them anything more on their persons than a light dress calculated only for the summer, or for a warmer climate.... In this destitute condition, they are wading in cold mud, or are hurried on over the frozen road, as the case may be. Many of them have in this way had their feet frost-bitten; and being unable to travel, fall in the rear of the main party, and in this way are left on the road to await the ability or convenience of the contractors to assist them. Many of them, not being able to endure this unexampled state of human suffering, die, and, it is said, are thrown by the side of the road, and are covered over only with brush, &c., where they remain until devoured by the wolves.

How long this state of things will exist is hard to conjecture. It is now past the middle of December, and the winter, though cold, is by no means at its worst stage; and when the extreme of winter does fall upon these most miserable creatures, in their present suffering and desperate condition, the destruction of human life will be most deplorable.

US Congress, *Register of Debates*, 24th Congress, 2nd session, vol. 13 (Washington DC: Gales and Seaton, 1837) 1539.

11. Osceola Vows to Fight for Seminole Land (1834)

A few Seminole chiefs were bullied into signing away their lands in Florida with the 1832 Treaty of Paynes Landing. But they hardly spoke for the nation as a whole. Osceola made that clear when he and other Seminole leaders met with federal agent Wiley Thompson at the Seminole agency in October 1834. A year later Seminoles attacked the agency and killed Thompson.

My Brothers! The white people got some of our chiefs to sign a paper to give our lands to them, but our chiefs did not do as we told them to do; they did wrong. We must do right. The agent tells us we must go away from the lands we live on—our homes and the graves of our fathers—and go over the big river [Mississippi] among bad Indians. When the agent tells me to go from my home, I hate him, because I love my home, and will not go from it.

My Brothers! When the Great Spirit tells me to go with the white man, I go; but he tells me not to go. The white man tells me I shall go, and he will send people to make me go. But I have a rifle, and I have some powder and lead. I say we must not leave our homes and lands. If any of our people want to go west, we won't let them; and I tell them they are our enemies, and we will treat them so, for the Great Spirit will protect us.

Thomas L. M'Kenney, *Memoirs, Official and Personal; with Sketches of Travels among the Northern and Southern Indians, Vol. 1* (New York: Paine and Burgess, 1846) 280.

12. Major Hitchcock Calls the Seminoles "Right in Defending Their Homes" (1840–1841)

Major Ethan Allen Hitchcock was assigned to help subdue the Florida Seminoles, though he felt that he was on the wrong side of the fight, as these excerpts from his journal and letters to Secretary of War John Bell make clear. Hitchcock came to understand that the Seminoles could not be subdued and recommended withdrawal.

The government is in the wrong, and this is the chief cause of the persevering opposition of the Indians, who have nobly defended their country against our attempt to enforce a fraudulent treaty. The natives used every means to avoid a war, but were forced into it by the tyranny of our government....

The Treaty of Payne's Landing was a fraud on the Indians: They never approved of it or signed it. They are right in defending their homes and we ought to let them alone.... The army has done all that it could. It has marched all over the upper part of Florida. It has burned all the towns and destroyed all the planted fields. Yet, though the Indians are broken up and scattered, they exist in large numbers ....

To carry on such a war seems an idle, if not wicked waste of life and treasure... Not a single [Seminole] war party, after striking a blow, has been captured by us, so far as I know, out of the multitude of instances of pursuit since this war began. Flight with them has become a science....

The conclusion, then, is this: that the government will actually gain time and save money, lives, and reputation, by conceding something to the Indians...acknowledging their possession (by a truce, not a treaty) of as much of the country as will satisfy them....

There is now a tendency on the part of the Indians to abstain from acts of war. Let this be fostered by pacific communications. Some will come in and be induced to emigrate. Others will gradually lay aside the rifle, and the war will die a natural death. It may require some time to accomplish this amicably; but it is certain that force cannot effect it in a much longer time if at all.

Ethan Allen Hitchcock, *Fifty Years in Camp and Field*, edited by W. A. Croffut (New York: G.P. Putnam's Sons, 1909) 120, 121–22, 129.

13. John Ross Denies Georgia's Claim to Cherokee Land (1828)

Principal Chief John Ross vigorously defended Cherokee rights, warning Georgia against claiming Cherokee land. Nevertheless, in December 1828, the Georgia General Assembly passed an act extending its authority over the Cherokee Nation as of June 1830.

The pretended claim of Georgia to a portion of our lands, is alleged on the following principles. First, by discovery. Secondly, by conquest. Thirdly, by compact.

We shall endeavor briefly to elucidate the character of this claim. In the first place, the Europeans by the skill and enterprise of their Navigators, discovered this vast Continent, and found it inhabited exclusively by Indians of various Tribes, and by pacific courtesy and designing stratagems, the aboriginal proprietors were induced to permit a people from a foreign clime to plant colonies, and without the consent or knowledge of the native Lords, a potentate of England, whose eyes never saw, whose purse never purchased, and whose sword never conquered the soil we inhabit, presumed to issue a parchment, called a "Charter," to the Colony of Georgia, in which its boundary was set forth, including a great extent of country inhabited by the Cherokee and other Indian nations.

Secondly, after a lapse of many years when the population of their Colonies had become strong, they revolted against their sovereign, and by success of Arm, established an Independent Government, under the name of "the United States." It is further alleged that the Cherokee Nation prosecuted a war at the same time against the colonies.

3dly. Several years after the Treaties of peace, friendship and protection, which took place between the U.S. and Cherokee Nation, and by which the faith of the United States was solemnly pledged to guarantee to the Cherokee Nation forever, their title to their lands, a Compact [of 1802] was entered into between the United States and the State of Georgia, by which the United States promised to purchase for the use of Georgia certain lands belonging to the Cherokee Nation so soon as it could be done on *reasonable* and *peaceable terms*.

Thus stands the naked claim of Georgia to a portion of our lands. The claim advanced under the plea of discovery is preposterous. Our ancestors from time immemorial possessed this country, not by a "Charter" from the hand of a mortal King, who had no right to grant it, but by the Will of the King of Kings, who created all things and liveth for ever and ever.

The claim advanced on the second head, on the ground of conquest, is no less futile than the first, even admitting that the Cherokees waged a war with the Colonies, at the time they fought for their independence. The Cherokees took part in the war, only as the allies of Great Britain, and not as her subjects, being an independent nation.... At the termination of the war, the United States negotiated with the Cherokees on the terms of peace as an independent nation, and...solemnly pledged their faith that our title should be guaranteed to our nation forever.

The third pretension is extremely lame. The United States enters into a compact with Georgia that they will purchase certain lands, which belong to us, for Georgia, so soon as they can do it on *peaceable* and *reasonable terms*. This promise was made on the part of the United States without knowing whether this nation would ever consent to dispose of those lands on any terms whatever; and the Cherokees not being a part of the compact, their title cannot be affected in the slightest degree.

Cherokee Phoenix (New Echota, Cherokee Nation), 22 October 1828.

14. John Ross and the Cherokee Council Call the Treaty of New Echota a Fraud (1836)

After the US Senate ratified the Treaty of New Echota, Chief John Ross and the Cherokee Council petitioned Congress to repudiate the document as a fraud, pointing out that Major Ridge and other Cherokee treaty signers had no authority to make such an agreement.

We are overwhelmed; our hearts are sickened; our utterance is paralyzed, when we reflect on the condition in which we are placed by the audacious practices of unprincipled men, who have managed their stratagems with so much dexterity as to impose on the Government of the United States, in the face of our earnest, solemn, and reiterated protestations.

The instrument in question is not the act of our nation. We are not parties to its covenants. It has not received the sanction of our people. The makers of it sustain no office nor appointment in our nation, under the designation of chiefs, headmen, or any other title, by which they hold, or could acquire, authority to assume the reins of government, and to make bargain and sale of our rights, our possessions, and our common country. And we are constrained solemnly to declare that we cannot but contemplate the enforcement of the stipulations of this instrument on us, against our consent, as an act of injustice and oppression, which, we are well persuaded, can never knowingly be countenanced by the Government and people of the United States, nor can we believe it to be the design of these honorable and high-minded individuals, who stand at the head of the Government, to bind a whole nation by the acts of a few unauthorized individuals. And therefore we, the parties to be affected by the result, appeal with confidence to the justice, the magnanimity, the compassion, of your honorable assemblies, against the enforcement on us of the provisions of a compact, in the formation of which we have had no agency....

On your kindness, on your humanity, on your compassion, on your benevolence, we rest our hopes.

US House of Representatives, *Memorial of a Delegation of the Cherokee Nation*, 25th Congress, 2nd session, document no. 99, 12–13.

15. The Cherokee Trail of Tears (1839)

Here a white traveler describes the sad, deplorable condition of Cherokee exiles traveling through Kentucky on their way west in the winter of 1838-39. The writer noted that "if there be a God who avenges the wrongs of the injured," he would not want to be the object of their silent prayers for all the land in Georgia.

On Tuesday evening we fell in with a detachment of the poor Cherokee Indians.... about eleven hundred...sixty wagons—six hundred horses, and perhaps forty pairs of oxen. We found them in the forest camped for the night by the road side...under a severe fall of rain accompanied by heavy wind. With their canvas for a shield from the inclemency of the weather, and the cold wet ground for a resting place...many of the aged Indians were suffering extremely from the fatigue of the journey, and the ill health consequent upon it...several were then quite ill, and one aged man we were informed was then in the last struggles of death.

...The sick and feeble are carried in wagons...a great many ride on horseback and multitudes go on foot—even aged females, apparently nearly ready to drop into the grave, were traveling with heavy burdens attached to the back—on the sometimes frozen ground, and sometimes muddy streets, with no covering for the feet except what nature had given them.... We learned from the inhabitants on the road where the Indians passed, that they buried fourteen or fifteen at every stopping place, and they make a journey of ten miles per day only on an average.

...One lady passed on in her hack in company with her husband...she was a mother too and her youngest child about three years old was sick in her arms, and all she could do was to make it comfortable as circumstances would permit.... she could only carry her dying child in her arms a few miles farther, and then she must stop in a stranger-land

and consign her much loved babe to the cold ground, and that too without pomp or ceremony, and pass on with the multitude....

...When I passed the last detachment of those suffering exiles and thought that my native countrymen had thus expelled them from their native soil and their much loved homes, and that too in this inclement season of the year in all their suffering, I turned from the sight with feelings which language cannot express and wept like childhood then.

"The Suffering Exiles: A Traveler's View of One of the Last Emigrant Parties," *New York Observer*, 26 January 1839, in Grant Foreman, *Indian Removal* (Norman: University of Oklahoma Press, 1932) 305–307.

4

Widening Gaps: Planters, Plain Folk, and the Enslaved

The Rise of King Cotton

The push for NativeAmerican expulsion was driven not only by overt racism but also by the value of native lands. What gave that land its value was the extent to which it could produce wealth, especially in the form of cotton, which was fast becoming the South's leading cash crop. By 1860, cotton was the leading export product for the entire United States, accounting for nearly half the total. Southern cotton output amounted to twice that of the rest of the world combined. Little wonder that the South was called the Cotton Kingdom.

The rise of King Cotton had been relatively recent. In 1791 the nation produced just 5,000 bales. Slaveholders devoted little of their labor force to cotton because it took too long to separate the seeds from the fibers by hand. Then came the cotton engine, commonly called a "gin" for short, which did the job mechanically and much more quickly. Eli Whitney, a Connecticut man employed as a tutor on Catherine Greene's Georgia plantation, is usually credited with the cotton gin's invention. Though there were simpler versions of the gin dating to as early as the fifth century in India, the gin Whitney patented in 1793, using a second cylinder to clean fibers off the first, was considerably more efficient.

There is some controversy over the origins of Whitney's gin. Whitney may have gotten the design, or at least the idea, from Catherine Greene. Or the idea may have come from conversations Whitney had with enslaved Africans on the Greene plantation. There is even some evidence that an Augusta mechanic named Hodgen Holmes had his own gin in the works at the same time Whitney was developing his. We do know that in 1796, Holmes patented an improved version that used saw teeth in place of Whitney's metal spikes on a rotating cylinder, making it easier for the cotton fibers to be removed by the second cylinder.

The gin's impact on cotton production was dramatic. By 1801 the nation's output was up to 100,000 bales. In 1833 it was more than ten times that amount at 1,099,500. By 1859, production had ballooned to 5,868,000 bales. That production reflected the high price of cotton. Those prices encouraged producers to buy up as much good cotton land as they could. Most of that land lay in a broad swath running from South Carolina to Texas, often called the Black Belt both for its rich soil and its slave population. Rice was still the major crop along the Carolina-Georgia coast. Tobacco dominated in the upper South, as did sugar cane in southern Louisiana. But cotton far out-distanced other cash crops. What money did not go into land went mostly into slaves to work it.

With so much of the South's investment capital going into land and slaves, little was left for industrialization, a trend reflected in the South's overwhelmingly rural population. In 1860, though the slave states had a population of just over 12 million, more than a third of the nation's total of over 31 million, it accounted for about 15 percent of US industry. Much of that industry was related to cotton in the form of transporting, ginning, pressing bales, and textile manufacturing.

Transportation, which was vital to the South's cash-crop economy, initially centered on its rivers as much from necessity as convenience. Southern dirt roads, a few improved with wooden planks and nearly all locally maintained, were poorly kept. Some were impassable for much of the year. According to one account, they were most often "indebted for their improvement to nothing but the wheels that run over them."

Though water transport was preferred to roads, it was fairly dangerous. River pilots were always on the lookout for hidden boulders, sand bars, and downed trees. During dry spells, stranded boats were either dug out by hand or left for weeks. Another danger was steam power itself, with boiler explosion more than occasional. Accidents were so common that insurance rates for river cargoes ran as high as 3 percent of the freight's value. By contrast, ocean-going cargoes could be insured for half that rate.

High insurance rates and the dangers of navigation were major reasons that many cotton growers and merchants began to see railroads

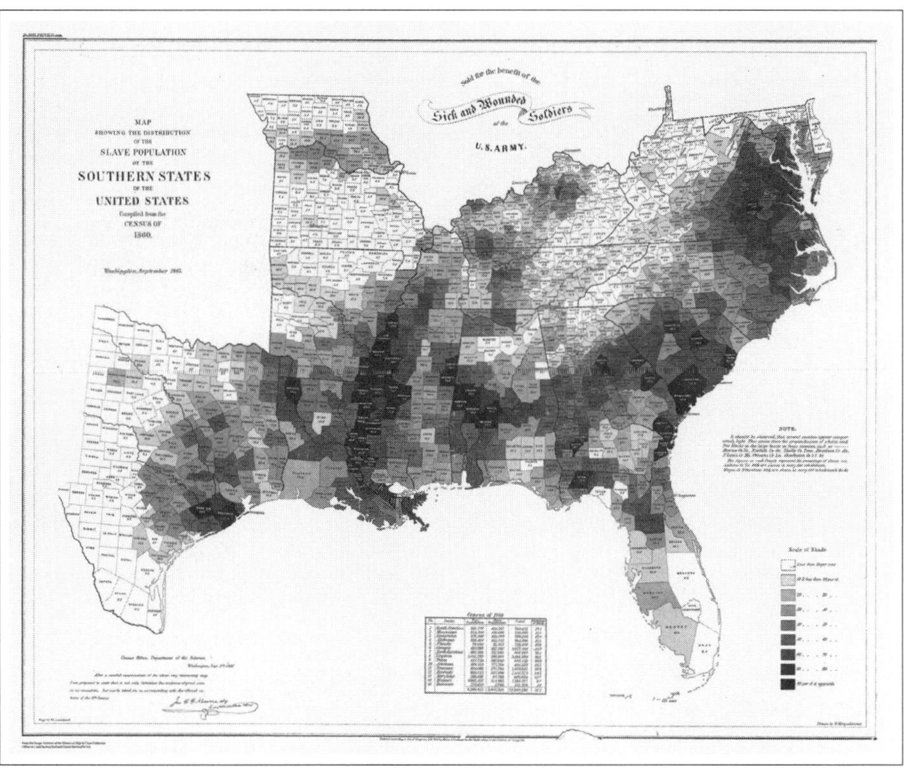

Distribution of the South's enslaved population by county. Darker areas represent heavier concentrations of enslaved people as a percentage of total population. Cotton cultivated by slave labor predominated in the Deep South, tobacco in the Upper South, sugar cane in southern Louisiana, and rice along the coasts of Georgia and the Carolinas.

Prepared from the 1860 census. U.S. Department of the Interior, 1861.

as a cheaper alternative. Construction began on several lines in the 1830s. In 1833, a 136-mile rail line opened running from Charleston to Hamburg, South Carolina, just across the Savannah River from Augusta. Aimed at diverting cotton traffic to Charleston, it was at the time the world's longest rail line. The Panic of 1837 and resulting economic depression put so many Southern banks out of business that capital for railroad construction was difficult to raise. But it was going strong again by the mid-1840s. By 1860 the South had close to 10,000 miles of track, just under half that of the North.

Whether it was trade, manufacturing, or transportation, much of the South's economic activity was directly or indirectly driven by cash-crop agriculture, mostly cotton and tobacco. The towns depended on the plantations and served the needs of planters. Local cotton fed the cotton mills that were beginning to spring up. Workers at train depots and river docks loaded cotton and tobacco. Wagoneers, steamer crews, and railroad workers hauled the product. Carpenters and masons built cotton and tobacco warehouses. Merchants and manufacturers sold their goods to the townspeople and to the plantations. Cotton and tobacco brokers, for an average 2.5 percent commission, provided planters with access to textile mills and cigar factories of the North and Europe.

Diverging Fortunes of Planters and Plain Folk

Though cotton and tobacco brought great wealth to the South, that wealth was concentrated in the hands of a very few. By 1860, only one-fourth of white Southerners owned slaves. Of those, about half owned less than five. The richest 5 percent of whites owned 53 percent of the region's wealth. The bottom half owned only 1 percent. It was but one reflection of what had become a rigid socioeconomic scale headed by planters, along with a few industrialists and financiers. At the bottom were poor whites and slaves.

Planters are generally defined as people who owned twenty or more slaves. That was roughly the level at which a slaveholder could afford to hire an overseer to manage the plantation and its slave labor force. Planters and their families comprised about 225,000 people, or nearly 3 percent of the South's approximately 8 million whites. Seventy percent of planters owned less than fifty slaves. Planters who owned 50 or more numbered just over 10,000. Only 2,265 owned more than 100.

For sheer ostentation, the big planters were hard to beat. The most affluent modeled themselves after the landed gentry of Britain. Many, like the Shacklefords of Early County, Georgia, were renowned for the extravagance they displayed at every opportunity. One overnight guest at "The Pines," as the Shackleford plantation was called, arrived by horseback at dusk and was "ushered to a room where a body servant prepared his bath and laid out fresh linen. Downstairs, candles and an open fire illuminated a large room with French windows opening onto a veranda. There were comfortable chairs, tables for reading by lamplight, a secretary for writing, a piano piled high with music. A dinner table [was] laid with the finest silver, china and crystal."

Most planters did not live in such lavish surroundings as the Shacklefords. Their residences were most often eight- to ten-room homes made of clapboard planks, usually painted with whitewash. Some did not even reside on their plantations, preferring the comforts and conveniences of town life. Most were educated, but they often lacked the social and cultural refinement so often associated in popular media with the planter class. The great majority, especially the smaller planters, viewed themselves mainly as businessmen whose wealth happened to confer upon them a degree of social prestige.

On the next rung down the South's social ladder stood a comfortably well-to-do class made up of prosperous slaveholding farmers owning between five and nineteen slaves, together with a smattering of merchants and urban professionals. These slaveholders and their families totaled about 815,000, or 40 percent of all slaveholders. Their primary cash crop was cotton, but many also raised livestock and grew oats and corn for market. They lived in moderate homes of five or six rooms and were better fed, clothed, and usually better educated than the yeomen and poor whites.

Roughly 4,960,000 Southerners, 62 percent of the free population, comprised the yeoman class of small land-holding farm families. Nearly a million of these folk were members of small slaveholding households, owning less than five slaves. The other four million belonged to families owning no slaves at all.

Yeomen generally lived in two- to four-room homes made of unpainted clapboard planks or squared, rough-hewn logs. Few had much if any formal education. Many were functionally illiterate. They usually grew some form of cash crop, but much of their acreage was devoted to subsistence farming. This was especially true for nonslaveholding yeomen. Many depended more on small herds of free roaming (or open range) livestock than produce, particularly in the Appalachian and Ozark uplands and pine barrens of the coastal plains.

Whatever the family's economic focus, their main concern was having enough food on the table from day to day. For most yeomen, cotton and tobacco did not figure prominently in that effort. With few hands to work their land, concentration on cash crops was a luxury they could not afford. It was unlikely that they ever would. There was only so much good farmland to go around, and by the 1840s most of it was already owned by planters and more affluent slaveholders. Land prices were so high that chances of moving into the planter class or even reaching the ranks of the comfortably well-off were not good, especially among lesser yeomen.

These lesser yeomen were sometimes only marginally better off than landless or near-landless poor whites, often called "white trash" by planters and more prosperous slaveholders. About 2 million Southerners were poor whites, making up a quarter of the South's free population. They included tens of thousands of urban laborers and their families who one observer described as "in such a condition that, if temporarily thrown out of employment, great numbers of them are at once reduced to a state of destitution, and are dependent upon credit or charity for their daily food."

Most poor whites belonged to rural families of tenants and farm laborers who did not own enough land to support their families, or owned no land at all. Some hired themselves out to landholders for meager wages. Others worked for a share of the crop. They lived mostly in plank or log structures with one or two rooms and plank or dirt floors. What vegetables they had were grown with their own hands in small gardens. What meat there was came largely from hunting or fishing. Literacy rates were low among these people. Like most yeomen, few of the South's tenants and sharecroppers could ever hope to improve their condition.

Opportunities for upward mobility had been better only a generation before. Land prices earlier in the century had been relatively low as Native American land was becoming available. Wealthy men from the increasingly crowded East bought much of the better land, but small farmers had little trouble getting loans with which to purchase land and sometimes slaves. Cotton prices were on the rise, and there was every expectation that loans could be repaid. Farmers who had enough good land might even hope to become affluent slaveholders or even planters.

But a severe economic depression, the Panic of 1837, put an end to the hopes of millions. Cotton and tobacco prices fell dramatically and continued falling into the early 1840s. Aspiring yeomen found it impossible to keep up with loan payments. Their land and slaves were repossessed and sold at auction, usually to better-established slaveholders. Some farmers were able to keep a few acres and eke out a living as lesser yeomen. Many, however, lost everything and fell into tenancy and sharecropping. When the cotton market finally recovered in the 1840s, planters and the more affluent slaveholders held nearly all the South's better agricultural lands. By that time, most Southern farmers found themselves trapped in a poverty from which few could ever escape.

The gap between rich and poor continued to grow through the 1850s. Larger slaveholders bought up more and more land, forcing a rapid rise in land prices and making it nearly impossible for smaller farmers to increase their holdings—or for tenant farmers to buy any land at all. Wealth in terms of slaveholding was also becoming concentrated in fewer hands. During the 1850s, the proportion of slaveholders in the free population dropped by 20 percent. Georgia historian Numan Bartley notes that "only the division of land and slaves of deceased planters among heirs prevented social mobility from being considerably more closed than it was." Economic circumstances beyond their control were forcing so many yeomen into landless tenancy that the editor of one newspaper predicted the complete disappearance of small independent farmers in the South.

Slavery without Submission

At the bottom of the social scale in a caste of their own, separate and distinct from the white class structure, were African Americans. Numbering about 4.25 million, they made up over a third of the South's population. Most were held as slaves. In the 1860 census, only a quarter-million were listed as "free colored." Yet these folk were not entirely free. They could not vote, testify against whites in court, or even hold property in their own names. Their property was held by a white person designated as their "guardian." To support the slaveholder argument that blacks could not take care of themselves, free blacks, even those who held no property, were required by state law to have white guardians.

Restrictions on blacks held as slaves were even tighter. In addition to those applying to free blacks, state slave codes dictated that no slave could carry a gun, travel without a pass, or learn to read or write. Slave marriages had no legal standing. Slave gatherings, even for religious services, were forbidden without a white person present.

Such restrictions were born both of fear and a drive for control. Despite slaveholder claims to the contrary, the "wise master," as historian Kenneth Stampp put it, "did not take seriously the belief that Negroes were natural-born slaves. He knew better. He knew that Negroes freshly imported from Africa had to be broken into bondage; that each succeeding generation had to be carefully trained. This was no easy task, for the bondsman rarely submitted willingly. Moreover, he rarely submitted completely. In most cases there was no end to the need for control—at least not until old age reduced the slave to a condition of helplessness." Control of elderly slaves was hardly ever a concern in any case. Less than four percent ever lived to see age sixty.

Slave resistance took a variety of forms ranging from work slowdowns to running away. Suicide was not unheard of. Some slaves were treated so badly that death was a welcomed relief. In 1856, one enslaved woman took her own life by swallowing strychnine. Sometimes slaves took their owners' lives as well. When the overseer on a Georgia plantation began beating a young slave girl with a sapling tree, one of the older slaves grabbed an axe and killed him.

More often slaves were on the receiving end of violence. They were defined as property both by slave-state courts and finally, in the *Dred Scott* case of 1857, by the United States Supreme Court. As personal property, slaves were subject to the absolute authority of their owners and to whatever controls they chose to employ. As one member of the Georgia state Supreme Court said, "subordination can only be maintained by the right to give moderate correction—a right similar to that which exists in the father over his children." But that was little protection for the enslaved. The definition of "moderate correction" was left entirely to slaveholders. "Should death ensue by accident, while this slave is thus receiving moderate correction," recalled one observer, "the constitution of Georgia kindly denominates the offence justifiable homicide." Other slave states' constitutions offered a similar view.

Because slaves had monetary value, death as a direct result of discipline was unusual. The objective of physical torture was to inflict as much pain as possible without doing permanent damage. Scarring or mutilation might decrease the slave's resale value or ability to work. Physical abuse was, nevertheless, extremely common. Owners or overseers frequently administered beatings in the "buck" or "rolling jim" positions. In each case the slave was stripped naked and bound tight. Rias Body, a former slave, remembered the buck as "making the Negro squat, running a stout stick under his bended knee, and then tying his hands firmly to the stick—between the knees. Then the lash was laid on his back parts."

Another common method of abuse was to string slaves up by their thumbs with only their toes touching the ground and whip them. The slave might be "further tormented by having his wounds 'doctored' with salt and red pepper." Former slave Rhodus Walton belonged to an owner "whose favorite form of punishment was to take a man (or woman) to the edge of the plantation where a rail fence was located. His head was then placed between two rails so that escape was impossible and he was whipped until the overseer was exhausted. This was an almost daily occurrence, administered on the slightest provocation." After recalling the variety of tortures inflicted on slaves, one freedman told an interviewer in the 1930s, "Sir, you can never know what some slaves endured." Little wonder that slaveholders lived in constant fear of

Ellen and William Craft, an enslaved couple from Bibb County, Georgia, devised an escape plan in which Ellen would dress in men's clothing and pose as a slaveholder with William as her slave. That Ellen's light complexion allowed her to "pass" for white says much about the sexual oppression that enslaved women so often experienced. It also makes clear that slavery was not entirely a race-based institution.

Engraving from William Still, *The Underground Rail Road* (1872).

slave rebellion. To mitigate that fear, they frequently hired poor whites to ride on slave patrols, designed to guard against insurrection. Slaves found away from their owners' premises without written permission could be given up to twenty lashes or more.

The Sorest Spot

Besides the constant threat of physical punishment, slaveholders found that the most effective means of intimidating slaves was by threatening their families. Any slave might be pushed to the point of disregard for his or her own safety and attempt to fight back or escape. But when owners threatened loved ones, slaves were more likely to hold their anger in check. Slave marriages were, therefore, encouraged even though they had no recognition in law. Such recognition would have established a state-sanctioned bond between members of the slave family, implicitly infringing on the "property" rights of the owner—specifically the right to deal with and dispose of his property as he saw fit. To further stress their power, slaveholders used a variety of means to drive home the point that even within the slave family, the owner was still in control. Some personally presided over the marriage ceremony. Others did not even allow parents to name their own children. They reserved that privilege for themselves.

In naming the children of slave women, many slaveholders were actually exercising their own parental rights. For a planter to have any number of mistresses among his slaves was quite normal. Some slaveholders viewed rape as another method of enforcing psychological dominance within the slave community. Others did it simply because they viewed slaves as property to be used at their pleasure. The first sexual experience a planter's son had was usually with a female slave. Robert Ellett, enslaved in King William County, Virginia, recalled that "in those days if you was a slave and had a good looking daughter, she was taken from you. They would put her in the big house where the young masters could have the run of her." Pregnancy often followed. Little wonder that slaves of light complexion were present on nearly every plantation. William Craft, formerly enslaved in Georgia, wrote after his escape that "slavery in America is not at all confined to persons of any particular complexion; there are a very large number of slaves as white as anyone." By law, the mother's slave status was passed on to her children regardless of the father's status.

Mary Chesnut, wife of a prominent South Carolina planter/politician, wrote of slavery and the sexual oppression it promoted as "a monstrous system." "Like the patriarchs of old," she complained, "our men live all in one house with their wives and their concubines, and the mulattoes one sees in every family exactly resemble the white children. And every lady tells you who is the father of all the mulatto children in everybody's household, but those in her own she seems to think drop from the clouds, or pretends so to think."

Though slaveholders constantly spoke of blacks as sub-human, their own urges and actions demonstrated otherwise. Thomas Jefferson called blacks "inferior to the whites in the endowments both of mind and body," wondering aloud whether they might be a "different species of the same genus." Yet for decades Jefferson kept an enslaved mistress, Sally Hemings, and fathered several children by her. Fanny Kemble noted the same phenomenon among slaveholders generally, and its accompanying hypocrisy, from a Georgia plantation owned by her husband Pierce Butler: "Mr. Butler, and many others, speak as if there were a natural repugnance in all whites to any alliance with the black race; and yet it is notorious that almost every Southern planter has a family more or less numerous of illegitimate colored children."

With the legal status of white women only marginally better than that of slaves, they had little choice but to endure the infidelity of their husbands. In referring to Harriet Beecher Stowe's *Uncle Tom's Cabin,* which described many of slavery's brutalities, Mary Chesnut suggested that the author "did not hit the sorest spot. She makes [Simon] Legree a bachelor." When the slaves finally gained their freedom, an Alabama planter's wife said of Abraham Lincoln, "he has freed us, too."

Some enslaved people used their light skin to good advantage. In 1833, one Southern newspaper ran an advertisement offering twenty dollars for the return of an escaped slave named Mabin. The paper described him as "a bright mulatto, with grey eyes—hair straight and sandy.... He will pass for a white man where he is not known." Such descriptions of runaway slaves were common. Ellen Craft, daughter of a slave mother and her white owner, also used her light complexion to escape. In December 1848, she and her husband William both escaped from slavery in Bibb County, Georgia. With Ellen posing as a slaveholder and William as her slave, they boarded a train in Macon and headed for Savannah. Traveling several legs of their long and dangerous journey by steam ship and railroad, they reached freedom by train in Philadelphia on Christmas morning.

No matter how the children were sired, slaveholders usually encouraged slave women to have as many as possible. More children, of course, meant more field hands, but they also gave the owner an effective tool of control. Not only did slaves fear abuse of family members, there was also the concern that they might be sold off at any time. As the slaves well knew, an owner's threat to sell spouses or children was no idle one. One traveler who visited a slave market in Columbus, Georgia, wrote that "such separations as these are quite common, and appear to be no more thought of, by those who enforce them, than the separation of a calf from its brute parent."

A Georgia woman recalled slave traders driving groups of children to market "the same as they would a herd of cattle." Slaves constantly feared having their families put through such misery. They were also less likely to run away since that too would mean permanent separation from their loved ones. Of the many thousands of slaves who escaped bondage in the early nineteenth century, most were young, single, and childless.

The most celebrated escapes followed various routes known collectively as the Underground Railroad. Harriet Tubman, most famous of the railroad's "conductors," led upwards of 300 escapees to freedom. Rewards offered for her capture totaled as much as $40,000 but she was never caught. Neither was Arnold Gragston, an enslaved Kentuckian who ferried hundreds of fellow bondsmen and women across the Ohio River before making his own escape. Thanks to Tubman, Gragston, and so many others like them, well over 100,000 enslaved people, and perhaps many more, escaped north during the antebellum era.

Not all escape routes ran northward. Spanish Florida was a haven for refugees in the Deep South until it became a US territory in 1821. In the Southwest, Mexico proved attractive for those escaping bondage. "In

Mexico you could be free," recalled a former slave. "They didn't care what color you was, black, white, yellow or blue."

Regardless of distance or direction, escaping slavery was dangerous work. Slave catchers and bloodhounds were hot on the heels of every escapee. Captured refugees could have several toes or even half a foot cut off to prevent further escapes. One slave was whipped so badly after a failed attempt that he died three days later.

"The fear of being pursued with guns and blood-hounds, and of being killed or captured" weighed heavily on Henry Bibb's mind before he fled Kentucky for freedom in Detroit. But the heaviest burden on his heart was his strong attachment to friends and family. For most enslaved people, the greatest deterrent to escape was the near-certainly that they would never see loved ones again. Henry had planned to buy his wife out of slavery, but his former owner sold her away before Henry could raise the money. Most slaves did not want to take such a risk. "My pappy tried to get away," recalled Mary Ella Grandberry, whose family was held in Alabama, "but he couldn't see how to take all us children with him, so he had to stay with us."

For those torn between the burdens of slavery and the absence of family, local escapes were sometimes resorted to. Some escapees lived in small isolated groups and raided farms and plantations for hogs, chickens, corn, and vegetables. Others set up camp deep in the woods, swamps, and mountains, and lived off the land. It was not unheard of for these refugees, commonly referred to as maroons, to have communities with dozens of members. A few, such as those in the Great Dismal Swamp on the border of North Carolina and Virginia, and those among the Seminoles in the Florida Everglades numbered in the hundreds.

Some communities survived for generations, occasionally fighting back attempts to enslave them. In 1856, a posse of North Carolina slave catchers succeeded only in getting one of their number killed when they found a settlement of black refugees hiding in a swamp. Frederick Douglass, escapee from Maryland who became the nineteenth century's most prominent spokesman for freedom and civil rights, applauded such resistance. "Every slave-hunter who meets a bloody death in his infernal business," wrote Douglass, "is an argument in favor of the manhood of our race."

The Root of All Evil: Expanding Profits, Constricting Attitudes

Despite constant resistance in varying degrees, by the early nineteenth century slavery based on African ancestry was a firmly established Southern institution, the South's "peculiar institution" in the language of the day. But it had not always been so. Two centuries earlier there had been no distinctions in law or custom between white and black servants. In fact, the term "slave" was applied to whites as well as to blacks. Like white servants, blacks typically gained freedom after serving a number of years in what was legally defined as indentured servitude.

In the Western world generally, the eighteenth century was a time of rising arguments against slavery. The Scientific Revolution had shown that there were natural laws governing the physical universe. Some reasoned that there were also natural laws governing human interaction. Perhaps people had natural rights. John Wesley, a resident of colonial Savannah who helped lay the foundations of the Methodist Church, was certain of it. "Liberty," he insisted, "is the right of every human creature...and no human law can deprive him of that right which he derives from the law of nature."

Though race-based slavery was long established by the time of the Revolution, Thomas Jefferson nonetheless wrote in the Declaration of Independence that "life, liberty, and the pursuit of happiness" were "unalienable rights" endowed by the Creator. If true, was not slavery a violation of natural rights? The question troubled even slaveholders of Jefferson's generation, schooled as so many were in Enlightenment philosophy. Most were unwilling to give up slavery, Jefferson included, but they did see it as an unnatural institution destined to end one day. Some, like George Washington, freed their slaves in their wills. Others freed their slaves long before their deaths. Southern court records from the late eighteenth century are filled with manumission documents freeing hundreds of slaves.

Aside from the moral issues involved, most Americans of the Revolutionary era tended to view slavery as an economic dead end. The institution thrived only in the tobacco fields of the Chesapeake region and the rice country of coastal Carolina and Georgia. As the nation expanded, slavery would become proportionally less important to the nation's economy and would eventually die a natural death. But the cotton gin changed all that and became the vehicle by which slavery was carried westward across the Deep South. Not surprisingly, slaveholder attitudes changed with slavery's increasing profitability.

That change did not occur overnight. Antislavery sentiment in the South remained vigorous well into the nineteenth century. Any number of abolitionist societies were active across the South. Robert Finley, president of the University of Georgia, was a founder of the American Colonization Society in 1816. While some supported the society as a means of ridding the South of free blacks, many early members such as Finley had genuine antislavery motives. To discourage the use of slave labor, some societies paid above-market prices for cotton produced by free labor. James G. Birney started an abolitionist newspaper in Alabama. In 1827 the Alabama legislature passed a law prohibiting the importation of slaves from other states, and at every session throughout the decade members proposed legislation favoring gradual emancipation. As late as 1831, the Virginia legislature considered gradual emancipation.

But this was also the era of Native American removal, which completed the transition in slaveholder attitudes begun a generation earlier by the cotton gin. Not only did they have the technology and labor force with which to make cotton king, they now had the land on which to do it. Slaveholders began to view slavery as a necessary and perpetual institution. Senator John C. Calhoun wrote in 1837 that "the relation existing in the slaveholding states is, instead of an evil, a good—a positive good." Attitudes of the Founding Fathers toward slavery, slaveholders now argued, were erroneous. Benjamin Hill, one of Georgia's leading planter-politicians, wrote that "in our early history the Southern statesmen were antislavery in feeling...Washington, Jefferson, Madison, Randolph, and many of that day who never studied the argument of the cotton gin, nor heard the eloquent productions of the great Mississippi Valley. Now our people not only see the justice of slavery, but its providence too."

The slaveholders' new position presented them with a difficulty. Just a quarter of Southern whites owned slaves. Outside the southern United States chattel slavery survived only in Brazil, Cuba, Puerto Rico, Dutch Guiana, and parts of Africa. How were they to guarantee the survival of

Southern clergymen such as Patrick Hues Mell of Georgia, president of the Southern Baptist Convention, led the South toward a literalist view of the Bible with their insistence that scripture justified slavery. Such efforts went a long way toward establishing the South as the nation's more religiously conservative "Bible Belt."

Illustration from P.H. Mell, Jr., *The Life of Patrick Hues Mell* (1895).

slavery in a society where most voters did not own slaves and in a world where slaveholders were a dying breed?

The Southern Slaveocracy Justifies Itself

In the 1830s slaveholders launched a campaign designed to educate their fellow Southerners, and the world, on the virtues of slavery. In the first place, the world could not do without Southern cotton. Textile mills in Britain and the North depended too much upon it. Benjamin Hill insisted that "the world can never give up slavery until it is ready to give up clothing." Besides, slaveholders argued, people of African descent were content in slavery because it was, as Georgia planter-politician Alexander H. Stephens put it, their "natural and normal condition." Dr. Samuel A. Cartwright of New Orleans claimed that their supposed child-like state of mind was due to a disease that he called *dysesthesia*, which Cartwright defined as "defective atmospherization of the blood conjoined with a deficiency of cerebral matter in the cranium." If slaves were content in slavery, why did so many try to escape? Cartwright had an answer for that too—*drapetomania*, or simply an insane urge to run away.

There was also the Biblical defense. How could slavery be an evil institution when the patriarchs of the Old Testament had owned slaves? Were these not men ordained by God? Was not slavery the result of Noah's curse on his younger son Ham and all his descendants, whose dark complexion was assumed to be a result of the curse? Georgian Patrick Hues Mell, later president of the Southern Baptist Convention, stressed that point in his *Slavery. A Treatise, Showing that Slavery Is Neither a Moral, Political, nor Social Evil* (1844): "From Ham were descended the nations...that now constitute the African or negro race. Their inheritance, according to prophecy, has and will *continue to be* slavery." Mell took it literally as gospel that "God, by the mouth of Noah...instituted slavery...it cannot be an immorality."

The Virginia Baptist preacher Thornton Stringfellow, in his *Scriptural and Statistical Views in Favor of Slavery* (1856), argued that the Bible "recognized this institution as one that was lawful among men." Stringfellow cited 1 Timothy 6 in which the Apostle Paul, after counting masters as "worthy of all honor," warns that "if any man teach otherwise...he is proud, knowing nothing, but doting about questions and strifes of words, whereof cometh envy, strife, railings, evil surmisings." There could be no question about it for Stringfellow. Slavery was a hallowed institution ordained by God. Opposition to it could be nothing more than "evil surmisings."

Throughout the South, clergymen emerged as some of the most active and influential of slavery's defenders. Those ministers who held that scripture must be taken literally had been for some time disturbed by a strong opposing trend in Christianity. By the early nineteenth century, science had shown that the Bible contained many factual errors and omissions. In the eighteenth century, influential clergymen and laity began to argue that the Bible must be understood symbolically, not literally. But if the Bible was to be interpreted symbolically, what might that mean for its treatment of slavery? Was that to be taken symbolically as well? Could Paul have been using the relationship of servant to master as a metaphor for the relationship of humanity to God? No, said some, such symbolism would not do. If the scriptures were to be used effectively as a moral defense of slavery, they must be taken literally, and not just in part but in whole. As the slaveholding South changed its attitude toward slavery's morality in the early nineteenth century, it became increasingly tied to a literalist view of the Bible.

"Whoever doubts that it is a blessing," wrote one apostle of slavery to Alabama's *Montgomery Advertiser*, "has no right to hold any opinion at all on the subject." Other proslavery men said the same, and meant it. By the 1830s it was becoming dangerous to hold antislavery sentiments in the South. Those who opposed slavery either kept their views hidden or were driven out. The Grimké sisters of South Carolina, Sarah and Angelina, fled to the North where they were active in both the abolitionist and women's rights movements. James G. Birney left Alabama to form the Liberty Party, the nation's first antislavery political organization. In 1840 he became its first presidential candidate.

Intolerance on the slavery question had a particularly chilling effect on Southern institutions of higher learning. One Southern newspaper editor boldly declared that "the professorships should be sifted and weeded of those who may covertly circulate opinions not in sympathy with our social institutions." Slavery's defenders were happy to comply. Horace Holley, president of Kentucky's Transylvania University and a religious liberal, was removed from his post. The free-thinking President Thomas Cooper of South Carolina College (now the University of South Carolina), was also driven from office. Professor Benjamin Hedrick lost the chair of agricultural chemistry at his alma mater, the University of North Carolina, because he dared express unorthodox views on slavery. The university's governing board justified Hedrick's removal on the grounds that his "political opinions...are not those entertained by any member of this body." Even the University of Virginia, founded as a haven of free thought and inquiry, introduced religious exercises mainly to bolster slavery.

In less than a generation, Southern academia lost many of its finest intellectuals. Those who remained dared not challenge the view that slavery was a positive good and that the King James Bible was God's literal word. To the contrary, men like Matthew Fontaine Maury of Virginia—naval officer, pioneer oceanographer, and professor at Virginia Military Institute—upheld the Bible as the greatest book of science there was. In response to critics who viewed the Bible as "no authority in matters of science," Maury proclaimed that "the Bible is authority for everything it touches."

Perhaps the most effective tactic adopted by slaveholders in defending slavery was their encouragement of racist fears. By playing on such fears, slavery's defenders hoped to make all whites feel they had a stake in preserving the slave system whether they owned slaves or not. Poor whites were encouraged to think of what slavery's end might mean for them. No longer would they be in a position of social superiority to blacks, or anyone else for that matter. A writer in Georgia's *Columbus Times* stated the case clearly: "It is African slavery that makes every white man in some sense a lord.... Here the division is between white free men and black slaves, and every white is, and feels that he is a *man*." A correspondent of the *Southern Recorder* in Milledgeville, Georgia, agreed. It was slavery that gave "dignity to the poor man of the South." Without slavery, the rights guaranteed to whites would have to be shared with blacks, including perhaps even the right to vote.

Political Control in the Slaveocracy

Though all adult white males could vote, and most did, there was little for them to decide in a general sense. Then as now, any successful bid for high political office depended as much on wealth as votes, and planters held most of the wealth. In Southern state politics, both major parties, Whig and Democratic, centered as much on personalities as issues, and both represented slaveholding interests. Whigs tended to attract larger slaveholders, whose wealth and wider investments gave them broader national concerns. Smaller slaveholders gravitated toward the Democratic Party, which often differed with the Whigs on issues such as banking, infrastructure, and how best to use state revenues. But party leaders were united when it came to slavery. Promoting racist fear—that traditional staple of Southern politics—was always a central campaign objective.

The influence of slaveholder wealth in politics was not lost on plain folk. As one Tennessee farmer observed, the slaveholder, or slaveholder-backed candidate, "used money whenever he could. This fact usually elected him." The effect was easy to see. During the 1850s, though the proportion of slaveholders in the general population was falling, their numbers in Southern state legislatures were on the rise.

Legislative apportionment had much to do with slaveholder dominance in state legislatures. Each county usually elected one state senator and one or more house representatives depending on population. But blacks, who could not vote, were counted as three-fifths of a person in awarding state house representation. As a result, voters in high slaveholding counties carried much greater weight in state legislatures.

The poll tax gave slaveholders an edge as well. Though poll taxes might keep poor men from voting, they could also be used as a tool of political control. Landless whites and even yeomen who depended on larger landholders either for credit or employment or both could usually be counted on for political support, sometimes with the big landholder paying their poll tax. It was not difficult to know who voted for whom in an era before the secret ballot was in common use.

Wealthy slaveholders also held huge barbeques at election time, when good food and fine liquor proved politically influential. A similar scheme operated in urban centers, where a practice known as "penning" was sometimes used. Campaign workers would round up men off the streets, get them drunk, and march them to the polls. The party with the largest "pen" usually won. In his extensive study of the Deep South's political culture, Donald DeBats concluded that "far from encouraging citizen participation in the party system, the leaders of both parties discouraged grassroots politics.... Beyond the simple casting of a ballot, the role of the citizen in the party system was passive by design."

Slaveholder control of Southern state politics was near absolute. One North Carolina citizen observed that although the majority of those eligible to vote owned no slaves, "they have never yet had any part or lot in framing the laws under which they live. There is no legislation except for the benefit of slavery and slaveholders." While it is true that some nonslaveholders held high public office, they were nearly always backed directly or indirectly by slaveholder money. Some married into planter families. With their web of inter-family connections and economic dominance, it seemed that slaveholder control of the South was secure and that slavery as an institution was secure as well. But even as slaveholders consolidated their political power, cracks began to appear at the base of the South's social pyramid. As wealth became concentrated in fewer hands and opportunities for economic advancement were increasingly closed to yeomen and poor whites, those cracks began to grow.

Threats to the Slaveocracy from Within

Antislavery sentiment never completely died in the South despite efforts to wipe it out. Some continued to view slavery as a moral evil. Others opposed it on economic grounds. Still others disliked slavery simply because they were too poor ever to own slaves. Certainly the enslaved opposed slavery, and showed it by rising resistance and increasing escape attempts.

One source of unease among whites was the attitude of many slaveholders toward plain folk. As one Tennessee farmer put it:

"Slaveholders always acted as if they were of a better class, and there was always an unpleasant feeling between slaveholders and those working themselves." A South Carolina planter, in a private letter to a friend, wrote of poor whites: "Not one in ten is superior to a negro."

Most planters tried to keep such opinions concealed lest their hypocrisy be exposed. Occasionally, though, suggestions of planter arrogance slipped into print. In his 1854 defense of slavery, *Sociology for the South, or The Failure of Free Society*, George Fitzhugh not only insisted that slavery was "the best form of society yet devised for the masses" but also "that slavery, *black or white*, was right and necessary." Could whites be enslaved should the slave system continue? Some were beginning to fear the possibility.

Whatever the reasons, discomfort with the slave regime was on the rise among nonslaveholding whites in the late antebellum era. Some were even willing to speak out or take action. In 1859, one poor Georgia laborer confided to an acquaintance that if it came to a war over slavery, he was going to "black himself" and fight to end it. Without slavery, perhaps he could get better wages. That same year, a farmer was convicted of hiding a runaway slave for three months. Other whites were arrested for writing fake passes for slaves. A white man in Greene County, Georgia, was arrested for teaching slaves "to write and cipher." In South Carolina, a poor white woman, Elizabeth Blackwell, was accused of helping runaway slaves. Poor whites living in and around the Great Dismal Swamp of Virginia and North Carolina commonly harbored black fugitives.

The most outspoken opponent of slavery among Southern whites was Hinton Rowan Helper. Born the son of a yeoman farmer in North Carolina, Helper wrote what historian George M. Fredrickson called "the most important single book, in terms of its political impact, that has ever been published in the United States." In *The Impending Crisis of the South*, published in 1857, Helper argued vigorously that the "lords of the lash are not only absolute masters of the blacks...but they are also the oracles and arbiters of all nonslaveholding whites, whose freedom is merely nominal, and whose unparalleled illiteracy and degradation is purposely and fiendishly perpetuated." Slavery, Helper pointed out, benefited few except slaveholders. Its very existence, funneling investment capital not

Hinton Rowan Helper, born to a nonslaveholding North Carolina farm family, pointed out that the slave system discouraged economic development and kept most Southerners in poverty. Such attitudes among plain folk caused deep concern for slaveholders.

Engraving from Hinton Rowan Helper, *The Impending Crisis of the South* (enlarged edition, 1860).

into industrial development but into purchasing more land and slaves, kept most white Southerners in poverty. Slavery made the South little more than a colony of the North, providing raw materials and buying back manufactured goods.

Helper was hardly alone in pointing out the economic drawbacks of slavery. James Stirling, a British traveler who passed through the South in the late 1850s, wondered why the Southern states were lagging behind in "development and prosperity." He could find only one answer—slavery. "When Southern statesmen count up the gains of slavery," warned Stirling, "let them not forget also to count its cost. They may depend upon it, there is a heavy 'per contra' to the profits of niggerdom." Many native Southerners too recognized slavery's retarding influence, though few spoke of it openly. One who did was Roswell King, Jr., for nineteen years an overseer on the Butler plantations near Darien, Georgia. He confided to Pierce Butler's wife Fanny Kemble: "I hate slavery with all my heart; I consider it an absolute curse wherever it exists. It will keep those states where it does exist fifty years behind the others in improvement and prosperity."

Not only did slavery hinder economic growth, but the resulting concentration of cotton and tobacco on the South's most productive lands forced it to import foodstuffs. Georgia's comptroller-general lamented in 1860 that, with regard to food, this state was "every day becoming more dependent upon those 'not of us.'" Livestock production was declining. The corn crop was stagnant. In just ten years, the oat crop had dropped by more than half. One newspaper editor in Eufaula, Alabama, complained about huge shipments of high-priced foodstuffs from the Midwest coming up the Chattahoochee River. He blamed planters who, more concerned with cotton, preferred to import food rather than grow it. Other Southern editors urged planters to grow more corn and less cotton. Such pleas accomplished little. By 1860 the South was importing more food than ever.

Rising discontent within the Cotton Kingdom caused increasing panic among slaveholders. As if to confirm Hinton Rowan Helper's arguments, one Carolina planter asked, "If the poor whites realized that slavery kept them poor, would they not vote it down?" Many were beginning to suspect it. How could support for slavery be maintained among poor whites if they owned no slaves and had no prospects of ever owning any? Some suggested state laws mandating that each white family be given at least one slave. Others demanded a slave for every white person. One editor suggested reopening the slave trade from Africa, with or without the approval of Congress, to bring the price of slaves down. If slavery was constitutional, he reasoned, then so was the slave trade, and any law restricting it should be ignored.

Those who took a larger view realized that discontent among lower-class whites was not simply the expense of slaves but also the lack of land. There was only so much prime farmland to go around, and the more affluent slaveholders already had most of it. Slavery's defenders saw the future security of slavery in terms of territorial expansion. The hope of cheap land in expanding slave states could help keep nonslaveholders supporting slavery. More slave states would also mean fewer lands to which increasing numbers of escaping slaves might flee. To slaveholders it was clear—slavery must expand or die. The issue of slavery's expansion into the territories would dominate national politics for more than a decade and finally lead to the Civil War.

Documents

1. Frederick Law Olmsted on Life among Southern Plain Folk (1850s)

Olmsted was a New York journalist who traveled through the South in the 1850s and recorded his impressions of the people he met. In passage A, he gives us a picture of life for urban workers in Georgia. Passages B–D all concern the same Mississippi farm family with whom Olmsted spent one rainy night. In passage C, the conversation Olmsted has with his hosts at breakfast makes clear the ambivalent and conflicted attitudes of common whites toward blacks and slavery. Passage D describes some of the economic difficulties of small farmers.

A. The Precarious Life of Urban Workers

At Columbus [Georgia], I spent several days. It is the largest manufacturing town, south of Richmond, in the Slave States. It is situated at the Falls, and the head of steamboat navigation of the Chattahoochee, the western boundary of Georgia. The water-power is sufficient to drive two hundred thousand spindles, with a proportionate number of looms. There are, probably, at present from fifteen to twenty thousand spindles running. The operatives in the cotton-mills are said to be mainly "Cracker girls" (poor whites from the country), who earn, in good times, by piece-work, from $8 to $12 a month. There are, besides the cotton-mills, one woollen-mill, one paper-mill, a foundry, a cotton-gin factory, a machine-shop, etc. The laborers in all these are mainly whites, and they are in such condition that, if temporarily thrown out of employment, great numbers of them are at once reduced to a state of destitution, and are dependent upon credit or charity for their daily food. Public entertainments were being held at the time of my visit, the profits to be applied to the relief of operatives in mills which had been stopped by the effects of a late flood of the river. Yet Slavery is constantly boasted to be a perfect safeguard against such distress.

B. A Night with a Farm Family

...A planter, at whose house I called after sunset, said it was not convenient for him to accommodate me, and I was obliged to ride till it was quite dark. The next house at which I arrived was one of the commonest sort of cabins. I had passed twenty like it during the day, and I thought I would take the opportunity to get an interior knowledge of them. The fact that a horse and wagon were kept, and that a considerable area of land in the rear of the cabin was planted with cotton, showed that the family were by no means of the lowest class, yet, as they were not able even to hire a slave, they may be considered to represent very favorably, I believe, the condition of the poor whites of the plantation districts....

It was raining and nearly nine o'clock. The door of the cabin was open, and I rode up and conversed with the occupant as he stood within. He said that he was not in the habit of taking in travelers, and his wife was about sick, but if I was a mind to put up with common fare, he didn't care. Grateful, I dismounted and took the seat he had vacated by the fire, while he led away my horse to an open shed in the rear—his own horse ranging at large, when not in use, during the summer.

The house was all comprised in a single room, twenty-eight by twenty-five feet in area, and open to the roof above. There was a large fireplace at one end and a door on each side—no windows at all. Two bedsteads, a spinning-wheel, a packing case, which served as a bureau, a cupboard, made of rough hewn slabs, two or three deer-skin seated chairs, a Connecticut clock, and a large poster of Jayne's patent medicines, constituted all the visible furniture, either useful or ornamental in purpose. A little girl, immediately, without having had any directions to do so, got a frying-pan and a chunk of bacon from the cupboard, and cutting slices from the latter, set it frying for my supper. The woman of the house sat sulkily in a chair tilted back and leaning against the logs.... A baby lay crying on the floor. I quieted it and amused it with my watch till the little girl, having made "coffee" and put a piece of corn-bread on the table with the bacon, took charge of it.

I hoped the woman was not very ill.

"Got the headache right bad," she answered. "Have the headache a heap, I do. Knew I should have it to-night. Been cuttin' brush in the cotton this afternoon. Knew't would bring on my headache. Told him so when I begun."

As soon as I had finished my supper...the little girl put the fragments of the dishes in the cupboard, shoved the table into a corner, and dragged a quantity of quilts from one of the bedsteads, which she spread upon the floor, and presently crawled among them out of sight for the night.... The baby having fallen asleep was laid away somewhere, and the woman dragged off another lot of quilts from the beds, spreading them upon the floor. Then taking a deep tin pan, she filled it with alternate layers of corn-cobs and hot embers from the fire. This she placed upon a large block, which was evidently used habitually for the purpose, in the center of the cabin. A furious smoke arose from it, and we soon began to cough. "Most *too* much smoke," observed the man. "Hope 'twill drive out all the gnats, then," replied the woman. (There is a very minute flying insect here, the bite of which is excessively sharp.)

The woman suddenly dropped off her outer garment and stepped from the midst of its folds, in her petticoat; then, taking the baby from the place where she had deposited it, lay down and covered herself with the quilts upon the floor. The man told me that I could take the bed which remained on one of the bedsteads, and kicking off his shoes only, rolled himself into a blanket by the side of his wife. I ventured to take off my cravat and stockings, as well as my boots, but almost immediately put my stockings on again, drawing their tops over my pantaloons. The advantage of this arrangement was that, although my face, eyes, ears, neck, and hands, were immediately attacked, the vermin did not reach my legs for two or three hours. Just after the clock struck two, I distinctly heard the man and the woman, and the girl and the dog scratching, and the horse out in the shed stamping and gnawing himself. Soon afterward the man exclaimed, "Good God Almighty—mighty! mighty! mighty!" and jumping up pulled off one of his stockings, shook it, scratched his foot vehemently, put on the stocking, and lay down again with a groan. The two doors were open, and through the logs and the openings in the roof, I saw the clouds divide and the moon and stars reveal themselves. The woman, after having been nearly smothered by the smoke from the pan which she had originally placed close to her own pillow, rose and placed it on the sill of the windward door, where it burned feebly and smoked lustily.... Fortunately the cabin was so open that it gave little annoyance, while it seemed to answer the purpose of keeping all flying insects at a distance.

C. Nonslaveholder Attitudes toward Slavery

When, on rising the next morning, I said that I would like to wash my face, water was given me for the purpose in an earthen pie-dish. Just as breakfast, which was exactly the same materials as my supper, was ready, rain again began to fall, presently in such a smart shower as to put the fire out and compel us to move the table under the least leaky part of the roof.

At breakfast occurred the following conversation:—

"Are there many niggers in New York?"

"Very few."

"How do you get your work done?"

"There are many Irish and German people constantly coming there who are glad to get work to do."

"Oh, and you have them for slaves?"

"They want money and are willing to work for it. A great many American-born work for wages, too."

"What do you have to pay?"

"Ten or twelve dollars a month."...

"Ain't niggers all-fired sassy at the North?"

"No, not particularly."

"Ain't they all free there? I hearn so."

"Yes."

"Well, how do they get along when they's free?"

"I never have seen a great many, to know their circumstances very well. Right about where I live they seem to me to live quite comfortably; more so than the niggers on these big plantations do, I should think."

"O! They have a mighty hard time on the big plantations. I'd ruther be dead than to be a nigger on one of these big plantations."

"Why, I thought they were pretty well taken care of on them."

The man and his wife both looked at me as if surprised, and smiled.

"Why, they are well fed, are they not?"

"Oh, but they work 'em so hard. My God, sir, in pickin' time on these big plantations they start 'em to work 'fore light, and they don't give 'em time to eat."

"I supposed they generally gave them an hour or two at noon."

"No, sir; they just carry a piece of bread and meat in their pockets and they eat it when they can, standin' up. They have a hard life on 't, that's a fact. I rekon you can get along about as well withouten slaves as with 'em, can't you, in New York?"

"In New York there is not nearly so large a proportion of very rich men as here. There are very few people who farm over three hundred acres, and the greater number—nineteen out of twenty, I suppose—work themselves with the hands they employ. Yes, I think it's better than it is here, for all concerned, a great deal. Folks that can't afford to buy niggers get along a great deal better in the free states, I think; and I guess that those who could afford to have niggers get along better without them."

"I [have] no doubt that's so. I wish there warn't no niggers here. They are a great curse to this country, I expect. But 'twouldn't do to free 'em; that wouldn't do no how!"...

"Are there many people here who think slavery a curse to the country?"

"Oh, yes, a great many. I reckon the majority would be right glad if we could get rid of the niggers. But it wouldn't never do to free 'em and leave 'em here. I don't know anybody, hardly, in favor of that. Make 'em free and leave 'em here and they'd steal every thing we made. No body couldn't live here then."

These views of slavery seem to be universal among people of this class. They were repeated to me at least a dozen times.

D. Economic Difficulties of Small Farmers

Hereabouts the plantations were generally small, ten to twenty negroes on each; sometimes thirty or forty. Where he used to live [Alabama] they were big ones—forty or fifty, sometimes a hundred on each. He had lived here ten years. I could not make out why he had not accumulated wealth, so small a family and such an inexpensive style of living he had. He generally planted twenty to thirty acres, he said; this year he had sixteen in cotton and about ten, he thought, in corn. Decently cultivated, this planting should have produced him five hundred dollars' worth of cotton, besides supplying him with bread and bacon—his chief expense, apparently. I suggested that this was a very large planting for his little family; he would need some help in picking time. He ought to have some now, he said; grass and bushes were all overgrowing him; he had to work just like a nigger; this durnation rain would just make the weeds jump, and he didn't expect he should have any cotton at all. There warn't much use in the man's trying to get along by himself; every thing seemed to set in agin him. He'd been trying to hire somebody, but he couldn't, and his wife was a sickly kind of woman.

His wife reckoned he might hire some help if he'd look round sharp.

My horse and dog were as well cared for as possible, and a "snack" of bacon and corn-bread was offered me for noon, which has been unusual in Mississippi. When I asked what I should pay, the man hesitated and said he reckoned what I had had wasn't worth much of anything; he was sorry he could not have accommodated me better. I offered him a dollar, for which he thanked me warmly. It is the first instance of hesitation in charging for a lodging which I have met with from a stranger at the South.

Frederick Law Olmsted, *The Cotton Kingdom*, 2 vols. (New York: Mason Brothers, 1861–1862) 1:273–74; 2:105–12.

2. Women Recall Resistance to Slavery (ca. 1850s)

In the 1930s, interviewers from the Federal Writers' Project traveled the South recording the many ways in which aging freed people remembered slavery. In 1945, B. A. Botkin, a folklorist and scholar, became the first to publish a collection of those memories. Among them were the following recollections of resistance by enslaved women.

A.

Her boss [Pennington] went off deer hunting once for a few weeks. While he was gone, the overseer tried to whip her. She knocked him down and tore his face up so that the doctor had to 'tend him. When Pennington came back, he noticed his face all patched up and asked him what was the matter with it. The overseer told him that he went down in the field to whip the hands and that he just thought he would hit Lucy a few licks to show the slaves that he was impartial, but she jumped on him and like to tore him up. Old Pennington said to him, "Well, if that is the best you could do with her, damned if you won't just have to take it."

B.

One day when an old woman was plowing in the field, an overseer came by and reprimanded her for being so slow—she gave him some back talk, he took out a long closely woven bull whip and lashed her severely. The woman became sore and took her hoe and chopped him right across the head, and, child, you should have seen how she chopped this man to a bloody death.

C.

Early Hurt had an overseer named Sanders. He tied my sister Crecie to a stump to whip her. Crecie was stout and heavy. She was a grown young woman and big and strong. Sanders had two dogs with him in case he would have trouble with anyone. When he started laying that lash on Crecie's back, she pulled up that stump and whipped him and the dogs both.

B. A. Botkin, editor, *Lay My Burden Down: A Folk History of Slavery* (University of Chicago Press, 1945) 175.

3. Harriet Jacobs Remembers Abuse as a Slave Girl (ca. 1828)

In 1842, when she was nearly thirty years old, Harriet Jacobs escaped from slavery in North Carolina and became an antislavery activist. Here she recalls her abuse under slavery.

I now entered on my fifteenth year—a sad epoch in the life of a slave girl. My master began to whisper foul words in my ear. Young as I was, I could not remain ignorant of their import.... He peopled my young mind with unclean images, such as only a vile monster could think of. I turned from him with disgust and hatred. But he was my master. I was compelled to live under the same roof with him—where I saw a man forty years my senior daily violating the most sacred commandments of nature. He told me I was his property; that I must be subject to his will in all things. My soul revolted against the mean tyranny. But where could I turn for protection? No matter whether the slave girl be as black as ebony or as fair as her mistress. In either case, there is no shadow of law to protect her from insult, from violence, or even from death; all these are inflicted by fiends who bear the shape of men. The mistress, who ought to protect the helpless victim, has no other feelings towards her but those of jealousy and rage. The degradation, the wrongs, the vices, that grow out of slavery, are more than I can describe.

...I cannot tell how much I suffered in the presence of these wrongs, nor how I am still pained by the retrospect. My master met me at every turn, reminding me that I belonged to him. If I went out for a breath of fresh air, after a day of unwearied toil, his footsteps dogged me. If I knelt by my mothers grave, his dark shadow fell on me even there. The light heart which nature had given me became heavy with sad forebodings. The other slaves in my master's house noticed the change. Many of them pitied me; but none dared to ask the cause. They had no need to inquire. They knew too well the guilty practices under that roof; and they were aware that to speak of them was an offence that never went unpunished....

I once saw two beautiful children playing together. One was a fair white child; the other was her slave, and also her sister. When I saw them embracing each other, and heard their joyous laughter, I turned sadly away from the lovely sight. I foresaw the inevitable blight that would fall on the little slave's heart.

Harriet A. Jacobs, *Incidents in the Life of a Slave Girl*, edited by L. Maria Child (Boston MA: published for the author, 1861) 44–48.

4. William and Ellen Craft Reach Freedom on Christmas Day (1848)

William and his light-complected wife Ellen both escaped from enslavement in Bibb County, Georgia, in December 1848, William posing as his wife's slave. He later wrote an account of their flight published under the title Running a Thousand Miles for Freedom. *After a harrowing, days-long, multi-legged journey by land and sea, they finally arrive in Philadelphia on Sunday, Christmas Day. They could not travel together because blacks and whites were not allowed to ride in the same car.*

I also met with a coloured gentleman on this train, who recommended me to a boarding-house that was kept by an abolitionist, where he thought I would be quite safe, if I wished to run away from my master. I thanked him kindly, but of course did not let him know who we were. Late at night, or rather early in the morning, I heard a fearful whistling of the steam-engine; so I opened the window and looked out, and saw a large number of flickering lights in the distance, and heard a passenger in the next carriage—who also had his head out of the window—say to his companion, "Wake up, old horse, we are at Philadelphia!"

The sight of those lights and that announcement made me feel almost as happy as Bunyan's Christian must have felt when he first caught sight of the cross. I, like him, felt that the straps that bound the heavy burden to my back began to pop, and the load to roll off. I also looked, and looked again, for it appeared very wonderful to me how the mere sight of our first city of refuge should have all at once made my hitherto sad and heavy heart become so light and happy. As the train speeded on, I rejoiced and thanked God with all my heart and soul for his great kindness and tender mercy, in watching over us, and bringing us safely through.

As soon as the train had reached the platform, before it had fairly stopped, I hurried out of my carriage to my master, whom I got at once into a cab, placed the luggage on, jumped in myself, and we drove off to the boarding-house which was so kindly recommended to me. On leaving the station, my master—or rather my wife, as I may now say—who had from the commencement of the journey borne up in a manner that much surprised us both, grasped me by the hand, and said, "Thank God, William, we are safe!" then burst into tears, leant upon me, and wept like a child. The reaction was fearful. So when we reached the house, she was in reality so weak and faint that she could scarcely stand alone. However, I got her into the apartments that were pointed out, and there we knelt down, on this Sabbath, and Christmas-day—a day that will ever be memorable to us—and poured out our heartfelt gratitude to God, for his goodness in enabling us to overcome so many perilous difficulties, in escaping out of the jaws of the wicked.

William Craft, *Running a Thousand Miles for Freedom* (London: William Tweedie, 1860) 78–80.

5. Robert Glenn Remembers Being Sold away from his Parents (ca. late 1850s)

Robert Glenn, born in North Carolina in 1850, was eighty-seven years old when he told a Federal Writers' Project worker about being sold, as hundreds of thousands were, away from his family. One observer wrote that "such separations as these are quite common, and appear to be no more thought of, by those who enforce them, than the separation of a calf from its brute parent."

They sold me away from my father and mother and I was carried to the state of Kentucky. I was bought by a Negro speculator by the name of Henry Long who lived not far from Hurdles Mill in Person County....

Father knew it was all off, mother was frantic but there was nothing they could do about it. They had to stand and see the speculator put me on his horse behind him and ride away without allowing either of them to tell me goodbye.... He took me to his home, but on the way he stopped for refreshments, at a plantation, and while he was eating and drinking he put me into a room where two white women were spinning flax. I was given a seat across the room from where they were working. After I had sat there awhile wondering where I was going and thinking about mother and home, I went to one of the women and asked, "Missus when will I see my mother again?" She replied, "I don't know child, go and sit down." I went back to my seat and as I did so both the women stopped spinning for a moment, looked at each other, and one of them remarked. "Almighty God, this slavery business is a horrible thing. Chances are this boy will never see his mother again." This remark nearly killed me, as I began to fully realize my situation. Long, the Negro trader, soon came back, put me on his horse and finished the trip to his home. He kept me at his home awhile and then traded me to a man named William Moore who lived in Person County. Moore at this time was planning to move to Kentucky, which he soon did, taking me with him. My mother found out by the "Grapevine telegraph" that I was going to be carried to Kentucky. She got permission and came to see me before they carried me off. When she started home I was allowed to go part of the way with her but they sent two Negro girls with us to ensure my return. We were allowed to talk privately, but while we were doing so, the two girls stood a short distance away and watched as the master told them when they left that if I escaped they would be whipped every day until I was caught. When the time of parting came and I had to turn back, I burst out crying loud. I was so weak from sorrow I could not walk, and the two girls who were with me took me by each arm and led me along half carrying me.

Robert Glenn, Interview, 1937, in *Slave Narratives, Vol. 11: North Carolina Narratives*, Federal Writers' Project, 1936–1938, Manuscript Division, Library of Congress, Washington DC, part 1, 329–32.

6. Rev. Thornton Stringfellow Uses the Bible to Defend Slavery (1850)

The Reverend Thornton Stringfellow, a Baptist preacher in Virginia, was one of the Old South's staunchest defenders of slavery. Here he interprets Old Testament practice to justify enslaving people "of another nation."

Has God ingrafted hereditary slavery upon the constitution of government he condescended to give his chosen people—that people, among whom he promised to dwell, and that he required to be holy? I answer, he has. It is clear and explicit. He enacts, first, that his chosen people may take their money, go into the slave markets of the surrounding nations, (the seven devoted nations excepted), and purchase men-servants and women-servants, and give them, and their increase, to their children and their children's children, forever; and worse still for the refined humanity of our age—he guarantees to the foreign slaveholder perfect protection, while he comes in among the Israelites, for the purpose of dwelling, and raising and selling slaves, who should be acclimated and accustomed to the habits and institutions of the country. And worse still for the sublimated humanity of the present age, God passes with the right to buy and possess, the right to govern, by a severity which knows no bounds but the master's discretion. And if worse can be, for the morbid humanity we censure, he enacts that his own people may sell themselves and their families for limited periods, with the privilege of extending the time at the end of the 6th year to the 50th year or jubilee, if they prefer bondage to freedom. Such is the precise character of two institutions, found in the constitution of the Jewish commonwealth, emanating directly from Almighty God. For the 1,500 years, during which these laws were in force, God raised up a succession of prophets to reprove that people for the various sins into which they fell; yet there is not a reproof uttered against the institution of *involuntary slavery*, for any species of abuse that ever grew out of it. A severe judgment is pronounced by Jeremiah, (chapter xxxiv. see from the 8th to the 22d verse), for an abuse or violation of the law, concerning the *voluntary* servitude of Hebrews; but the prophet pens it with caution, as if to show that it had no reference to any abuse that had taken place under the system of *involuntary slavery*, which existed by law

Southern clergymen generally saw the Bible as a justification for slavery. Angelina Grimké, member of a prominent South Carolina slaveholding family, disagreed. Pointing out that scriptural "servants" were more akin to employees than slaves, she argued that the Bible, far from giving sanction to slavery, was a strong argument against it.

Engraving from the Library of Congress.

among that people; the sin consisted in making hereditary bond-men and bond-women of Hebrews, which was positively forbidden by the law, and not for buying and holding one of another nation in hereditary bondage, which was as positively allowed by the law.

Thornton Stringfellow, *A Brief Examination of Scripture Testimony on the Institution of Slavery* (Washington DC: Congressional Globe Office, 1850) 8.

7. Angelina Grimké Uses the Bible to Denounce Slavery (1836)

Angelina Grimké was born into a prominent slaveholding family in Charleston, South Carolina. Like her sister Sarah, she grew to hate slavery. Angelina moved to the North at age twenty-two and became an active abolitionist. In her 1836 Appeal to the Christian Women of the South, *she refuted the notion that the Bible justified Southern slavery. She did so in part by citing two verses that slavery's defenders generally ignored.*

1. "Thou shall not deliver unto his master the servant that is escaped from his master unto thee. He shall dwell with thee, *even* among you, in that place which he shall choose, in one of thy gates, where it liketh him best: thou shalt not oppress him." Deut. xxiii, 15, 16.

2. "And ye shall hallow the fiftieth year, and proclaim *Liberty* throughout *all* the land, unto *all* the inhabitants thereof: it shall be a jubilee unto you." Livit. xxv, 10.

Here, then, we see that by this first law, the *door of Freedom was opened wide to every servant who* had any cause whatever for complaint; if he was unhappy with his master, all he had to do was to leave him, and *no man* had a right to deliver him back to him again, and not only so, but the absconded servant was to *choose* where he should live, and no Jew was permitted to oppress him. He left his master just as our Northern servants leave us; we have no power to compel them to remain with us, and no man has any right to oppress them; they go and dwell in that place where it chooseth them, and live just where they like. Is it so at the

South? Is the poor runaway slave protected *by law* from the violence of that master whose oppression and cruelty has driven him from his plantation or his house? No! no! Even the free states of the North are compelled to deliver unto his master the servant that is escaped from his master into them....

But by the second of these laws a still more astonishing fact is disclosed.... On the great day of atonement every fiftieth year the Jubilee trumpet was sounded throughout the land of Judea, and *Liberty* was proclaimed to *all* the inhabitants thereof. I will not say that the servants' *chains* fell off and their *manacles* were burst, for there is no evidence that Jewish servants *ever* felt the weight of iron chains, and collars, and handcuffs; but I do say that even the man who had voluntarily sold himself and the *heathen* who had been sold to a Hebrew master, were set free, the one as well as the other. This law was evidently designed to prevent the oppression of the poor, and the possibility of such a thing as *perpetual servitude* existing among them.

Where, then, I would ask, is the warrant, the justification, or the palliation of American Slavery from Hebrew servitude? How many of the Southern slaves would now be in bondage according to the laws of Moses; Not one. You may observe that I have carefully avoided using the term *slavery* when speaking of Jewish servitude; and simply for this reason, that *no such thing* existed among that people; the word translated servant does *not* mean *slave*, it is the same that is applied to Abraham, to Moses, to Elisha and the prophets generally. *Slavery* then *never* existed under the Jewish Dispensation at all, and I cannot but regard it as an aspersion on the character of Him who is "glorious in Holiness" for any one to assert that "*God sanctioned, yea commanded slavery* under the old dispensation." I would fain lift my feeble voice to vindicate Jehovah's character from so foul a slander. If slaveholders are determined to hold slaves as long as they can, let them not dare to say that the God of mercy and of truth *ever* sanctioned such a system of cruelty and wrong. It is blasphemy against Him.

Angelina Grimké, *Appeal to the Christian Women of the South* (New York: American Anti-Slavery Society, 1836) 9–11.

8. Slaveholders Cheat Plain Folk Out of Their Land

Relations between lower-class whites and blacks had been strained by design since the colonial era. In this insightful passage from the Slave Narratives, *a former slave illustrates one of many ways in which the wealthy encouraged racism, kept nonslaveholding whites supporting slavery, and personally profited by it.*

We didn't think much of the poor white man. He was down on us. He was driven to it by the rich slave owner. The rich slave owner wouldn't let his Negroes associate with poor white folks. Some of the slave owners, when a poor white man's land joined theirs and they wanted his place, would have their Negroes steal things and carry them to the poor white man and sell them to him. Then the slave owner, knowing where the stuff was (of course the slave had to do what his master told him) would go and find his things at the poor white man's house. Then he would claim it, and take out a writ for him, but he would give him a chance. He would tell him to sell out to him, and leave, or take the consequences. That's the way some of the slave owners got such large tracts of lands.

Sam T. Stewart, interview, 1937, in *Slave Narratives, Vol. 11: North Carolina Narratives,* Federal Writers' Project, 1936–1938, Manuscript Division, Library of Congress, Washington DC, part 2, 319.

9. John Conrad Keysaer on Politics and Class Relations (ca. 1850s)

Between 1914 and 1922, Civil War veterans living in Tennessee were sent a questionnaire asking about their early lives, war-time experience, and later years. It also asked about class relations in the pre-war period. One respondent was John Conrad Keysaer, a native Virginian, who was raised in a nonslaveholding farm family. He served in the Confederate army, 10th Virginia Regiment, for four years and was wounded twice.

Question: Did the men who owned slaves mingle freely with those who did not own slaves, or did slaveholders in any way show by their actions that they felt themselves better than respectable, honorable men who did not own slaves?

Answer: Slave holders always acted as if they were of a better class and there was always an unpleasant feeling between slave holders and those working themselves.

Question. At the churches, at the schools, at public gatherings in general, did slaveholders and nonslaveholders mingle on a footing of equality?

Answer: The slave holders always seemed to act above the working class and for the most part were clannish.

Question: Was there a friendly feeling between slaveholders and nonslaveholders in your community, or were they antagonistic to each other?

Answer: There was always a kind of feeling, though not antagonistic, just "uppish."

Question: In a political contest, in which one candidate owned slaves and the other did not, did the fact that one candidate owned slaves help him any in winning the contest?

Answer: Usually, the slave holder was elected. He used money to get votes whenever he could. This fact usually elected him.

Question: Were the opportunities good in your community for a poor young man, honest and industrious, to save up enough to buy a small farm or go in business for himself?

Answer: The opportunities for a poor young man were very poor. Wages low, very little could be saved. A great many from my community went west after the war to get a better start. I was one of them.

Adapted from Gustavus W. Dyer and John Trotwood Moore, compilers, *The Tennessee Civil War Veterans Questionnaires, Vol. 3* (Easley SC: Southern Historical Press, 1985) xv–xvii, 1284–86.

10. George Fitzhugh Advocates Enslaving Whites (1854)

Slavery's apologists generally focused on supposed black inferiority as a defense. But by the late antebellum period slaveholders were increasingly touting slavery as the best labor system the world had ever known. Black slaves enjoyed the care of benevolent masters, and they had no worries about unemployment. Poor whites, George Fitzhugh argued, could benefit from that system as well.

The free laborer rarely has a house and home of his own; he is insecure of employment; sickness may overtake him at any time and deprive him of the means of support; old age is certain to overtake him, if he lives, and generally finds him without the means of subsistence; his family is probably increasing in numbers, and is helpless and burdensome to him. In all this there is little to incite to virtue, much to tempt to crime, nothing to afford happiness, but quite enough to inflict misery. Man must be more than human, to acquire a pure and a high morality under such circumstances....

We find slavery repeatedly instituted by God, or by men acting under his immediate care and direction, as in the instances of Moses and Joshua. Nowhere in the Old or New Testament do we find the institution condemned, but frequently recognized and enforced.... It is probably no cause of regret that men are so constituted as to require that many should be slaves....

We have endeavored to show, heretofore, that the negro slave, considering his indolence and unskilfulness, often gets his fair share, and sometimes more than his share, of the profits of the farm, and is exempted, besides, from the harassing cares and anxieties of the free laborer. Grant, however, that the negro does not receive adequate wages from his master, yet all admit that in the aggregate the negroes get better wages than free laborers; therefore, it follows that, with all its imperfections, slave society is the best form of society yet devised for the masses....

Free society is theoretically impracticable, because its friends admit that "in all old countries the supply of labor exceeds the demand." Hence a part of the laboring class must be out of employment and starving, and in their struggle to get employment, reducing those next above them to the minimum that will support human existence....

Ten years ago we became satisfied that slavery, *black or white*, was right and necessary. We advocated this doctrine in very many essays.... We believe we are morally and religiously right....

"Every man for himself and devil take the hindmost," is the moral which liberty and free competition inculcate.

George Fitzhugh, *Sociology for the South, or the Failure of Free Society* (Richmond: A. Morris, Publisher, 1854) 38, 96, 162–63, 222, 225, 229.

11. Hinton Rowan Helper Urges Abolitionism among Southern Whites (1857)

Hinton Rowan Helper, born to a family of nonslaveholding North Carolina farmers, became one of the foremost Southern critics of slavery. In his 1857 book, The Impending Crisis of the South, *Helper pointed out that slavery discouraged industrialization, kept the South dependant on the North, kept most Southerners in poverty and political impotency, and he called on Southerners to abolish it. He also took Northerners to task for opposing only slavery's expansion, not the institution itself. Finally, and prophetically, he called on slaveholders to emancipate their slaves or see it done for them.*

The causes which have impeded the progress and prosperity of the South, which have dwindled our commerce, and other similar pursuits, into the most contemptible insignificance; sunk a large majority of our people in galling poverty and ignorance, rendered a small minority conceited and tyrannical, and driven the rest away from their homes; entailed upon us a humiliating dependence on the Free States; disgraced us in the recesses of our own souls, and brought us under reproach in the eyes of all civilized and enlightened nations—may all be traced to one common source, and there find the solution in the most hateful and horrible word, that was ever incorporated into the vocabulary of human economy—*Slavery!...*

Notwithstanding the fact that the white nonslaveholders of the South, are in the majority, as five to one, they have never yet had any part or lot in framing the laws under which they live. There is no legislation except for the benefit of slavery, and slaveholders.... A cunningly devised mockery of freedom is guaranteed to them, and that is all.... the only privilege extended to them is a shallow and circumscribed participation in the political movements that usher slaveholders into office....

The lords of the lash are not only the absolute masters of the blacks, who are bought and sold, and driven about like so many cattle, but they are also the oracles and arbiters of all nonslaveholding whites, whose freedom is merely nominal, and whose unparalleled illiteracy and degradation is purposely and fiendishly perpetuated....

It is expected that the stupid and sequacious masses, the white victims of slavery, will believe, and, as a general thing, they do believe, whatever the slaveholders tell them; and thus it is that they are cajoled into the notion that they are the freest, happiest, and most intelligent people in the world, and are taught to look with prejudice and disapprobation upon every new principle or progressive movement....

With regard to the unnational and demoralizing institution of slavery, we believe the majority of Northern people are too scrupulous. They seem to think that it is enough for them to be mere freesoilers, to keep in check the diffusive element of slavery, and to prevent it from crossing over the bounds within which it is now regulated by municipal law. Remiss in their *national* duties, as we contend, they make no positive attack upon the institution in the Southern States....

But, Sirs, knights of bludgeons, chevaliers of bowie-knives and pistols, and lords of the lash, we are unwilling to allow you to swindle the slaves out of all the rights and claims to which, as human beings, they are most sacredly entitled. Not alone for ourself as an individual, but for others also—particularly for five or six millions of Southern nonslaveholding whites, whom your iniquitous statism has debarred from almost all the mental and material comforts of life—do we speak, when we say, you *must* emancipate your slaves....

Frown, Sirs, fret, foam, prepare your weapons, threat, strike, shoot, stab, bring on civil war, dissolve the Union, nay, annihilate the solar system if you will—do all this, more, less, better, worse, anything—do what you will, Sirs, you can neither foil nor intimidate us; our purpose is as firmly fixed as the eternal pillars of Heaven; we have determined to abolish slavery, and, so help us God, abolish it we will!

Hinton Rowan Helper, *The Impending Crisis of the South* (New York: Burdick, 1857) 25, 42–45, 113–14, 185, 187.

5

A South Divided: Secession and the South's Inner Civil War

Slavery's Expansion Splits the Nation

The issue of slavery's expansion, though pressed with new urgency by slaveholders, was not new at all. It was older than the nation itself. Shortly after Georgia's founding in 1732, there had been an effort to halt slavery at the Savannah River. Proslavery pressure from Savannah merchants and South Carolina rice planters was constant, and slaves were smuggled into the colony despite Georgia's ban on slavery. Bowing to those pressures, Georgia's Trustees lifted the ban in 1750. Within twenty years, nearly half of Georgia's people were enslaved.

At the same time, slavery as a viable economic institution was dying in the North. But in the South, the cotton gin gave slavery an economic vitality that grew in strength with each new slave state added to the Union. Congress reached a temporary settlement of the question in 1820 with the Missouri Compromise. Missouri was admitted to the Union as a slave state and Maine as a free state, thus preserving the balance of free and slave states in the Senate. More significantly, a line extending westward from the southern border of Missouri established a boundary between slavery and freedom. All future states created north of the line would be free. Those south of the line would be slave.

The issue once more became unsettled as slaveholders began pushing into Mexico's northern province of Texas during the 1820s. Having just fought a revolution against the slave power of Spain, Mexico began to outlaw slavery and tried to prevent the further importation of slaves. Still, illegal Anglo immigrants keep coming, bringing slaves with them. Refusing to abide by Mexican law, the Anglos established their independence with the Texas Revolution of 1835–1836. They immediately requested admission to the Union as a slave state, but Congress was so reluctant to discuss the divisive issue of slavery's expansion that it ignored the request. It was another decade before the US finally instigated war with Mexico and took all its northern territories from Texas to California.

With the Mexican War's end in 1848, slavery was again thrust onto the nation's political stage. Mexico had begun to abolish slavery two decades earlier. Would it now be reintroduced in the new US territories? Many hoped the divisive issue of slavery could be avoided. But in 1849 California requested admission to the Union as a free state and Congress was forced to act. The next year California entered the Union under the Compromise of 1850, giving the free states a two-seat advantage in the Senate. In exchange, slaveholders got a Fugitive Slave Act mandating the return of slaves who escaped to the North. As for the remaining territories of the Mexican Cession, "popular sovereignty" would prevail. Voters in both the New Mexico and Utah territories would make the decision on slavery themselves.

Using opposition to the Compromise of 1850 as a pretext, pro-secessionists organized movements in Mississippi, Alabama, Georgia, and South Carolina. In all but South Carolina, Unionists quickly organized to oppose them. The turning point came in December with the Georgia Platform. Georgia's convention voted by more than ten-to-one to support compromise but declared the state ready to secede if slavery were ever restricted in the Western territories. The Georgia Platform also insisted that the Union's preservation depended on "faithful execution" of the Fugitive Slave Act. The Alabama and Mississippi state conventions supported the Georgia Platform, and newspapers across the country credited it with having saved the Union. But given its preeminence of slavery over the Union, the ambiguities of popular sovereignty, and the ambivalence of Northern law enforcement toward hunting down increasing numbers of fugitive slaves, the Georgia Platform was a sure formula for the Union's impending collapse.

Popular sovereignty's inherent complications became clear soon after Congress passed the Kansas-Nebraska Act in 1854. In exchange for Southern congressional votes favoring organization of these territories through which Northerners hoped to build the first transcontinental

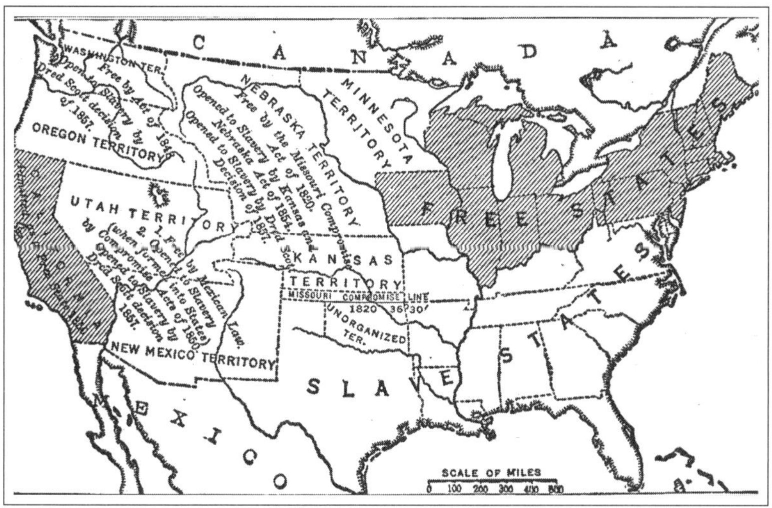

Slaveholders relentlessly pressed for slavery's expansion, gaining ground from the Compromise of 1820 onward. Within four decades, their efforts brought on a war that destroyed the very institution they sought to protect.

Map from Robert Hall, Harriet Smither, and Clarence Ousley, *A History of the United States* (1920).

railroad, the Nebraska and Kansas territories, both north of the Missouri Compromise line, were opened to slavery under popular sovereignty. It seemed to most Northern Congressmen a small price to pay. They were certain there was no real danger of Kansas or Nebraska becoming slave states since geography did not suit them to large-scale cotton or tobacco production.

But Kansas was just west of Missouri, a slave state, and Northerners feared the possibility of slavery's expansion. Even so, few white Northerners called themselves abolitionists. Most were by no means opposed to slavery where it existed since it kept most African Americans confined to the South. Racism played a large role in forming white attitudes in the North, as did economic fears. Laborers worried that freedom for slaves would enable them to migrate north and compete for already low-paying jobs. Northern industrialists and financiers worried that the end of slavery would mean the end of cheap Southern cotton, which fueled textile manufacturing, the North's leading industry. What most Northerners opposed, and all they opposed, was slavery's extension into territorial lands that they wanted for themselves. They hoped to keep those lands devoid of blacks, slave or free.

In the wake of Kansas-Nebraska, most Northern Whigs and many Democrats joined with Free Soilers and a smattering of abolitionists to form the Republican Party, dedicated to free land and free states in the West. They ran their first presidential candidate in 1856, John C. Frémont, calling for "free men, free land, and Frémont!" Ironically Frémont was a Southerner, born in Savannah and raised in Charleston, who as a young man had joined the army and made a name for himself as military governor of California and one of the state's first two senators. Fear of Frémont's antislavery leanings led Southern Whigs to join with Democrats or with the short-lived nativist American (Know Nothing) Party to keep Frémont out of the White House. Pennsylvania Democrat James Buchanan, who was no threat to slavery's expansion, won the election.

Still, the Kansas question remained unsettled. Free Soil activists rushed to get settlers into Kansas. Proslavery men did the same. Few slaveholders themselves made the move, but they did finance proslavery expeditions of Southern poor whites to Kansas, providing them with wagons, horses, oxen, and, most importantly, land. The controversy turned violent when a proslavery raid on the town of Lawrence left one man dead. An antislavery band led by John Brown, later of Harpers Ferry fame, retaliated by killing five proslavery men along Pottawatomie Creek. By the end of 1856, perhaps 200 settlers on both sides were dead.

The Supreme Court tried to settle the issue in 1857 with the *Dred Scott* case, calling enslaved blacks property that could be taken anywhere in the United States, including the territories. This decision pushed more Northerners into the Republican camp, all but ensuring that the next president would be a Republican. Fearing that result, leading Southern secessionists, called Fire-Eaters for their extremist rhetoric, tried to build support for their cause by labeling all Northerners, Republicans in particular, abolitionists bent on fomenting slave rebellion. The Fire-Eaters got a boost in October 1859 when John Brown led an attempt to seize the federal arsenal at Harpers Ferry, Virginia, and arm the state's slaves. His effort failed and a state court sentenced Brown to hang for treason. But Fire-Eaters now had an incident they could use to portray Northerners as abolition-supporting, rebellion-promoting "Black Republicans."

Fire-Eaters Press for Secession

This volatile atmosphere of panic and paranoia formed the backdrop of the presidential campaign in 1860. The Democrats split over slavery in the territories, with Northerners holding to popular sovereignty and Southerners clinging to the *Dred Scott* decision. Most Southern delegates left the convention and formed their own party, the Southern Rights Party, nominating John Breckinridge of Kentucky. The remaining Democrats nominated Stephen Douglas of Illinois, who selected former Georgia governor Herschel V. Johnson as his vice-presidential running mate.

Southern Whigs who refused to join the Southern Rights Party formed their own Constitutional Union Party, stressing their adherence to the Union, and nominated John Bell of Tennessee. Republicans, united on everything but a candidate, finally settled on a dark-horse from Illinois named Abraham Lincoln. In the November elections, as nearly everyone expected, Lincoln carried all the more populous free states and became president elect.

Despite Lincoln's poor showing in the slave states, where his name was not even allowed on the ballot, he did have strong Southern support, albeit mostly among enslaved people who could not vote. They attended so many public campaign rallies that some whites became alarmed by their "unusual interest in politics, and the result of the Presidential election." What blacks repeatedly heard from Southern Rights men was that Lincoln, despite his promise to the contrary, intended to free the slaves. Alabama freedman Louis Meadows remembered that slaves "hoped and prayed he would be elected. They wanted to be free and have a chance." In the lead-up to the election that year, rebellions and rumors of rebellions were rife across the South. With slaves expecting freedom, and taking it for themselves, a Lincoln presidency could only make slave control more difficult even if Lincoln himself was no direct threat to slavery.

With Lincoln poised to enter the White House, secessionists pushed hard for disunion. Most slaveholders would now almost certainly support such a move. If lesser yeomen and poor whites could be made to see Lincoln as a John Brown writ large, they too might support withdrawal from the Union. Secessionist leaders had to act quickly before Lincoln took office the next March or they might never have another chance.

Still, slaveholders were not entirely united behind secession. Lager slaveholders especially, who were more likely to have investments in the North, feared the economic disruption that war would surely bring. Others feared that such a war would divide Southerners and doom slavery. Alexander H. Stephens, ironically soon-to-be vice president of the Confederacy, agreed: "The election of no man, constitutionally chosen to that high office, is sufficient cause to justify any state to separate from the Union…to withdraw from it because any man has been elected, would put us in the wrong." Prophetically, Stephens also predicted an inner civil war among Southerners themselves. "The movement will before it ends I fear be beyond the control of those who started it," Stephens said, and Southerners would "at no distant day commence cutting one another's throats."

Secessionist leaders brushed such fears aside and urged voters to fear Lincoln instead. Though he knew better, Governor Joe Brown of Georgia repeated the secessionist drumbeat that Lincoln intended to free the slaves. And he encouraged plain folk to believe that both their pocket book and their pride would suffer for it. Blacks would, in Brown's words, "come into competition with [plain folk], associate with them and their children as equals—be allowed to testify in court against them—sit on juries with them, march to the ballot box by their sides, and participate in the choice of their rulers—claim social equality with them—and ask the hands of their children in marriage." Secessionists such as Brown hoped that playing on racist fears would swing popular opinion their way.

Divisions over secession set the stage for intense controversy at state secession conventions, at least in those states where secessionists had a strong voice. Though most slave states held elections for delegates to secession conventions, Southern popular opinion ran so strongly against breaking up the Union that in the upper South and border states, comprising over half the slave states, an overwhelming majority of voters dismissed secession out of hand. Only in the Deep South was secession an immediate threat. Even there voters were deeply divided. So worried were secessionist leaders over the possibility of secession being voted down that they used intimidation and violence in their efforts to control the ballot box wherever they could. Samuel Beaty, a farmer in Mississippi's Tippah County who was physically threatened because of his Union sentiments, dared not go to the polls. "It would," he said, "have been too dangerous." Secessionists threatened to hang James Cloud, a crippled farmer in Jackson County, Alabama, after he spoke up for the Union.

The Common People Forced to Follow

The balloting for state convention delegates makes clear that the South was badly divided. It also suggests that those divisions were largely class related. North Carolina's vote declining even to hold a convention showed the state's electorate more clearly divided along class lines than ever before. In Louisiana, nonslaveholding voters left little doubt that they saw the secession movement as an effort simply to maintain "the peculiar rights of a privileged class." All seventeen counties in northern Alabama, where relatively few voters held slaves, sent delegates to the state convention with instructions to oppose secession. In Lawrence County, voters elected anti-secessionist delegates by a 90-percent margin. Few counties outside Georgia's plantation belt sent secessionist delegates to its convention. And in Texas, where 81 percent of slaveholders voted for secessionist delegates, only 32 percent of nonslaveholders did so. Slaveholders across the South, who comprised barely a fourth of the electorate, consistently demonstrated much greater support for secession than did their nonslaveholding neighbors.

Nevertheless, slaveholders commanded a dominant voice at all the state conventions. In Georgia, while roughly a third of qualified voters held slaves, 87 percent of the convention delegates were slaveholders. Similar statistics across the Deep South virtually guaranteed secession regardless of the popular will. Beginning with South Carolina in December 1860, secessionists took Mississippi, Florida, Alabama, Georgia, and Louisiana out of the Union. Texas finally went on February 1, 1861. Three days later, representatives from the seceded states met in Montgomery, Alabama, to form the Confederate States of America with Jefferson Davis as its appointed president. One Texas politician conceded that ambitious colleagues had engineered secession without strong backing from "the mass of the people." Alfred Aldrich, a South Carolina legislator and staunch secessionist, admitted the same: "But whoever waited for the common people when a great move was to be made—We must make the move and force them to follow."

If most Southerners opposed secession, most Northerners opposed civil war. "It cannot be denied," wrote the *New York Times* on 21 March 1861, "that there is a growing sentiment throughout the North in favor of *letting the Gulf States go*." It was mainly business elites with economic ties to the South, especially those with cotton interests, who pressured Lincoln to hold the Union together by force if necessary. But he could not do that without an army. What Lincoln needed was an incident to fire Northern nationalism and draw volunteers. Lincoln got his incident on 12 April when, after he threatened to resupply Union-held Fort Sumter in South Carolina's Charleston Harbor, Confederate forces bombarded the garrison. The flag had now been fired upon and Lincoln called for 75,000 volunteers to defend it. Four days after the Sumter incident, New York's *Buffalo Daily Courier* wrote: "With the facts before us we cannot believe that Mr. Lincoln intended that Sumter should be held.... War is inaugurated, and the design of the administration is accomplished."

Lincoln helped accomplish Jefferson Davis's design as well. The certainty of invasion united white Southerners behind the Confederacy like nothing else could. Within a few weeks, four more slave states—Arkansas, Tennessee, North Carolina, and Virginia—left the Union. So many men volunteered for service that the Confederacy was hard pressed to arm them all. "The Union feeling *was strong* up to [Lincoln's] recent proclamation," wrote a North Carolina congressman in late April. "This War Manifest extinguishes it, and resistance is now on every man's lips and throbs in every bosom.... Union men are now such no longer."

But that was not entirely the case. Despite the passionate post-Sumter excitement, there were large cracks in the facade of Southern unity. Throughout the month of May, Unionists held anti-secession rallies all across Tennessee. In North Carolina, there were reports that "Guilford, Randolph and adjoining counties are unshaken in their devotion to the Stars and Stripes." Pickens County, Georgia, which voted overwhelmingly pro-Union, continued to fly the US flag at its courthouse for weeks after secession.

In Virginia, within days of the firing on Fort Sumter and Lincoln's call for volunteers, former governor Henry Wise and his secessionist allies demanded that the sitting governor, John Letcher, take the federal arsenal at Harpers Ferry and the Gosport Navy Yard at Norfolk. Letcher refused and reminded his friends that Virginia's convention had not taken the state out of the Union. In what amounted to a coup d'état, secessionist leaders took control of volunteer troops and ordered assaults on the federal installations. Letcher reluctantly sanctioned the action a day later. When secessionists intimidated the Virginia state convention into approving secession, western Virginia took steps to split off and stay with the Union. Other Upper South slave states were divided as well, but Missouri, Kentucky, Maryland, and Delaware ultimately rejected secession.

Conscription and Cotton in a Rich Man's War

Despite their general reluctance to secede, there was considerable enthusiasm for the war among Southern whites in the wake of Lincoln's call for volunteers to invade the South. Some still blamed slaveholders for bringing on the war, but, as one Tennessee colonel anxiously pleaded: "Our Southern soil must be defended. We must not stop to ask who brought about the war, who is at fault, but let us go and do battle." Whatever their misgivings about secession, plain folk were encouraged to believe that the honor of their men and the safety of their women was now at stake. And, despite Lincoln's promise to the contrary, "fear of Negro equality," as historian Georgia Lee Tatum put it, "caused some of the more ignorant to rally to the support of the Confederacy."

Even so, enlistments declined rapidly after July's First Battle of Manassas, or Bull Run as the North called it. Men were reluctant to leave their families in fall and winter 1861-62, and many of those already in the army deserted to help theirs. In October 1861, one worried Confederate wrote to his governor that "our people don't seem to be inclined to offer their services." That same month, a recruiter in Columbus, Georgia, reported to the War Department that it was almost impossible to find volunteers. In February 1862, W. H. Byrd of Augusta, Georgia, wrote that he had been trying for two weeks to raise a company in what he called "this 'Yankee City,' but I regret to say every effort has failed." That failure did not result from a lack of potential recruits. The *Augusta Chronicle and Sentinel* had noted a week earlier that "one who walks Broad Street and sees the number of young men, would come to the conclusion that no war...was now waging."

The Confederacy's response to its recruitment problem served only to weaken its support among plain folk. In April 1862 the Confederate Congress passed the first general conscription act in American history. Refusal to serve meant execution for treason. Attempts to escape to Union lines could lead to the same fate. There were ways to avoid the draft, especially for those with money. Wealthy men could hire a substitute or pay an exemption fee. Few but the most affluent could afford either option. And then there was the infamous twenty slave law, which exempted one white man of draft age for every twenty slaves owned. This meant that any planter could be excused from the draft. Though few seemed to realize it at the time, this law would come to define the war for Southern plain folk. Said Private Sam Watkins of Tennessee: "It gave us the blues; we wanted twenty negroes. Negro property suddenly became very valuable, and there was raised the howl of 'rich man's war, poor man's fight.'"

Planters justified being excused from the draft by pointing out that soldiers would need food, and so would their families back home. Who better to provide that food than the planters? They had the best land on which to grow food and the slave labor to produce it. Many planters agreed to "bonding" contracts that obligated them to contribute food to soldiers' families. As soldiers left for the front, they were told to have no worries where food was concerned. They and their families would be well fed.

But common folk quickly learned that planter patriotism was more apparent than real. Food production never came close to meeting demand because planters devoted far too much acreage to cotton and tobacco. In 1862, cotton production reached its second highest level on record to that time. In spring 1862, Frederick Burtz of southwest Georgia wrote to Governor Joe Brown about planters growing too much cotton, begging him to "stop those internal enemies of the country, for they will whip us sooner than all Lincolndom combined could do it."

The Confederacy never passed legislation restricting cotton or tobacco production. The Confederate Congress did nothing more than request that planters increase food production and decrease cotton exports. Planters generally ignored the request. Most states passed laws limiting production of non-food items, but enforcement was lax. With prices on the rise, cotton producers and dealers were getting richer than ever. Some bragged openly that the longer the war went on the more money they made.

The dire food shortage brought on by cotton and tobacco overproduction marked the beginning of a spiraling inflationary cycle that rendered Confederate currency nearly worthless. The problem was made worse by speculators, who bought as much food as they could and hoarded it waiting for prices to rise. E. H. Grouby, editor of Georgia's *Early County News*, called speculators "far greater enemies to the South and do more to injure her cause than ten times their number of Yankees in the field." Such people, said Grouby, "carry their patriotism in the *pocketbook*."

Rampant inflation made farmers less willing to exchange what food they had for Confederate money. By 1863, the Richmond government determined that what it could not buy it would take by force. That summer it passed a 10-percent confiscation tax, called impressment, on farm produce and livestock. But there was a loophole. Impressment agents could take as much as they wanted beyond 10 percent as long as they paid for it in Confederate currency or promissory notes, neither of which carried much value. When an impressment officer took two cows from a South Carolina farmer, the man thundered that "the sooner this damned Government fell to pieces the better it would be for us."

Rioting, Deserting, and Voting by Classes

The food shortage hit soldiers' families especially hard. With their husbands and fathers at the front and impressment officers confiscating what little food they had, it was difficult for soldiers' wives to provide for themselves and their children. Planters had promised to keep soldiers' families fed, but they never grew enough food to meet the need. Much of what food they did produce was sold to speculators, who hoarded it or priced it far beyond the reach of most plain folk.

Desperate to avoid starvation, thousands of women took action. As early as 1862, food riots began breaking out all over the South. Gangs of hungry women, many of them armed, ransacked stores, depots, and supply wagons searching for anything edible. Major urban centers like Richmond, Mobile, and Galveston saw the biggest riots. Every major city in Georgia—Atlanta, Columbus, Augusta, Savannah, and Macon—had such disturbances. Even smaller towns, like Georgia's Valdosta, Colquitt, and Marietta; North Carolina's High Point, Greensboro, and Salisbury; Sumter, South Carolina; Lafayette, Alabama; Archer, Florida; and Sherman, Texas, all saw women rioting for food.

In an open letter to the *Savannah Morning News,* one enraged Georgian was sure where the blame lay: "The crime is with the planters...as a class, they have yielded their patriotism, if they ever had any, to covetousness...for the sake of money, they are pursuing a course to destroy or demoralize our army—to starve out the other class dependent on them for provisions." The letter spoke for a great many plain folk. It seemed increasingly obvious to them that they were fighting a rich man's war, which made the problem of desertion that much worse. One Confederate officer from Florida wrote home to his wife that "discontent is growing rapidly in the ranks and I fear that unless something is done...we will have no army. The laws that have been passed generally protect the rich, and the poor begin to say it is the rich man's war and the poor man's fight, and they will not stand it." By the tens of thousands, soldiers continued leaving the army.

Deserters found plenty of neighbors willing to help them avoid further entanglements with the Confederacy. That was obvious even from distant Richmond. A disgusted head of the Bureau of Conscription complained that desertion had "in popular estimation, lost the stigma that justly pertains to it, and therefore the criminals are everywhere shielded by their families and by the sympathies of many communities." A resident of Bibb County, Georgia, wrote that the area around Macon was "full of deserters and almost every man in the community will feed them and keep them from being arrested." In Marshall County, Mississippi, a witness noted that "many deserters have been for months in this place without molestation.... Conscripts and deserters are daily seen on the streets of the town." When deserters were arrested in Alabama's Randolph County, an armed mob stormed the jail and set them free.

Desertion became so serious by summer 1863 that Jefferson Davis publicly begged absentees to return. If only they would, he insisted, the Confederacy could match Union armies man for man. But they did not return. A year later, Davis openly admitted that two-thirds of Confederate soldiers were absent, most of them without leave. Some deserted to the Union, joining other Southerners, mostly from the Upper South, who had enlisted early on. The Union armies eventually contained about 300,000 whites from the slave states. Most deserters went home to their families, forming mutual protection organizations sometimes called "Tory" or "layout" gangs.

Some deserters joined with other anti-Confederates in a shadowy antiwar movement, widely known as the Peace Society, to end the conflict with or without Southern independence. The Peace Society was one of the largest of the many secret or semi-secret organizations, such as the Peace and Constitutional Society in Arkansas and the Heroes of America in Appalachia, that sprang up across the South to oppose the war. Little is known of the Peace Society's early days. It probably formed in north Alabama or east Tennessee during spring 1862 and later spread south into Alabama and Georgia.

So great were elitist fears of rising disaffection that there were calls for class-based restrictions on voting rights. Some demanded an increase in the poll tax to discourage poorer men from casting ballots. Others suggested banning them from politics entirely with property qualifications for voting and office holding. Such efforts served only to inflame common folk and further undermine Confederate support. Several candidates for Georgia's General Assembly from Gilmer and surrounding counties ran on a "Union" ticket during the elections of fall 1863. So did candidates in northern Alabama. In parts of Mississippi, so numerous were Union men that cavalry units were posted to keep them away from the polls. Still, armed bands of deserters showed up at Mississippi polling places defying arrest and demanding their right to vote. In Floyd County, Virginia, Confederates guarded every precinct to prevent deserters from voting. Nevertheless, so many local deserters' relatives went to the polls that they elected a pro-Union sheriff, Ferdinand Winston, and several other Unionist county officials. In Mississippi's Tishomingo County, Confederate officials were so worried about a Union victory at the polls that they suspended elections entirely.

Fear, intimidation, and despondency kept many alienated voters away from the polls in 1863. And because the Confederate Constitution gave presidents a six-year term, Jefferson Davis was in no danger of losing his office. Even so, the election returns brought discouraging news for the Davis administration. In North Carolina, candidates for the Conservative Party, composed mainly of long-time Unionists, won nine of ten congressional seats—eight of them in favor of ending the war with or without Southern independence. In Texas, half the incumbent congressmen lost their seats. Of Georgia's ten congressional representatives, only one was reelected. The state's 90-percent freshman rate was the highest in the Confederacy. Eight of Georgia's new representatives ran on an anti-Davis platform. A Columbus newspaper reported that people were "voting by classes" and that the working men's ticket carried local elections by a large margin. Alabama ousted its staunchly pro-Davis governor. Four of the state's new congressmen were said to be outright Unionists. One Alabamian wrote that the election results showed a "decided wish amongst the people for peace."

In all, about half the Confederate Congress was turned out during the 1863 elections. Two-thirds of the newly elected members had opposed secession. The congressional freshman rate would likely have been much higher had it not been for the large block of essentially reappointed members representing districts under Union control.

The South's Inner Civil War

Rising class resentment, reflected to a considerable extent in the election results, was the very thing that slaveholders had tried to avoid for so long and what had, in large part, led many to push for secession in the first place. "Ironically," as historian Charles Bolton points out, "by engineering disunion, slaveowners fostered the growth of the kind of organizations they had long feared: class-based groups that pitted nonslaveholders against the interests of slaveowners."

Nowhere was that more evident than in the lowcountry of North Carolina. Planters in the region were terrified to learn that, as one wrote, Unionists among the lower classes had "gone so far as to declare [that they] will take the property from the rich men and divide it among the poor men." It was no idle threat. From near the war's beginning, bands of Unionists had been raiding coastal plantations. Formed initially to protect themselves from conscription and Confederate raiders, their objectives eventually expanded to include driving planters from their land and dividing it among themselves. Farther west in North Carolina's interior, class antagonism was also a strong motive for resistance. Many members of the Heroes of America were poor men who, as one contemporary recalled, were "induced to join the organization by the promise of a division here after among them of the property of the loyal Southern citizens."

Though their motives were not always the same, the one thing nearly all armed resisters had in common was that they were men of modest means. In eastern Tennessee, Unionist guerillas were mainly small farmers, artisans, and laborers. By contrast, pro-Confederates held three times as much real estate and twice as much personal property. In the North Fork district of western North Carolina's Ashe County, a comparison of thirty-four Union and forty-two Confederate volunteers shows that holdings in real and personal property among Confederates was more than twice that of their Union counterparts. In eastern North Carolina, the difference was even more dramatic. In Washington County, which supplied nearly an equal number of troops to the Union and the Confederacy, Union soldiers were fourteen times poorer than those in the Confederate army. Such figures reflect a class-based Unionism that made itself felt all across the South.

In 1863, as Union armies pushed their way south, a newspaper editor in the central Georgia town of Milledgeville was more concerned about the war at home. In an essay discussing the many ways in which white Southerners were working against the Confederacy, the editor wrote: "We are fighting each other harder than we have ever fought the enemy." Samuel Knight agreed. After touring southwest Georgia in late fall and winter 1863-64, he wrote to Governor Joe Brown of "strong Union feeling" in that part of the state. Knight concluded that white Southerners were "as bitterly divided against each other" as they had ever been against Northerners.

Armed resistance had been going on for some time. As early as summer 1862, there were newspaper reports of layout gangs in Calhoun County, Florida, just west of Tallahassee, that had "armed and organized themselves to resist those who may attempt their arrest." They were already in contact with the Union blockading fleet and receiving arms from it. At one point they even hatched a plot to kidnap Governor Milton and turn him over to the Federals. A pro-Confederate citizen learned of the scheme and warned Milton, who stayed in Tallahassee to avoid capture.

Just east of Florida's capital, deserter bands raided plantations in Jefferson, Madison, and Taylor counties. Along Florida's western Gulf coast, armed deserters and layouts were abundant in Lafayette, Walton, Levy, and Washington counties. In southwestern Florida between Tampa and Fort Myers, they ranged virtually unchallenged. On Florida's Atlantic coast, the counties Volusia, Duval, Putnam, and St. John's saw running battles between anti-Confederate bands and soldiers trying to bring them in.

Bands of deserters also ranged over southern Mississippi's Simpson County. When the sheriff arrested several of them, their friends broke them out of jail. That entire area of Mississippi was, in fact, largely controlled by deserters and resisters who killed or drove off anyone connected with the Confederacy. One of the most effective layout gangs operated in southeast Mississippi's Jones County and was led by Newton Knight, a slaveless farmer who left the Confederate army soon after conscription began. Upset that wealthy men could avoid the draft, Knight deserted and took up with others of his community who had done the same. "We stayed out in the woods minding our own business," Knight said, "until the Confederate Army began sending raiders after us with bloodhounds.... Then we saw we had to fight." So successfully did they subvert Confederate control in Jones County that some called it the Free State of Jones.

"Free State" was a phrase also widely applied to north Alabama's Winston County. Soon after Alabama seceded from the Union, Winston was said to have seceded from the state. A December 1861 letter to Alabama's governor warned that "if they had to fight for anybody, they would fight for Lincoln." And they did. Twice as many Winston County men served in the Union army as in the Confederate. Even many of those who initially signed on with the Confederacy soon had a change of heart. By summer 1863 there were at least ten thousand deserters and conscripts in the Alabama hill country formed into armed bands. Along the Florida line in southeast Alabama, a Confederate captain sent to catch deserters called the region "one of the greatest dens for Tories and deserters from our army in the world."

In Louisiana, James Madison Wells, though a man of means himself, denounced the Confederate secession effort as a rich man's war and organized a guerrilla campaign against it. From his Bear Wallow stronghold in Rapides Parish, Wells led deserters and other resisters in raids against Confederate supply lines and depots. In the state's Cajun parishes, bands of anti-Confederates did the same. One group that ranged west of Washington Parish, known locally as the "Clan," numbered more than 300. Commanded by a Cajun named Carrier, it drove off pro-Confederate home guards and forced plunder from all who opposed them.

In Bandera County, Texas, just west of San Antonio, residents formed a pro-Union militia, refused to pay taxes to the Confederate state government, and threatened to kill anyone who tried to make them do so. At the state's northern extreme near Bonham, several hundred anti-Confederates established three large camps close enough so that the entire force could assemble within two hours. In the central Texas county of Bell, deserters led by Lige Bivens fortified themselves in a cave known as Camp Safety. From there they mounted raids against the area's pro-Confederates.

In Arkansas and Missouri, the Ozark uplands were prime recruiting ground for Union companies of "mountain Feds." Among the most active was Williams's Raiders, formed around the Williams family of Arkansas's Conway and Van Buren counties and led by fifty-one-year-old Thomas Jefferson (Jeff) Williams. Williams and his neighbors were small farmers who at first wanted nothing to do with the war. But when Confederate draft officers came calling in 1862, Williams—along with his four sons, three sons-in-law, two brothers, a brother-in-law, four nephews, and twenty-five other men—formed an independent company of local Unionists to fight back. For the next few years Williams's Raiders fought with considerable success against Confederate authority in the Ozarks.

Deserters and resisters alike in the North Carolina mountains formed defensive militias and set up warning networks. Wilkes County was home to a band of 500 deserters organized as a guerrilla force who openly challenged Confederates to come and take them. Wilkes County's Trap Hill gang was especially aggressive in harassing local pro-Confederates. In Cherokee County, about 100 layouts formed a resistance force that disarmed Confederate soldiers and terrorized Confederate loyalists.

South Carolina's hill country also saw its share of resistance. Centered in Greenville, Pickens, and Spartanburg counties, deserter bands had designated assembly areas and an organized system of signals to warn of trouble on the way. "Every woman and child," according to one report, was "a watch and a guard for them." Deserter bands went on the offensive too. Operating in groups of between ten and thirty, they chased off conscript companies, raided supply depots, and looted and burned the property of anyone who openly supported the Confederacy.

Much the same was true in southwestern Virginia, where J. E. Joyner noted large numbers of deserters with weapons, which they vowed to use "against the Confederacy if there is any attempt to arrest them." Montgomery, Floyd, and Giles counties especially were home to numerous bands of deserters. Local Unionists too, aroused by Confederate home guard depredations, formed armed militias. One such unit, headed by "Captain" Charles Huff of Floyd County, regularly backed up local deserters and ambushed home guard patrols. The job was made easier by Joseph Phares, a double agent who kept Huff informed of the home guard's plans while feeding its officers disinformation.

The Confederacy's keystone state of Georgia was one of the most divided in the South. Anti-Confederate gangs operated in every part of the state. Some areas were so hostile to the Confederacy that army patrols dared not enter them. The pine barrens region of southeast Georgia was a favorite hideout for those trying to avoid Confederate entanglements. Soldier Camp Island in the Okefenokee Swamp was home to as many as a thousand deserters.

From Georgia's mountain county of Fannin, a letter arrived on the governor's desk in July 1862 warning that "a very large majority of the people now here, perhaps two-thirds, are disloyal." Anti-Confederates became so aggressive in Fannin that one man called it a "general uprising among our Torys of this County." That same month came news from Gilmer County, just north of Fannin, of "tories and traitors who have taken up their abode in the mountains." September found neighboring Lumpkin County overrun by Tories and deserters, robbing pro-Confederates of guns, money, clothes, and provisions. One Confederate sympathizer wrote that "the Union men—Tories—are very abusive indeed and says they will do as they please."

Slave Resistance and Self-Emancipation

So many soldiers were leaving the ranks and joining deserter gangs that the Confederacy's remaining supporters began to seriously consider what until then had been unthinkable—arming the slaves. As early as 1863, high-ranking Confederate officials began advocating such a move. Tens of thousands of blacks—eventually around 200,000–were already serving in the Union's army and navy, roughly 80 percent of them native Southerners. And they were proving to be very effective warriors. As prospects for Confederate victory became ever more dim, support among pro-Confederates for arming blacks began to grow. Even Jefferson Davis and Robert E. Lee became strong supporters of the effort.

Not surprisingly, most slaveholders fiercely resisted any suggestion that blacks be placed in the army. They feared not only the loss of their "property" but also what slave conscription would mean for slavery's future, dead though it nearly was in any case. General Howell Cobb summed up the prevailing slaveholder view when he insisted that "the day you make soldiers of them is the beginning of the end of the revolution. If slaves will make good soldiers, our whole theory of slavery is wrong."

There was also the question of whether giving guns to slaves would make them Confederates. It was an unlikely assumption. From the war's outset, blacks thought that Lincoln intended to free them. How could they think otherwise with Southern Fire-Eaters preaching it from every political stump. "The idea seems to have gotten out extensively among [the slaves] that they are soon all to be free," wrote one worried slaveholder in April 1861, "that Mr. Lincoln and his army are coming to set them free."

But enslaved blacks were not simply waiting to be given freedom. They were taking it for themselves. Though Lincoln's Emancipation Proclamation is often cited as having freed the slaves, it applied only to those behind Confederate lines. Even then, it only grudgingly recognized what blacks themselves had already forced on Lincoln's government.

During the war's early months, knowing that most Northerners were not abolitionists, Lincoln repeated that he had no intention of ending slavery. In his March 1861 inaugural address, in an effort to call back the seceded states, Lincoln supported a thirteenth amendment to the Constitution, the Corwin Amendment, that would have guaranteed slavery in the slave states forever. Citing the Fugitive Slave Act, Lincoln also instructed the army to return any escaped slaves to their owners. In July 1861, Congress, which had earlier passed the Corwin Amendment and sent it to the states in a failed attempt at ratification, backed Lincoln up with a resolution making clear that this was a war to preserve the Union, not to free the slaves. Nevertheless, tens of thousands of escaping slaves took freedom for themselves, refused to be re-enslaved, and forced Lincoln to alter his policy, a fact that blacks well understood.

Former Maryland slave Frederick Douglass, in an 1865 speech before the Massachusetts Anti-Slavery Society, stressed the impact that escaping slaves had on forcing an end to slavery. The Civil War began, he said, "in the interest of slavery on both sides."

> The South was fighting to take slavery out of the Union, and the North was fighting to keep it in the Union...both despising the negro, both insulting the negro. Yet, the negro, apparently endowed with wisdom from on high, saw more clearly the end from the beginning .... When our generals sent their underlings in shoulder-straps to hunt the flying negro back from our lines into the jaws of slavery, from which he had escaped, the negroes thought that a mistake had been made, and that the intentions of the Government had not been rightly understood by our officers in shoulder-straps, and they continued to come into our lines, threading their way through bogs and fens, over briers and thorns, fording streams, swimming rivers, bringing us tidings as to the safe path to march, and pointing out the dangers that threatened us.

"It is a matter of notoriety," lamented a Confederate official, "in the sections of the Confederacy where raids are frequent that the guides of the enemy are nearly always free negroes and slaves." In March 1863, seven escapees described as "bright and intelligent" arrived at Union lines in Mississippi with word of artillery positions around Vicksburg. A fugitive from the same area told of Confederate cavalry operations below Jackson. Jim Williams, an escaped former slave from Carroll Parish,

Louisiana, led federal troops in an ambush of Confederate forces, during which he killed one Rebel and captured two more. In Missouri, information from escaping slaves saved Union troops at Jefferson City from a surprise attack. In July 1864, as a Union raiding party approached the outskirts of Auburn, Alabama, a group of local blacks hurried out to warn its commander, Colonel William Hamilton, of Rebels hidden among the thickets ahead. In a charge that "could be better heard than seen," Hamilton and his men rushed the surprised Confederates, who, as Hamilton reported, "broke on our first fire and scattered in every direction."

Southern blacks assisted Southern whites as well in resisting the Confederacy. Deserters escaping the Confederate army could rely on slaves to give them food and shelter on the journey back home. Some blacks joined Tory gangs in their war against the Confederacy. Two slaves in Dale County, Alabama, helped John Ward, leader of a local deserter gang, kill their owner in his bed. Three white citizens of Calhoun County, Georgia, were arrested for supplying area slaves with firearms in preparation for a rebellion. Slaves in nearby Brooks County conspired with a local white man, John Vickery, to take the county and hold it for the Union.

Hundreds of thousands of slaves fled their enslavers in what historian W. E. B. DuBois called a general strike against the Confederacy. Every slave taken as servants to the front by Georgia's Troup Artillery escaped to Union lines. One Georgia slave was hanged for attempting to organize a mass exodus of local blacks to Federals on the Gulf coast. Many, like Susie King Taylor of Savannah, escaped to Union forces operating along the Atlantic coast. Taylor served one of the Union army's first black regiments, cooking for the men, doing their laundry, and acting as nurse. She also served as a teacher, having secretly learned to read and write while enslaved. She eventually married one of the soldiers and after the war opened a school for black children in Savannah.

Enslaved blacks in the interior for whom escape was more difficult nevertheless found various ways to resist. In areas of the Black Belt from which many of the white males had gone off to war, slaves were particularly defiant. In August 1862, slaveholder Laura Comer wrote in her diary: "The servants are so indolent and obstinate it is a trial to have anything to do with them." Slaves feigned ignorance or illness, sabotaged equipment, and roamed freely in defiance of laws requiring them to carry a pass.

What work slaves did, they did grudgingly. Some refused to work at all. Others used the threat of escape to force wage payments from their owners. Even if escape did not result, slaves were largely taking freedom by degrees. In summer 1863, an Alabama newspaper complained of blacks becoming "so saucy and abusive that a police force has become positively necessary as a check to this continued insolence." In Georgia, legislators had already introduced a bill "to punish slaves and free persons of color for abusive and insulting language." Along with freedom of speech, blacks were taking freedom of assembly as well. In Blakely, Georgia, the *Early County News* reported that blacks were "almost nightly running around where they have no business." A slaveholder in Columbus, Georgia, feared that blacks were forgetting their second-class status. "It is not uncommon," he wrote, "to see two or three in one whiskey shop." One woman wrote to her husband: "We are doing as best we know, or as good as we can get the Servants to do; they learn to feel very independent."

When independence led to escape and they could not make it to Union lines, fugitive slaves often gathered in small, isolated communities. Sometimes these settlements were multiracial. They were so numerous in the Southern coastal plain that one source called it "the common retreat of deserters from our army, tories, and runaway negroes." Like their white counterparts, groups of self-emancipated blacks sustained themselves by making raids on local towns and plantations. One white man complained in a letter to his governor that escaped former slaves were "killing up the stock and stealing every thing they can put their hands on."

Trying to stem the rising tide of resistance among slaves, state legislatures made several additions to their penal codes. They made arson punishable by death. They reinforced laws forbidding slaves to travel without passes and canceled all exemptions for slave patrols. Such efforts did little to restrain slaves. They had long since begun to anticipate freedom, even taking it for themselves, and were more and more ignoring the patrols. Some even fought back. They often tied ropes or vines neck-high across a dark stretch of road just before the patrollers rode by. According to a former slave, these traps were guaranteed to unhorse at least one rider. When patrollers raided a prayer meeting near Columbus, Georgia, one slave stuck a shovel in the fireplace and threw hot coals all over them. Instantly the room "filled with smoke and the smell of burning clothes and white flesh." In the confusion, every slave got away.

Try as they might, slaveholders found it impossible to maintain their accustomed control. It was with good reason that, as one Texas slaveholder wrote, "a great many of the people are actually afraid to whip the negroes." In Choctaw County, Mississippi, slaves turned the tables on their owner, Nat Best, subjecting him to 500 lashes. Texas bondsmen killed an overseer known for his "meanness over the slaves." In Virginia, a band of slaves armed with shotguns killed two planters. After Mississippi slaveholder Jim Rankin returned from the army "meaner than before," as one freedman told it, a slave "sneaked up in the darkness and shot him three times." Rankin lingered in agony the rest of the night before he died the next morning. "He never knowed who done it," the freedman recalled. "I was glad they shot him down."

Defeated by the People at Home

With slave resistance so widespread, it seems little wonder that slaveholders opposed placing firearms in the hands of slaves. Nevertheless, on 13 March 1865 the Confederate Congress finally passed legislation authorizing recruitment of up to 300,000 slaves. But there was no promise of freedom for those who agreed to serve. It hardly mattered in any case. By then the Confederacy was nearly spent. In April, the last major Confederate armies ceased to exist and chattel slavery died with them.

In a sense, the Confederacy's existence as a national entity was questionable from the start. Most Southerners had opposed secession in the first place and increasingly came to view the struggle as a rich man's war. On 5 April 1865, only days before the Confederacy's collapse, Georgia's *Early County News* expressed a resentment that had long since become common among Southern plain folk when it wrote: "This has been 'a rich man's war and a poor man's fight.' It is true there are a few wealthy men in the army, but nine tenths of them hold positions, always get out of the way when they think a fight is coming on, and treat the privates like dogs....There seems to be no chance to get this class to carry muskets."

Most texts tend to suggest that the North's greater population and industry explain Union victory. Yes, the North had more factories. But the South imported and produced munitions enough to keep its troops well supplied. Never did any Confederate army lose a major battle for lack of arms. What it lacked was men enough to carry those arms and food enough to feed them. Certainly the North's population was greater, twice as great in fact. But Confederate armies were outnumbered two-to-one mainly because so many Southerners refused to serve—or served on the Union side. Of about 200,000 blacks under federal arms, eight out of ten were native Southerners. Together with roughly 300,000 slave-state whites who did the same, Southerners who served in the Union military totaled nearly 500,000, or about a quarter of all federal men in arms.

There was dissent in the North as well. It was Northern draft resistance and anti-war sentiment generally that go a long way toward explaining how a Confederacy at war with itself was able to survive for as long as it did. But Northern dissent pales in comparison to dissent in the South. The Confederacy could nearly have met the Union man for man had it not been for rampant desertion and widespread draft evasion, problems that were far greater for the Confederates than the Federals.

The myth of war-time Southern unity, romanticized as the Lost Cause, arose only after the war as rampant racism worked to keep former slaves "in their place." White supremacy became a far greater unifying force for Southern whites than the Confederacy had ever been. That during the war white Southerners had "cursed the Southern Confederacy"—that they had fought each other "harder than we have ever fought the enemy"—all mattered little in the postwar era. What did matter was that the fiction of kind masters, contented slaves, and happily supportive plain folk vindicated the Confederacy and bolstered white supremacy. It was in fact this newly idealized Confederate South, not the Confederacy as it had been, that was firmly planted in the popular mind and became both a justification and a euphemism for white supremacy.

Lost Causers went to great lengths to preserve their rosy image of the past. They erected Confederate monuments all over the South. They named parks, buildings, towns, and counties after Confederate heroes. They enshrined Confederate ideology and icons in novels, in movies, at public events, and on Southern state flags. In doing so, they tried to bury the memory of dissent in a divided Civil War South, as one Mississippi Lost Causer put it, "so deep that the hand of time may never resurrect it."

The Lost Cause and its myth of Southern unity were perhaps most firmly cemented in the popular mind with the epic 1939 movie *Gone with the Wind*, based on the novel by Atlanta writer Margaret Mitchell. The film won ten Academy Awards and became one of the most enduring and widely viewed motion pictures in cinema history. Though the film contains no hint of the internal divisions that fatally undermined the Confederate war effort, for many people all over the world *Gone with the Wind* defines the Civil War South to this day.

On the whole, Lost Cause mythmakers helped perpetuate a system of class and race oppression that made the New South much like the Old South. In fact, the postwar South was hardly a New South at all. Though the Civil War is still viewed by many as *the* pivotal event in Southern history, little changed in a practical way as a result of the war. Planters remained the South's ruling class both politically and economically. Agriculture, particularly cotton agriculture, remained the region's dominant economic force. And though the Civil War did end chattel slavery, most former slaves, along with many whites, were forced into the economic bondage of sharecropping and tenancy, or as some called it, "the new slavery."

Significant change began only in the 1920s after the boll weevil wiped out most of the South's cotton crop. No longer needed to pick cotton, masses of tenant farmers, black and white, were driven off the land and released from the debt slavery that was so pervasive with tenancy. It would take decades more for federal programs from the New Deal onward, expanding economic and educational opportunities, farm mechanization, and the Civil Rights Movement to propel the region toward anything like a "new" South.

Most Southerners realized well before the Civil War ended that the postwar South would hardly be a new one. Their lives would go on much as they always had whether ruled from Richmond or Washington. Cornelia McDonald of Winchester, Virginia, wrote that common people "knew that they would be as well-off under one government as another." In fact, most Southerners eventually came to feel that they would be better off with the war over and the Union restored. To them, the Confederacy was the real enemy.

Viewing the war from a home front perspective leaves little wonder that so many Southerners turned against the Confederacy. It conscripted their men, impressed their supplies, and starved them out. It favored the rich and oppressed the poor. It made war on those who withheld their support and made life miserable for the rest. That dawning reality led more and more plain folk all across the South to oppose the Confederacy, or withhold support from it, as the war dragged on. Their attitudes and actions, along with widespread slave resistance, contributed in large part to the Confederacy's downfall, a fact that was well known to Southerners at the time. Some had even predicted it. In fall 1862, an Atlanta newspaper put it bluntly: "If we are defeated, it will be by the people at home." And so the Confederacy was defeated, not only by the Union army—in which close to half a million Southerners served—but also by sustained and violent resistance on the home front.

Documents

1. Mexico Tries to Stop Illegal Immigration and Slave Smuggling into Texas (1830)

After Mexico gained independence in the 1820s, it gradually began to end slavery. As part of that process, with its Decree of 1830, Mexico forbade further importation of slaves. Southern slaveholders ignored the law and kept crossing illegally into the Mexican province of Texas, bringing slaves with them and sparking the Texas Revolution.

Article 9. The introduction of foreigners across the northern frontier is prohibited under any pretext whatever, unless the said foreigners are provided with a passport issued by the agents of this Republic at the point whence the said foreigners set out.

Article 10. No change shall be made with respect to the slaves now in the states, but the federal government and the government of each state shall most strictly enforce the colonization laws and prevent the further introduction of slaves.

Article 11. It is prohibited that emigrants from nations bordering on this Republic shall settle in the states or territory adjacent to their own nation. Consequently, all contracts not already completed and not in harmony with this law are suspended.

Dublan y Lozno, *Legislacion Mexicana, Vol. 2*: 238–40, in Alleine Howren, "Causes and Origin of the Decree of April 6, 1830," *Southwestern Historical Quarterly* 16,4 (1912–1913): 416.

2. Dangerfield Newby Dies at Harpers Ferry Trying to Free His Family (1859)

The first man to die in the October 1859 Harpers Ferry Raid was Dangerfield Newby, a former Virginia slave. Found in his vest pocket were several letters from his wife, enslaved along with their children in Prince William County, just 40 miles from Harpers Ferry. The last, dated 16 August, brought urgent and disturbing news.

Dear Husband,

Your kind letter came duly to hand and it gave me much pleasure to hear from you and especially to hear you are better of your rheumatism and hope when I hear from you again you may be entirely well. I want you to buy me as soon as possible, for if you do not get me somebody else will.... It is said Master is in want of money. If so, I know not what time he may sell me, and then all my bright hopes of the future are blasted, for there has been one bright hope to cheer me in all my troubles, that is to be with you. For if I thought I should never see you, this earth would have no charms for me.... Do all you can for me, which I have no doubt you will. I want to see you so much. The children are all well. The baby cannot walk yet.... You must write soon and say when you think you can come.

Your affectionate Wife
Harriet Newby

Governor's Message and Reports of the Public Officers of the State (Richmond: William F. Ritchie, 1859) 116–17.

3. Virginians "Stand by the Constitution and the Union" (1861)

A few weeks before Virginia's vote for delegates to the state's secession convention, a mass meeting of working class men in Portsmouth drafted and unanimously approved a resolution.

Dangerfield Newby, a native Virginian born into slavery, was the first of John Brown's comrades to die on the Harpers Ferry raid of October 1859. Newby had joined the effort in hope of rescuing his wife and children from slavery in nearby Prince William County.

Photo from the National Park Service.

We look upon any attempt to break up this Government or dissolve this Union as an attack upon the rights of the people of the whole country, and tending to destroy the position of equality assumed by us all.... We hold that the Constitution of the United States is not a league or compact between the States in their sovereign capacity, but a Government proper, founded on the adoption of the people creating direct relations between the citizens and itself.... no power short of a Convention of the people of the whole Union, assembled according to the provisions of the Constitution, has power to absolve the citizen from his allegiance to the United States.... We look upon secession as having one meaning, viz. treason.... [We] stand by the Constitution and the Union.

Daily National Intelligencer (Washington DC), 17 January 1861.

4. James Bell of Alabama Begs His Son Not to Commit Treason (1861)

James Bell had six grown children in 1861, all loyal to the Union except one son, Henry, who moved to Mississippi and joined the Confederate army with his cousin, Andrew Lowrimore. It is to Henry that James Bell addressed this letter, three months after Alabama left the Union. Sadly, the family never had an opportunity to reconcile. While Henry joined the Confederate army, four of his brothers enlisted on the Union side. Three did not survive the war. Henry succumbed to disease in Chattanooga. His father James died at home in September 1862.

Ethridge, Alabama, April 27, 1861

Dear Son, it is with pleasure that I seat my self this morning to let you know that we are all well at present hoping when these few lines comes to hand that they may find you all well and doing well. I received a letter from you and Andrew Lowrimore this morning and was glad to hear that you are well but it was disgusting to me to think that I had raised a child that would secede from under the government that he was borned and raised under. It is something strange to me that people can forget the groans and cries of our forefathers in the Revolution so quick. Henry, just think back to the time when our forefathers walked over the frozen ground bare foot leaving their blood on the ground when fighting for the liberties that you have enjoyed ever since you have had a being in the world. God forbid that I ever should even be called a Secessionist. I had just as soon be called a Tory as to commit treason against the government that was sealed with the blood of my fathers. The Scripture informs us that a house divided against itself cannot stand. The Scriptures informs us that the Israelites divided in to Northism and Southism's and She was in bondage in less than ten years. Henry, you are out in a seceding country and they have got you puffed up with secessionism as tight as a toad. I don't see what you need to care, for you aint got no Slaves. All they want is to get you puffed up and go to fight for their infernal negroes and after you do their fighting you may kiss their hind parts for all they care. Henry, you wrote that if we was in a enlightened country that we could see better. I want you to understand that we aint in a heathen land, or wasn't until Alabama went out of the Union.... There is as smart men in this country as there is in Mississippi and as intelligent gentlemen as lives anywhere. Henry, may time hasten to roll around when you can see your own interest and turn your back upon the cursed question called Secessionism and return like the prodigal son and then come over and we will kill the fated calf. So I will close my few remarks hoping when you see these few lines that you will no longer [be] a secessionist.

James Bell, Letter to Henry Bell, 27 April 1861, Governor A.B. Moore Papers, Alabama Department of Archives and History, Montgomery.

5. Rev. John Aughey and a "Multitude" Evade the Draft in Mississippi (1862)

John Aughey was a Presbyterian minister who was nearly killed for supporting the Union. Mississippi authorities arrested Aughey and were about to execute him for treason when, with the help of sympathetic friends, he escaped and made his way to Union lines. From there he traveled north and in 1863 published a book recounting his experiences.

I, in common with many others, found it difficult to evade the conscript law. Knowing that in a multitude of councellors there is wisdom, we held secret meetings, in order to devise the best method of resisting the law. We met at night, and had our countersigns to prevent detection. Often our wives, sisters, and daughters met with us. Our meeting-place was some ravine, or secluded glen, as far as possible from the haunts of secessionists; all were armed; even the ladies had revolvers, and could use them too. The crime of treason we were resolved not to commit. Our counsels were somewhat divided, some advocating, as a matter of policy, the propriety of attending the militia muster, others opposing it for conscience' sake, and for the purpose of avoiding every appearance of evil. Many who would not muster as conscripts, resolved to escape to the Federal lines; and making the attempt two or three at a time, succeeded in crossing the Tennessee River, and reaching the Union army, enlisted under the old flag, and have since done good service as patriotic warriors. Some who were willing to muster as conscripts, were impressed into the Confederate service, and I know not whether they ever found an opportunity to desert. Others, myself among the number, were saved by the timely arrival of the Federal troops, and the occupation of the country by them, after Beauregard's evacuation of Corinth.

John H. Aughey, *The Iron Furnace: or, Slavery and Secession* (1863; Philadelphia: James S. Claxton, 1865) 64.

6. Oliver Sanders of Louisiana Refuses "to Fight For the Rich Man's Negroes" (ca. 1862)

Captain Dennis E. Haynes, a Louisiana Unionist who late in the war commanded a unit of federal scouts, recalled in his memoir a Confederate home guard company led by "Bloody Bob" Martin that terrorized draft evaders in western Louisiana.

One of the first of "Bloody Bob's" murders was the killing of Oliver Sanders. He lived about eight miles southeast of Manny [in] Sabine Parish. He was a poor man, and had a wife and eight children.... Sanders said that before he would go to fight for the rich man's negroes, and leave his family to suffer, while the rich man stayed at home—as he could do, according to the exemption in the conscript act—if he had to die fighting at all he would die fighting at home. "Bloody Bob," hearing of this, went to test the truth of his statement; but, coward as he is in his heart—for I never knew a bloodthirsty villain to be anything else—he took a company of his vampires with him. Sanders was at home; but before he could prepare to meet them with any hopes of success, they had made a charge on the house and surrounded it. Sanders jumped for his rifle, which lay on a rack over the door facing the road, and in his attempt to get hold of it he exposed his body to the full view of his enemies, who poured in a volley on him, with dreadful effect to poor Sanders. He staggered and fell—fell across a sick child on the bed, pierced with eight bullets—a lifeless corpse.... His wife and some neighboring women had to bury him, for the men were either in the army or in the woods.... These cruelties were not only sanctioned, but applauded by the sensitive, the elite aristocracy of western Louisiana.

D. E. Haynes, *A Thrilling Narrative of the Sufferings of Union Refugees, and the Massacre of the Martyrs of Liberty in Western Louisiana* (Washington DC: McGill and Witherow, 1866) 66–67.

7. Draft Evaders "Dispatched with Great Cruelty" in Tennessee (1863)

Anti-Confederates organized a network of underground railroads to shuttle escaping Unionists to federal lines. They laid out routes, established safe houses, and used conductors to guide refugees on their way. One guide, Daniel Ellis of Carter County, Tennessee, piloted perhaps 4000 people out of the Confederacy. In March 1863, five draft evaders whom Ellis had agreed to escort to Kentucky were spotted by a Confederate patrol along the Watauga River.

When the rebels first fired, poor Taylor surrendered; they continued to shoot at him...shooting the top of his head off with a musket.... Tatum was killed nearly at the same time that Taylor was, he being first wounded in the shoulder, and then dispatched with great cruelty. The other three men ran some distance, while the rebels were shooting at them as fast as they could; at length they surrendered.... these poor men were hung up to torture, and suffer a thousand pangs of death; for they were hung so as not to break their necks, but rather to be chocked to death by degrees .... While they were suspended by their necks, and before life was extinct, they were treated with the greatest brutality, by their reckless murderers beating them with their guns. Captain Roby Brown, a citizen of Johnson County, Tennessee, and one ot the home guards in that county, enjoyed himself very much at this miserable feast of blood. He had a complete frolic around them while they were struggling in all the agonies of a terrible death. He knocked them with his gun, and would then dance up to them, and turn them around violently, telling them to "face their partner." He would say to them that "he did not like to dance with any person that would not face him;" while they, with tongues as black as ink protruding out of their mouths, and their eyes bursting from their sockets, exhibited a spectacle of horror which was enough to strike terror to the very soul of any person who was not perfectly hardened in villainy and crime, and callous to the most wretched displays of human suffering, and steeped in the deepest depths of infamy.

Daniel Ellis, *Thrilling Adventures of Daniel Ellis* (New York: Harper and Brothers, 1867) 106–109.

8. Cotton Planters and Speculators Undermine the Confederate War Effort (1862)

In Mach 1862, as the South entered its second year of war, food production was declining and prices were rising. Primary contributing factors were cotton growing and speculation, as laid out in this letter from Frederick Burtz of Albany, Georgia, begging Governor Joseph E. Brown to intervene.

Dear Sir,

Under the circumstances, I hope you will suffer me to intrude a little upon your time and attention, which I know is already heavily taxed, but we are in great danger of *subjugation* to the hated government that we are resisting, *not* by the army of demons invading our country, but by the *avarice* and *menial subjects* of King Cotton. Notwithstanding...the *resolutions* of a great many county meetings not to plant cotton, and to plant a *provision* crop this year, common sense reasoning in every crowd of men, and a famine now staring us in the face, there are yet many planters who persist in planting cotton!...

Those unpatriotic men in our midst who are engaged in buying up and holding the necessaries of life, and who fears no God nor sympathize with humanity, have priced nearly all kinds of provisions so high, that the poor cannot buy them, and continue to *advance* in the price...in the midst of this knowledge, even here in this small county, of two Militia districts, I hear of one planter who is pitching 900 acres in cotton, the overseer of another told me he is going to plant 300 acres, another...90 acres...another 300 acres, and two others full crops of cotton! And so it will be all over the state....

I hope your Excellency will adopt some plan to stop those internal enemies of the country, for they will whip us sooner than all Lincolndom combined could do it.

Frederick Burtz, Letter to Joseph E. Brown, 29 March 1862, Governor's Incoming Correspondence, Georgia Department of Archives and History, Morrow.

9. A North Carolina Private Recounts Hardships of Soldiers and Their Families (1863)

In February 1863, Private O. Goddin of the 51st North Carolina Regiment wrote to Governor Zebulon Vance about his own discontent and that of his fellow soldiers. They were especially concerned for their families back home.

Dear Sir

Please pardon the liberty which a poor soldier takes in thus addressing you as when he *volunteered* he left a wife with four children to go to fight for his country. He cheerfully made the sacrifices thinking that the government would protect his family, and keep them from starvation. In this he has been disappointed for the government has made a distinction between the rich man (who had something to fight for) and the poor man who fights for that he never will have. The exemption of the owners of 20 negroes and allowing of substitutes clearly proves it. Healthy and active men who have furnished substitutes are grinding the poor by speculation...unrestrained speculation has put provisions up in this market as follows: meal $4 to 5 per bushel, flour $50 to 60 per barrel, lard 70 cents per lb by the barrel, bacon 75 cents per lb by the load, and every thing else in proportion.

Now Governor, do tell me how we poor soldiers who are fighting for the "rich man's negro" can support our families at $11 per month? How can the poor live? I dread to see summer as I am fearful there will be much suffering and probably many deaths from starvation. They are suffering now....

The majority of our soldiers are poor men with families who say they are tired of the rich man's war and poor man's fight. They wish to get to their families and fully believe some settlement could be made were it not that our authorities have made up their minds to prosecute the war regardless of all suffering.... A man's first duty is to provide for his own household. The soldiers wont be imposed upon much longer. If we hear our families are suffering and apply for a furlough to go to them, we are denied. And if we go without authority we are arrested and punished as deserters.... You do not know how it is to be a poor man serving your country faithfully while your family are crying for bread because those who are enjoying their property for which you are fighting are charging such high prices for provisions and the necessaries of life and still holding on for higher prices.....

O. Goddin, Letter to Zebulon Vance, 27 February 1863, Governor's Papers, North Carolina Division of Archives and History, Raleigh, in Paul D. Escott et al., editors., *Major Problems in the History of the American South, Volume 1: The Old South* (New York: Houghton Mifflin, 1999) 365–66.

10. The South's Rioting Women (1863)

At the time this editorial appeared in April 1863, women all across the South were taking matters into their own hands and rioting for food and other basic goods. Though cotton over-production lay at the heart of food shortages, speculation made the situation much worse, as this writer makes clear. And, as the writer also predicts, women's riots continued though the end of the war.

The tendency to mob violence is becoming really alarming. In Atlanta and Salisbury, N.C., there have recently been forcible seizures of provisions and goods *by women*.... We hope no more scenes like those at Atlanta and Salisbury may occur, though we fear they will become frequent, as want presses harder upon the country.

It is a notorious fact that many selfish and unpatriotic men are hoarding large amounts of provisions in every community and refusing to sell at any price, even to the families of those who are fighting to secure for them their property and their other rights! As long as this continues, we shall expect to witness scenes of violence.

In the name of our beloved country—in the name of outraged humanity—in the name of that religion they profess to reverence—in the name of the God they pretend to fear—we call upon these men to change their policy before it shall be too late!

Southern Watchman (Athens GA), 8 April 1863.

11. Soldiers' Families in Miller County, Georgia, Call to Jefferson Davis for Help (1863)

Rural women were also feeling the hardships of food shortage. Here, soldiers' wives and mothers in Miller County, Georgia, write to President Jefferson Davis asking for help. But no help came. Conditions only worsened. In February

Women in Miller County, Georgia, wrote to President Jefferson Davis warning that God would "send down his fury and judgment" if the Confederacy continued to allow soldiers' families to suffer. But they were not waiting for God or Davis. With a fury of their own, women from Virginia to Texas—including those in Miller County—rioted for food.

Engraving from *Frank Leslie's Illustrated Newspaper,* 1863.

1865, fifty soldiers' wives armed with axes broke open the government depot in Colquitt, seat of Miller County, and took 100 bushels of corn.

Our crops is limited and so short...cannot reach the first day of march next.... our fencing is unanimously almost decayed.... But little [food] of any sort to rescue us and our children from a unanimous starvation.... We can seldom find [bacon] for none has got [any] but those that are exempt from service by office holding and old age, and they have no humane feeling nor patriotic principles.... An all wise god who is slow to anger and full of grace and mercy and without respect of persons and full of love and charity that he will send down his fury and judgment in a very great manner [on] all those our leading men and those that are in power if there is no more favors shown to those the mothers and wives and of those who in poverty has with patriotism stood the fence battles.... I tell you that with out some great and speedily alterating in the conducting of affairs in this our little nation god will frown on it and that speedily.

Soldiers' wives and mothers of Miller County, Georgia. Letter to Jefferson Davis, 8 September 1863, Letters Received by the Confederate Secretary of War, National Archives Microfilm Publications (Washington DC) M437, roll 80, 776–80.

12. Voting by Classes (1863)

In Columbus, Georgia, common folk organized and offered a slate of candidates for city office on the "Mechanics' and Working Men's Ticket" during the fall 1863 elections. According to the Columbus Enquirer, *the new party "prevailed by a very large majority." Its success sent shock waves through the ranks of the city's political establishment. On 9 October, the editor of the* Enquirer *voiced upper-class fears when he chastised plain folk for their "antagonistic" attitude and condemned the "causeless divisions of our citizens into classes." On 13 October, a competing city paper, the* Daily Sun, *ran a letter it received from a local man signing himself "Mechanic."*

I notice in the Enquirer, of Friday evening, an article complaining bitterly of the people voting by classes, in which both classes are accused of clannishness, but the burden of his complaint seems to rest on mechanics and working men. He says, "there is certainly no ground for any antagonism in the city." In this the Enquirer is mistaken; for any man, woman or child can see that the people are dividing into two classes, just as fast as the pressure of the times can force them on. As for example: class No. 1, in their thirst for gain, in their worship of Mammon, and in their mighty efforts to appropriate every dollar on earth to their own account, have lost sight of every principle of humanity, patriotism, and virtue itself, and seem to have forgotten that the very treasures they are now heaping up are the price of blood, and unless this mania ceases, will be the price of liberty itself; for we know something of the feeling which now exits in the army, as well as in our work-shops at home. The men know well enough that their helpless families are not cared for, as they were promised at the beginning of the war.... They know, too, that every day they remain from home, reduces them more and more in circumstances, and that by the close of the war a large majority of the soldiery will be unable to live; in fact, many of them are ruined now, as many of their homes and other effects are passing into the hands of speculators and extortioners, for subsistence to their families. Thus you see, that all the capital, both in money and property, in the South, is passing into the hands of class No. 1, while class No. 2 are traveling down, soon to take their station among the descendants of Ham. You can easily see who are class No. 2. The soldiery, the mechanics, and the workingmen, not only of Columbus, but of all the Confederate States. In view of these things, is it not time that our class should awake to a sense of their danger, and in the mildest possible manner begin the work of self-defense, and endeavor to escape a bondage more servile than that imposed by the aristocracy of England on their poor peasantry? Then we claim the right, as the first alternative, to try and avert the great calamity, by electing such men to the councils of the nation as we think will best represent our interests. If this should fail, we must then try more potent remedies....

But, notwithstanding the mechanics and working men can barely sustain animal life, their condition is much better than the poor soldiers',

In 1864, Jefferson Davis publicly admitted that two-thirds of the Confederate army had deserted. When they reached home, many deserters joined layout gangs. They ambushed conscript patrols, attacked supply depots, and made war on Confederate authority wherever they found it. So violent did this inner civil war become that a Georgia newspaper wrote in 1863, "We are fighting each other harder than we have ever fought the enemy."

Engraving from R.M. Devens, *The Pictorial Book of Anecdotes and Incidents of the War of the Rebellion* (1866).

who are fighting the rich man's fight, for they suffer all of the privations and hardships incident to the life of a soldier, with a perfect knowledge of the sufferings of their families at home, who are (many of them) without a comfortable shelter....True, they are sometimes offered assistance at the sacrifice of their honor, and that by men who occupy high places both in church and State. Then is there not an "organization of hostility" against the interests of our class, which justice and honor demand that we should guard with unceasing vigilance?...

Daily Sun (Columbus GA), 13 October 1863.

13. Samuel Knight Finds "Strong Union Feeling" in Southwest Georgia (1864)

Following a trip through southwestern Georgia in the late fall and winter 1863-64, Samuel Knight wrote to Governor Joseph E. Brown of war-weariness and its impact among common folk.

My dear sir

Permit me the liberty of writing you these few lines in regard to the state of our country at this time through the Second Congressional District [southwest Georgia] and no doubt but many other portions of the state. I have been traveling through this district for the last three months and mingling freely with the common people and have found with much regret that among that class generally there is a strong Union feeling .... I also learn from good authority that the same feeling exists among the soldiers in the field to an alarming extent....

There is also a loud cry raised against so many enrolling officers in the country, and the general talk is that, if they need men in the army, why don't they take back these loafering enrolling officers who is doing the country more harm than that many Yankees could do, for there [are] more than twice as many enrolling officers as conscripts and so on and also that poor people has to pay all the tax and do all the fighting while the gentleman and their sons are loafering over the country pretending to hunt conscripts. Such has become the common talk of the people....

There is many deserters now in Georgia that say they will die before they will go back to the service.... They had rather come under Lincoln....

Many of the soldiers families in this district are almost upon starvation at this time. Many of them are living entirely without meat and not half enough bread and there is not provisions in many of the settlements to keep the women and children from suffering and if there was they could not get it at the present prices....

And, kind sir, I do hope you will give this thing your most candid attention.... For it is a certain fact that the southern people are fast becoming as bitterly divided against each other as the Southern and Northern people ever has been. I have not written this letter to exaggerate these things. I only write such as I know to be true.

Samuel Knight, Letter to Joseph E. Brown, 22 February 1864, Governor's Incoming Correspondence, 1861–1865, Georgia Department of Archives and History, Morrow.

14. Deserters "Have Sympathizers All Through This Country" in Texas (1863)

Bonham, Tex., October 21, 1863

Maj. Gen. J. B. Magruder:

...Our domestic affairs are in a bad condition. I am now perfectly satisfied that there are not less than 1,000 deserters, from the army, conscription, and the militia, in the woods, ready to take to the brush in this sub-district. The largest number in any one place is 30 miles from here, where there are from 200 to 400 at three camps, within 10 miles, all of whom can concentrate within two hours. They keep every road picketed that goes into their vicinity so perfectly that not a man, woman, or child goes near them that [they] don't know it; they have sympathizers all through this country, and, if they can't be induced to come out peaceably, we will have trouble and bloodshed enough in this section to make our very hearts sick, and a war of the most wretched and savage character will be inaugurated.... but, if we have to kill them, let us do it for our country's sake.

Henry E. McDulloch,
Brigadier-General

War of the Rebellion: A Compilation of the Official Records of the Union and Confederate Armies (Washington DC: Government Printing Office, 1880–1901) series 1, volume 26, part 2, 344–45.

15. "Desertion Spreads and Enjoys Impunity" in North Carolina (1863)

Salisbury, N.C., September 2, 1863
Col. J. S. Preston
Superintendent of Conscription:

...The utter inadequacy now of any force that we can command without potential aid from the armies in the field will become apparent when it is realized that desertion has assumed [a] more formidable shape and development than could have been anticipated.... Deserters now leave the Army with arms and ammunition in hand. They act in concert to force by superior numbers a passage against bridge or ferry guards, if such are encountered. Arriving at their selected localities of refuge, they organize in bands variously estimated at from fifty up to hundreds at various points.... In Cherokee County a large body of deserters (with whom I class also those in resistance to conscription) have assumed a sort of military occupation, taking a town, and that in Wilkes County they are organized, drilling regularly, and entrenched in a camp to the number of 500. Indeed, the whole number of deserters in the latter county is said to be much larger. The reports of our patrols indicate 300 or 400 organized in Randolph County, and they are said to be in large numbers in Catawba and Yadkin, and not a few in the patriotic county of Iredell. These men are not only determined to kill in avoiding apprehension (having just put to death yet another of our enrolling officers), but their esprit de corps extends to killing in revenge as well as in prevention of the capture of each other. So far they seem to have had no trouble for subsistence.... Letters are being sent to the Army stimulating desertion and inviting the men home, promising them aid and comforts. County meetings are declaring in the same spirit and to hold back conscripts. As desertion spreads and enjoys impunity, in the same proportion do the enrolled conscripts hang back from reporting where there is not force enough to compel them, and the more dangerous and difficult becomes the position of our enrolling officers....

Geo W. Lay,

Lieutenant-Colonel and Inspector.

War of the Rebellion: A Compilation of the Official Records of the Union and Confederate Armies (Washington DC: Government Printing Office, 1880–1901) series 4, volume 2, 783–85.

16. Deserters "Swear Vengeance" in South Carolina (1863)

Greenville, S.C., August 7, 1863
Maj. C. D. Melton,

...A large number of deserters...have taken refuge in the mountain fastnesses and passes of the districts of Greenville, Pickens, and Spartanburg....

They are banded together in tens, twenties, and thirties, are bold, defiant, and even threatening.... They have spies and signals to indicate the approach of strangers, and are armed, many of them with Government arms with which they deserted.... They are unfortunately sustained in their conduct by many persons who have been heretofore regarded as good and loyal citizens.... They swear by all they hold sacred that they will die at home before they will ever be dragged forth again to do battle for such a cause....

Several bands of deserters...swear vengeance against any one who approaches with the intention of molesting them. The true and loyal citizens are afraid to turn out and aid the officers, as not only their lives, but the destruction of their homes and property is boldly threatened if they dare to give aid and assistance to the authorities in arresting them...

Jno. D. Ashmore,

Maj. and Chief Enrolling Officer

Southern blacks undermined the Confederate war effort whenever they could. As a grateful Union prisoner of war later wrote, "They were always ready to help anybody opposed to the Rebels. Union refugees, Confederate deserters, escaped prisoners—all received from them the same prompt and invariable kindness."

Engraving from Junius Henri Browne, *Four Years in Secessia* (1865).

War of the Rebellion: A Compilation of the Official Records of the Union and Confederate Armies (Washington DC: Government Printing Office, 1880–1901) series 4, volume 2, 771–73.

17. Women Defend Deserters with Hoes and Axes in Florida (1864)

"My men are deserting fast," wrote Captain Winston Stephens to his wife in January 1864. "The laws that have been passed generally protect the rich, and the poor begin to say it is the rich man's war and the poor man's fight, and they will not stand it." He went on to tell how that attitude among women as well as men made capturing deserters a dangerous undertaking.

...Corpl Smith returned from the east side of the St Johns [River] last night and gives a gloomy picture of affairs on that side, and an incident happened to him, that will illustrate the feelings on that side. He rode up to the house of one of my Deserters about daylight but the man was not at home, he then went on a few miles to another's home and there they saw both the men at work in the field, but the deserters saw them when they were about 1/4 mile from them and ran for the swamp close by, Corpl Smith and party charged their horses as fast as they could, and the women (about a dozen) came out with hoes and axes and tried to cut Smith off, but all the party were good horsemen but Smith and passed safely but his horse took fright and threw him in a bunch of palmettoes and the women shouted there's one of the d----d rascals off. Smith got up and the women blew the horn to let others know and told Smith if he would stay 15 minutes they would catch h--l, using all the time the most profane language they could think of. Some of the party would have gotten the deserters but they...got to the swamp before they could be overtaken, some of the party fired at them but missed. Smith says they have regular spies and that no party can go through the country without being found out by these persons on the watch.

Arch Fredric Blakey, Ann Smith Lainhart, and Winston Bryant Stephens, Jr., editors, *Rose Cottage Chronicles: Civil War Letters of the Bryant-Stephens Families of North Florida* (Gainesville: University Press of Florida, 1998) 311–12.

18. John Boston Frees Himself (1862)

In January 1862, John Boston, a refugee from Maryland who had fled to the Union army in Virginia, tried to get word of his successful escape to his wife Elizabeth, still in Maryland with their son Daniel. The Emancipation Proclamation was nearly a year away. Even then it would apply only in territory held by the Confederacy, not in Maryland. Yet Boston twice confidently refers to himself as a free man.

My Dear Wife. It is with great joy I take this time to let you know where I am. I am now in safety in the 14th Regiment of Brooklyn. This day I can address you, thank God, a free man. I had a little trouble in getting away, but as the Lord led the children of Israel to the land of Canaan, so he led me to a land where freedom will reign in spite of earth and hell. Dear, you must make your self content I am free from all the slavers' lash.... My Dear, I can't express my great desire that I have to see you. I trust the time will come when we shall meet again. And if we don't met on Earth, we will meet in heaven where Jesus reigns.... Dear Wife, I must close. Rest yourself contented I am free. I want you to write to me soon as you can without delay. Direct your letter to the 14th Regiment, New York State Militia, Uptons Hill, Virginia.... Your affectionate husband. Kiss Daniel for me.

John Boston

Ira Berlin, Barbara J. Fields, Thavolia Glymph, Joseph P. Reidy, and Leslie S. Rowland, editors, *Freedom: A Documentary History of Emancipation, Series 1, Vol. 1, The Destruction of Slavery* (Cambridge: Cambridge University Press, 1985) 357–58.

19. Susie King Taylor Flees to the Yankees (1862)

Susie King Taylor of Savannah, like so many other slaves in the Deep South, believed in spring 1862 that federal policy mandated their freedom. Although that was not yet the case, tens of thousands of slaves emancipated themselves by fleeing to Union lines, which eventually forced the Lincoln administration to recognize that indeed these people were free.

About this time I had been reading so much about the "Yankees" I was very anxious to see them. The whites would tell their colored people not to go to the Yankees, for they would harness them to carts and make them pull the carts around, in place of horses. I asked grandmother, one day, if this was true. She replied, "Certainly not!" that the white people did not want slaves to go over to the Yankees, and told them these things to frighten them.... I wanted to see these wonderful "Yankees" so much, as I heard my parents say the Yankee was going to set all the slaves free. Oh, how those people prayed for freedom! I remember, one night, my grandmother went out into the suburbs of the city to a church meeting, and they were fervently singing this old hymn,–

"Yes, we all shall be free,
Yes, we all shall be free,
Yes, we all shall be free,
When the Lord shall appear,"—

when the police came in and arrested all who were there, saying they were planning freedom, and sang "the Lord," in place of "Yankee," to blind any one who might be listening. Grandmother never forgot that night, although she did not stay in the guard-house, as she sent to her guardian, who came at once for her; but this was the last meeting she ever attended out of the city proper.

On April 1, 1862, about the time the Union soldiers were firing on Fort Pulaski, I was sent out into the country to my mother. I remember what a roar and din the guns made. They jarred the earth for miles. The fort was at last taken by them. Two days after the taking of Fort Pulaski, my uncle took his family of seven and myself to St. Catherine Island. We landed under the protection of the Union fleet, and remained there two weeks, when about thirty of us were taken aboard the gunboat P----, to be transferred to St. Simon's Island; and at last, to my unbounded joy, I saw the "Yankee."

Susie King Taylor, *Reminiscences of My Life in Camp* (Boston: Susie King Taylor, 1902) 7–9.

20. Enslaved Blacks Assist Whites Who Were "On Our Side" (ca. 1864)

Those enslaved people who did not escape slavery found many ways to work against the Confederacy. After the war, Nancy Johnson, enslaved near Savannah, told how she and her husband helped escaping Union prisoners and Confederate deserters.

There was a Yankee prisoner that got away and came to our house at night; we kept him hid in my house a whole day. He sat in my room. White people didn't visit our house then. My husband slipped him over to a man named Joel Hodges and he conveyed him off so that he got home.... The white people came hunting this man that we kept over night; my old master sent one of his own grandsons and he said if he found [him] that they must put my husband to death, and I had to tell a story to save [his] life. My old master would have had him killed. He was bitter. This was my master David Baggs. I told him that I had seen nothing of him. I did this to save my husband's life. Some of the rebel soldiers deserted and came to our house and we fed them. They were opposed to the war and didn't own slaves and said they would die rather than fight. Those who were poor white people, who didn't own slaves were some of them Union people. I befriended them because they were on our side.

Ira Berlin, Barbara J. Fields, Thavolia Glymph, Joseph P. Reidy, and Leslie S. Rowland, editors, *Freedom: A Documentary History of Emancipation, Series 1, Vol. 1, The Destruction of Slavery* (Cambridge: Cambridge University Press, 1985) 150–51.

21. Spotswood Rice Lays Claim to His Children (1864)

Spotswood Rice, who had been taught to read by his owner's son, escaped enslavement on a Missouri tobacco plantation and joined the Union army. He apparently tried and failed to take his children with him. On 3 September 1864, he wrote one letter (A) to his children letting them know he was coming for them, and another (B) to his former owner, Kittey (also Kaity) Diggs, saying much the same in a somewhat harsher tone.

A.

My Children, I take my pen in hand to write you a few lines to let you know that I have not forgot you and that I want to see you as bad as ever. Now my Dear Children I want you to be contented with whatever may be your lots. Be assured that I will have you if it cost me my life. On the 28th of the month 8 hundred white and 8 hundred black solders expects to start up the river to Glasgow and above there that's to generaled by a general that will give me both of you. When they come I expect to be with them and expect to get you both in return. Don't be uneasy my children. I expect to have you. If Diggs don't give you up, this Government will and I feel confident that I will get you. Your Miss Kaitty said that I tried to steal you. But I'll let her know that God never intended for man to steal his own flesh and blood.... And as for her Christianity, I expect the Devil has such in hell....

B.

I received a letter from Cariline telling me that you say I tried to steal to plunder my child away from you. Now I want you to understand that Mary is my Child and she is a God given right of my own and you may hold on to her as long as you can but I want you to remember this one thing that the longer you keep my Child from me the longer you will have to burn in hell and the quicker you'll get there. For we are now making up about one thousand black troops to come up through and want to come through Glasgow.... I offered once to pay you forty dollars for my own child but am glad now that you did not accept it. Just hold on now as long a you can and the worse it will be for you.... My Children is my own and I expect to get them... This whole Government gives cheer to me and you cannot help yourself.

Ira Berlin, Joseph P. Reidy, and Leslie S. Rowland, editors, *Freedom: A Documentary History of Emancipation, Series 2, The Black Military Experience* (Cambridge: Cambridge University Press, 1982) 689–90.

22. "To Go, or Not to Go" (1864)

In early summer 1864, as the Union army was advancing through northern Georgia toward Atlanta, Governor Joseph E. Brown issued a general call to arms. A newspaper in Milledgeville, then the state capital, published one Shakespeare-like response from an anonymous Georgia farmer.

To go or not to go, that is the question:
Whether it pays best to suffer pestering
By idle girls and garrulous old women,
Or to take up arms against a host of Yankees,
And by opposing get killed—To die, to sleep,
(Git eout) and in this sleep to say we "sink
To rest by all our Country's wishes blest"
And live forever—(that's a consummation
Just what I'm after). To march, to fight—
To fight! perchance to die, aye there's the rub!
For while I'm sleep, who'll take care Mary
and the babes—when Billy's in the low ground,
Who'll feed 'em, hey! There's the respect
I have for *them* that makes life sweet;
For who would bear the bag to mill,
Plough Dobbin,[1] cut the wheat, dig taters,
Kill hogs, and do all sorts of drudgery
If I am fool enough to get a Yankee
Bullet on my brain! Who'll cry for me!
Would patriotism pay my debts, when dead?
But oh! The dread of something after death—
That undiscovered fellow who'll court Mary,

[1]"Dobbin" is an old English term for a workhorse.

And do my huggin—that's agony,
And makes me want to stay home,
Specially as I aint mad with nobody.
Shells and bullets make cowards of us all,
And blamed my skin if snortin steeds,
And pomp and circumstance of War
Are to be compared with feather beds,
And Mary by my side.

Confederate Union (Milledgeville GA), 28 June 1864.

23. Sergeant William Andrews Reflects on the Confederacy at War's End (1865)

Even among soldiers who stuck with Confederacy to its end, most had little affection for the Richmond government. What loyalty they felt was more for their brothers in arms than anyone else. Still, Sergeant William Andrews understood why so many others had long since deserted. At one point in his diary he wrote, "Thank God I have no wife and children to suffer on account of an ungrateful government" (p. 39). As the war came to a close, Andrews blamed the Confederacy for widespread suffering and had little regret for its loss.

May 3, 1865.... No one but a soldier can imagine how we felt starting home. I have been in the army since February '61. Over four years hard service, never knowing what day would be my last. Now that is all over and we can look forward with the hopes of a brighter day coming, for we have seen nothing but dark ones during the war.

While it is a bitter pill to have to come back into the Union, don't think there is much regret for the loss of the Confederacy. The treatment the soldiers have received from the government in various ways put them against it. The army has been half clothed and half starved, besides they have received but little of the worthless money due them. Numbers of Confederate soldiers who went home to aid their starving families and were afterwards shot for desertion would most likely be with us today if the government had fulfilled its contract by paying them off so they could have sent the money home to their needy families.

William H. Andrews, *Footprints of a Regiment: A Recollection of the First Georgia Regulars, 1861–1865*, edited with introduction by Richard M. McMurry (Atlanta: Longstreet Press, 1992) 184.

This unique statue of a Civil War soldier in generic uniform, its left foot resting on the broken blade of its sword as a hopeful sign of peace, stands in front of the Winston County court house in Double Springs, Alabama. It honors soldiers on both sides of the conflict and serves as an impassive counterpoint to the myth of Southern unity. Winston County sent 239 men to the Union army and 112 to the Confederacy. Of them, 21 shared last names.

Photo by the author.

Further Readings

General Works

Boles, John B. *The South through Time: A History of an American Region, Vol. I.* 3rd edition. Upper Saddle River NJ: Pearson Prentice Hall, 2004.

Cooper, William J., Jr., and Thomas E. Terrill. *The American South: A History, Vol. I.* 4th edition. Lanham MD: Rowan and Littlefield, 2009.

Gallay, Alan, editor. *Voices of the Old South: Eyewitness Accounts, 1528–1861.* Athens: University of Georgia Press, 1994.

Harris, J. William. *The Making of the American South: A Short History, 1500–1877.* Malden MA: Blackwell Publishing, 2006.

Keith, Jeanette. *The South: A Concise History, Vol. I.* Upper Saddle River NJ: Prentice Hall, 2002.

Link, William A., and Marjorie Spruill Wheeler. *The South in the History of the Nation, A Reader, Vol. I: Through Reconstruction.* Boston: Bedford/St. Martin's, 1999.

McMillen, Sally G., Elizabeth Hayes Turner, Paul D. Escott, and David R. Goldfield. *Major Problems in the History of the American South, Volume I: The Old South.* 3rd edition. Boston: Wadsworth, 2011.

1. Clash of Cultures: Race, Class, and Conflict in the Colonial South

Axtell, James. *The Indians' New South: Cultural Change in the Colonial Southeast.* Baton Rouge: Louisiana State University Press, 1997.

Berlin, Ira. *Many Thousands Gone: The First Two Centuries of Slavery in North America.* Cambridge MA: Belknap Press, 1998.

Braund, Catherine Holland. *Deerskins and Duffels: The Creek Indian Trade with Anglo-America, 1685–1815.* Lincoln: University of Nebraska Press, 1996.

Brown, Kathleen M. *Good Wives, Nasty Wenches, and Anxious Patriarchs: Gender, Race, and Power in Colonial Virginia.* Chapel Hill: University of North Carolina Press, 1996.

Gallay, Alan. *The Indian Slave Trade: The Rise of the English Empire in the American South, 1670–1717.* New Haven CT: Yale University Press, 2002.

Hahn, Steven C. *The Invention of the Creek Nation, 1670–1763.* Lincoln: University of Nebraska Press, 2004.

Hashaw, Tim. *Children of Perdition: Melungeons and the Struggle of Mixed America.* Macon GA: Mercer University Press, 2007.

Hudson, Charles. *Knights of Spain, Warriors of the Sun: Hernando de Soto and the South's Ancient Chiefdoms*. Athens: University of Georgia Press, 1998.

———. *The Southeastern Indians*. Knoxville: University of Tennessee Press, 1976.

Jordan, Dan, and Michael Walsh. *White Cargo: The Forgotten History of Britain's White Slaves in America*. New York: New York University Press, 2008.

Juricek, John T. *Colonial Georgia and the Creeks: Anglo-Indian Diplomacy on the Southern Frontier, 1733–1763*. Gainesville: University Press of Florida, 2010.

Kelton, Paul. *Epidemics and Enslavement: Biological Catastrophe in the Native Southeast, 1492–1715*. Lincoln: University of Nebraska Press, 2007.

Morgan, Edmund S. *American Slavery, American Freedom: The Ordeal of Colonial Virginia*. New York: W.W. Norton, 1975.

Mullin, Gerald W. *Flight and Rebellion: Slave Resistance in Eighteenth-Century Virginia*. New York: Oxford University Press, 1972.

Ramsey, William L. *The Yamasee War: A Study of Culture, Economy, and Conflict in the Colonial South*. Lincoln: University of Nebraska Press, 2008.

Silver, Timothy. *A New Face on the Countryside: Indians, Colonists, and Slaves in South Atlantic Forests, 1500–1800*. Cambridge: Cambridge University Press, 1990.

Smith, Mark M. *Stono: Documenting and Interpreting a Southern Slave Revolt*. Columbia: University of South Carolina Press, 2005.

Smith, Marvin T. *Coosa: The Rise and Fall of a Southeastern Mississippian Chiefdom*. Gainesville: University Press of Florida, 2000.

Williams, Eric. *Capitalism and Slavery*. 1944. New introduction by Colin A. Palmer. Chapel Hill: University of North Carolina Press, 1994.

Wood, Betty. *Slavery in Colonial America, 1619–1776*. Lanham MD: Rowman and Littlefield, 2005.

Wood, Peter H., Gregory A. Waselkov, and M. Thomas Hatley, editors. *Powhatan's Mantle: Indians in the Colonial Southeast*. Lincoln: University of Nebraska Press, 1989.

Wright, J. Leitch, Jr. *Anglo-Spanish Rivalry in North America*. Athens: University of Georgia Press, 1971.

2. *Rebels, Tories, and Victims: The South's First Civil War*

Breen, T. H. *Tobacco Culture: The Mentality of the Great Tidewater Planters on the Eve of the Revolution*. Princeton: Princeton University Press, 1985.

Brown, Richard Maxwell. *The South Carolina Regulators*. Cambridge MA: Belknap Press, 1963.

Crow, Jeffrey J., and Larry E. Tise, editors. *The Southern Experience in the American Revolution*. Chapel Hill: University of North Carolina Press, 1978.

Frey, Silvia R. *Water from the Rock: Black Resistance in a Revolutionary Age*. Princeton: Princeton University Press, 1992.

Hall, Leslie. *Land and Allegiance in Revolutionary Georgia*. Athens: University of Georgia Press, 2001.

Hatley, Tom. *The Dividing Paths: Cherokees and South Carolinians through the Revolutionary Era*. New York: Oxford University Press, 1995.

Hoffman, Ronald, Thad W. Tate, and Peter J. Albert, editors. *An Uncivil War: The Southern Backcountry in the American Revolution*. Charlottesville: University Press of Virginia, 1985.

Holton, Woody. *Forced Founders: Indians, Debtors, Slaves, and the Making of the American Revolution in Virginia*. Chapel Hill: University of North Carolina Press, 1999.

Kars, Marjoleine. *Breaking Loose Together: The Regulator Rebellion in Pre-Revolutionary North Carolina*. Chapel Hill: University of North Carolina Press, 2001.

Kierner, Cynthia. *Southern Women in Revolution, 1776–1800*. Columbia: University of South Carolina Press, 1998.

MacLeod, Duncan J. *Slavery, Race, and the American Revolution*. Cambridge: Cambridge University Press, 1974.

Massey, Gregory D. *John Laurens and the American Revolution*. Columbia: University of South Carolina Press, 2000.

Morill, Dan. *Southern Campaigns of the American Revolution*. Baltimore: Nautical and Aviation Publishing Company of America, 1993.

O'Donnell, James H., III. *Southern Indians in the American Revolution*. Knoxville: University of Tennessee Press, 1973.

Peicuch, Jim. *Three People's, One King: Loyalists, Indians, and Slaves in the Revolutionary South, 1775–1782*. Columbia: University of South Carolina Press, 2008.

Pybus, Cassandra. *Epic Journeys of Freedom: Runaway Slaves of the American Revolution and Their Global Quest for Liberty*. Boston: Beacon Press, 2006.

Shy, John. *A People Numerous and Armed: Reflections on the Military Struggle for Independence*. Ann Arbor: University of Michigan Press, 1990.

Troxler, Carole Watterson. *Farming Dissenters: The Regulator Movement in Piedmont North Carolina*. Raleigh: North Carolina Office of Archives and History, 2011.

Weigley, Russell Frank. *The Partisan War: The South Carolina Campaign of 1780–1782*. Columbia: University of South Carolina Press, 1970.

Wilson, David K. *The Southern Strategy: Britain's Conquest of South Carolina and Georgia, 1775–1780*. Columbia: University of South Carolina Press, 2005.

3. The South Moves West: Expansion and the Tragedy of Indian Removal

Covington, James W. *The Seminoles of Florida*. Gainesville: University Press of Florida, 1993.

Foreman, Grant. *Indian Removal: The Emigration of the Five Civilized Tribes of Indians*. Foreword by Angie Debo. Norman: University of Oklahoma Press, 1972.

Green, Michael D. *The Politics of Indian Removal: Creek Government and Society in Crisis*. Lincoln: University of Nebraska Press, 1982.

Heidler, David S., and Jeanne T. Heidler. *Indian Removal: A Norton Casebook*. New York: W.W. Norton, 2007.

Hudson, Angela Pulley. *Creek Paths and Federal Roads: Indians, Settlers, and Slaves and the Making of the American South*. Chapel Hill: University of North Carolina Press, 2010.

King, Duane H., editor. *The Cherokee Indian Nation: A Troubled History*. Knoxville: University of Tennessee Press, 1979.

McGrath, C. Peter. *Yazoo: Law and Politics in the New Republic*. Providence RI: Brown University Press, 1966.

Missall, John. *The Seminole Wars: America's Longest Indian Conflict*. Gainesville: University Press of Florida, 2004.

Moulton, Gary E. *John Ross: Cherokee Chief*. Athens: University of Georgia Press, 1978.

Owsley, Frank Lawrence, Jr. *Struggle for the Gulf Borderlands: The Creek War and the Battle of New Orleans, 1812–1815*. Gainesville: University Press of Florida, 1981.

Owsley, Frank Lawrence, Jr., and Gene A. Smith. *Filibusters and Expansionists: Jeffersonian Manifest Destiny, 1800–1821*. Tuscaloosa: University of Alabama Press, 1997.

Perdue, Theda, editor. *Cherokee Editor: The Writings of Elias Boudinot*. Knoxville: University of Tennessee Press, 1983.

Saunt, Claudio. *A New Order of Things: Property, Power, and the Transformation of the Creek Indians, 1733–1816*. Cambridge: Cambridge University Press, 1999.

Wallace, Anthony F. C. *The Long, Bitter Trail: Andrew Jackson and the Indians*. New York: Hill and Wang, 1993.

Wickman, Patricia R. *Osceola's Legacy*. Tuscaloosa: University of Alabama Press, 2006.

Wilkins, Thurman. *Cherokee Tragedy: The Ridge Family and the Decimation of a People*. Norman: University of Oklahoma Press, 1986.

Williams, David. *The Georgia Gold Rush: Twenty-Niners, Cherokees, and Gold Fever*. Columbia: University of South Carolina Press, 1993.

4. *Widening Gaps: Planters, Plain Folk, and the Enslaved*

Aptheker, Herbert. *American Negro Slave Revolts*. New York: Columbia University Press, 1943.

Ashworth, John. *Slavery, Capitalism, and Politics in the Antebellum Republic.* 2 volumes. Cambridge: Cambridge University Press, 1995 and 2007.

Berlin, Ira. *Slaves without Masters: The Free Negro in the Antebellum South.* New York: Pantheon, 1974.

Bolton, Charles C. *Poor Whites of the Antebellum South: Tenants and Laborers in Central North Carolina and Northeast Mississippi.* Durham: Duke University Press, 1994.

Bynum, Victoria E. *Unruly Women: The Politics of Social and Sexual Control in the Old South.* Chapel Hill: University of North Carolina Press, 1992.

Cashin, Joan E. *A Family Venture: Men and Women on the Southern Frontier.* New York: Oxford University Press, 1991.

Cecil-Fronsman, Bill. *Common Whites: Class and Culture in Antebellum North Carolina.* Lexington: University of Kentucky Press, 1992.

Craft, William. *Running a Thousand Miles for Freedom: The Escape of William and Ellen Craft from Slavery.* 1860. Reprint, with new forward and biographical essay by R. J. M. Blackett, Baton Rouge: Louisiana State University Press, 1999.

Daly, John Patrick. *When Slavery Was Called Freedom: Evangelicalism, Proslavery, and the Causes of the Civil War.* Lexington: University of Kentucky Press, 2002.

DeBats, Donald A. *Elites and Masses: Political Structure, Communication, and Behavior in Ante-Bellum Georgia.* New York: Garland Publishing, 1990.

Douglass, Frederick. *Narrative of the Life of Frederick Douglass.* Boston: Bedford Books, 1993.

Dusinberre, William. *Them Dark Days: Slavery in the American Rice Swamps.* New York: Oxford University Press, 1996.

Eaton, Clement. *The Freedom-of-Thought Struggle in the Old South.* New York: Harper and Row, 1964.

Forret, Jeff. *Race Relations at the Margins: Slaves and Poor Whites in the Antebellum Southern Countryside.* Baton Rouge: Louisiana State University Press, 2006.

Franklin, John Hope, and Loren Schweninger. *Runaway Slaves: Rebels on the Plantation.* New York: Oxford University Press, 1999.

Haggard, Dixie Ray, editor. *African Americans in the Nineteenth Century: People and Perspectives.* Santa Barbara CA: ABC-CLIO, 2010.

Harris, J. William. *Plain Folk and Gentry in a Slave Society: White Liberty and Black Slavery in Augusta's Hinterlands.* Middletown CT: Wesleyan University Press, 1985.

Heyrman, Christine. *Southern Cross: The Beginnings of the Bible Belt.* Chapel Hill: University of North Carolina Press, 1997.

Genovese, Eugene. *Roll, Jordan, Roll: The World the Slaves Made.* New York: Pantheon, 1974.

Genovese, Eugene and Elizabeth Fox-Genovese. *Slavery in White and Black: Class and Race in the Southern Slaveholders' New World Order*. Cambridge: Cambridge University Press, 2008.

Johnson, Walter. *Soul by Soul: Life inside the Antebellum Slave Market*. Cambridge: Harvard University Press, 1999.

Mathews, Donald G. *Religion in the Old South*. Chicago: University of Chicago Press, 1977.

McMillen, Sally G. *Southern Women: Black and White in the Old South*. Arlington Heights IL: Harlan Davidson, 1992.

Owsley, Frank Lawrence, Sr. *Plain Folk of the Old South*. 1949. New introduction by John B. Boles. Baton Rouge: Louisiana State University Press, 2008.

Rothman, Adam. *Slave Country: American Expansion and the Origins of the Deep South*. Cambridge: Harvard University Press, 2007.

Smith, Michael Thomas. *A Traitor and a Scoundrel: Benjamin Hedrick and the Cost of Dissent*. Newark: University of Delaware Press, 2003.

Stampp, Kenneth. *The Peculiar Institution: Slavery in the Antebellum South*. New York: Knopf, 1956.

Stevenson, Brenda. *Life in Black and White: Family and Community in the Slave South*. New York: Oxford University Press, 1996.

Wright, Gavin. *The Political Economy of the Cotton South*. New York: W.W. Norton, 1978.

5. A South Divided: Secession and the South's Inner Civil War

Ashworth, John. *The Republic in Crisis, 1848-1861*. Cambridge: Cambridge University Press, 2012.

Bailey, Fred Arthur. *Class and Tennessee's Confederate Generation*. Chapel Hill: University of North Carolina Press, 1987.

Berlin, Ira, Barbara J. Fields, Steven F. Miller, Joseph P. Reidy, and Leslie S. Rowland, editors. *Free at Last: A Documentary History of Slavery, Freedom, and the Civil War*. New York: The New Press, 1992.

Berlin, Ira, Joseph Patrick Reidy, and Leslie S. Rowland. *Freedom's Soldiers: The Black Military Experience in the Civil War*. Cambridge: Cambridge University Press, 1998.

Buker, George E. *Blockaders, Refugees, and Contrabands: Civil War on Florida's Gulf Coast, 1861–1865*. Tuscaloosa: University of Alabama Press, 1993.

Bynum, Victoria E. *The Free State of Jones: Mississippi's Longest Civil War*. Chapel Hill: University of North Carolina Press, 2001.

———. *The Long Shadow of the Civil War: Southern Dissent and its Legacies*. Chapel Hill: University of North Carolina Press, 2010.

Channing, Steven A. *Crisis of Fear: Secession in South Carolina*. New York: Simon and Schuster, 1970.

Durden, Robert F. *The Gray and the Black: The Confederate Debate on Emancipation.* Baton Rouge: Louisiana State University Press, 1972.

Edwards, Laura. *Scarlett Doesn't Live Here Anymore: Southern Women in the Civil War Era*. Urbana: University of Illinois Press, 2000.

Escott, Paul D. *After Secession: Jefferson Davis and the Failure of Confederate Nationalism*. Baton Rouge: Louisiana State University Press, 1978.

———. *The Confederacy: The Slaveholders' Failed Venture*. Santa Barbara CA: Praeger, 2010.

Freehling, William W. *The South vs. the South: How Anti-Confederate Southerners Shaped the Course of the Civil War*. New York: Oxford University Press, 2001.

Freehling, William W., and Craig M. Simpson, editors. *Secession Debated: Georgia's Showdown in 1860*. New York: Oxford University Press, 1992.

Inscoe, John C., and Robert C. Kenzer, editors. *Enemies of the Country: New Perspectives on Unionists in the Civil War South*. Athens: University of Georgia Press, 2001.

Johnson, Michael P. *Toward a Patriarchal Republic: The Secession of Georgia*. Baton Rouge: Louisiana State University Press, 1977.

Jordan, Winthrop D. *Tumult and Silence at Second Creek: An Inquiry into a Civil War Slave Conspiracy*. Baton Rouge: Louisiana State University Press, 1993.

Kruman, Marc W. *Parties and Politics in North Carolina, 1836–1865*. Baton Rouge: Louisiana State University Press, 1983.

Link, William A. *Roots of Secession: Slavery and Politics in Antebellum Virginia.* Chapel Hill: University of North Carolina Press, 2003.

Marten, James. *Texas Divided: Loyalty and Dissent in the Lone Star State, 1856–1874.* Lexington: University of Kentucky Press, 1990.

McCurry, Stephanie. *Confederate Reckoning: Politics and Power in the Civil War South*. Cambridge: Harvard University Press, 2010.

McMillan, Malcolm C. *The Disintegration of a Confederate State: Three Governors and Alabama's Wartime Home Front, 1861–1865.* Macon GA: Mercer University Press, 1986.

Mobley, Joe A. *Weary of War: Life on the Confederate Home Front*. Westport CT: Praeger, 2008.

Pickering, David, and Judy Falls. *Brush Men and Vigilantes: Civil War Dissent in Texas*. College Station: Texas A&M University Press, 2000.

Sarris, Jonathan Dean. *A Separate Civil War: Communities in Conflict in the Mountain South*. Charlottesville: University of Virginia Press, 2006.

Storey, Margaret M. *Loyalty and Loss: Alabama's Unionists in the Civil War and Reconstruction*. Baton Rouge: Louisiana State University Press, 2004.

Sutherland, Daniel E., editor. *Guerrillas, Unionists, and Violence on the Confederate Home Front*. Fayetteville: University of Arkansas Press, 1999.

Tatum, Georgia Lee. *Disloyalty in the Confederacy*. 1934. Reprint, with new introduction by David Williams, Lincoln: University of Nebraska Press, 2000.

Taylor, Susie King. *Reminiscences of My Life in Camp*. 1902. Reprint, with new introduction by Catherine Clinton, Athens: University of Georgia Press, 2006.

Thornton, J. Mills, III. *Politics and Power in a Slave Society: Alabama, 1800–1860.* Baton Rouge: Louisiana State University Press, 1978.

Walther, Eric H. *The Fire-Eaters*. Baton Rouge: Louisiana State University Press, 1992.

Weitz, Mark A. *More Damning than Slaughter: Desertion in the Confederate Army*. Lincoln: University of Nebraska Press, 2005.

Williams, David, Teresa Crisp Williams, and David Carlson. *Plain Folk in a Rich Man's War: Class and Dissent in Confederate Georgia*. Gainesville: University Press of Florida, 2002.

Williams, David. *Bitterly Divided: The South's Inner Civil War*. New York: The New Press, 2008.

———. *I Freed Myself: African American Self-Emancipation in the Civil War Era.* Cambridge: Cambridge University Press, 2014.

Index

Index